PRAISE FOR WHAT WE TALK ABOUT WHEN WE'RE OVER 60

"This collection of stories provides a forum for voices that often go unheard. This book offers us witty, wise, and moving stories that need to be told in a culture prone to ignore elders, especially if they're female."
—Kay Heath, associate professor of English

"I am blessed that Peggy Womack did not give up on love because I am the man in her life. The universe intended for us to be together even if it took a hurricane (Katrina) to bring us to each other. Peggy is an intelligent, witty, talented woman and her writing showcases these qualities. To love is above all to be there and Peggy is always there for me."
—Rick Gray, PhD, Peggy's twin flame, horse trainer, and behavior health CEO.

"Maureen Burn's ability to find the wisdom in the everyday moments and then turn that wisdom into story is not only a treat for the reader but offers moments of transformation. Her gift for humor and reflection offers readers a unique view of their lives. Everyone can see themselves as the main character in Maureen's reflections."
—Camille Beecroft, managing editor, FAITH MAGAZINE

"My memory of meeting Lois and J.W. Brown many years ago is how beautiful she was and how handsome and kind he was. I couldn't piece together that 'wild' Jerry Lee Lewis was part of this down-to-earth family, or that their daughter, Myra, was just 13 years old and married to Jerry. In her chapter 'Rock-and-Roll Romance,' Myra pays tribute to her parents and their 70-year marriage. Lois and J.W.'s devotion to each other warms your heart and brings tears to your eyes. I love their story….."
—Elaine Orlando, co-founder of the Jerry Lee Lewis Fan Club

"Bonnie Ross Parker, in spite of personal heartbreaking loss, reaches out to teach and strengthen others. Some of her insights: 'We can find hope. We can move on even when facing challenges that feel like climbing Mt. Everest one step at a time.... We can only do our best, be our best, and have faith that our journey has purpose.' I invite you to read Bonnie's excellent excerpt with a willingness to experience a heart-shift. For indeed, that will happen if you are ready."
—Dr. Paula Fellingham, Founder and CEO of The WIN
(Women's Information Network)

"All those images of wicked stepmothers? Forget them. Mary Mattson's tender accounting of her relationship with two stepdaughters reads like an invitation

to be part of the family. She has a keen eye for details that tell her story of love and patience. Her essay makes us want to have stepmothers of our own."
—Elsa McDowell, editorial writer and former columnist for
THE POST and COURIER

"Brenda Cox has created a heartwarming Southern family story about three unique and unusual cousins. This is a wonderful, revealing read into their lives."
—Jimmie DeRamus, star of the History Channel's *Cajun Pawn Stars*

"'End stage winter poisoning' is a notion to which many cannot relate. But if you have spent time in Northern Michigan you know exactly what it is. Cheryl Reed shares a glimpse as to why anyone would endure ESWP. Her recollections of a full life well lived in all four Michigan seasons go deep and fleeting as gold light falling through tree limbs to a bank of trillium. Something pleasurable indeed she has shared, and that old winter really wasn't so long after all."
—John Shoemaker, cheese maker, Blue Moon Cheese

"Jan Odom's frank depiction of mental illness is both tough and humanizing, offering readers a wider landscape in which to examine and understand those inflicted with what is often held as a secret shame."
—Elizabeth Champlin, college English instructor, poet, and author

"Lottie Claiborne is a complete and utter joy. To read her story is to understand that Lottie the woman is so much more than Lottie the Body who performed on stage for over forty years. The warmth of her spirit and the wisdom she's gained through a life led on stages around the world resonates in her words in *What We Talk About…When We're over 60*. Everyone should read her inspirational story and have the pleasure of spending an afternoon with Lottie!!"
—Terri K. Zyskowski & Don Davenport, Owners and Photographers, Mission Detroit Photography

"A compelling reflection of life as experienced by a woman who is too young to be fulfilled, too old to be provincial, and too wise to accept complacency. Linda Hughes blends insight, humor, reality, and fantasy into a delightful account of aging at its best."
—Judy Ragan, Director of Marketing, Silver Sage Media, LLC.

For more endorsements, reviews, and chatting join us on Facebook:
www.facebook.com/whatwetalkabout

What We Talk About When We're Over 60

What We Talk About When We're Over 60

❧

Dear Debbie,
Enjoy!
Love,
Linda
11-15-16

Sherri Daley, Linda Hughes
& twenty-eight women who have something to say

DEEDS PUBLISHING | ATLANTA

Published by Deeds Publishing
Marietta, GA
www.deedspublishing.com

Printed in The United States of America

Library of Congress Cataloging-in-Publications Data is available upon request.

ISBN 978-1-941165-23-2

Books are available in quantity for promotional or premium use. For information, write Deeds Publishing, PO Box 682212, Marietta, GA 30068 or info@deedspublishing.com.

First Edition, 2014

10 9 8 7 6 5 4 3 2 1

ACKNOWLEDGMENTS & DEDICATION

OUR HEARTFELT THANKS TO THE INCREDIBLE WOMEN WHO SHARED their stories in this book. Their candor, humor, and camaraderie throughout this entire process have made this book come to life.

And our appreciation to the Babcocks of Deeds Publishing—Bob, Jan, and Mark. Without them, none of this would have been possible. They are the best!

* * *

What We Talk About... is dedicated to women over 60 everywhere.

CONTENTS

Foreword   xi

1: Men Are Like Handbags | Leslie, 60   1
2: Lost Love Found | Marj, 64   7
3: Rock-and-Roll Romance | Myra, 68   15
4: A Snitch Falls in Love | Gilda, 97   25
5: The Old Boyfriend Tour | Sherri, 66   29
6: A Work in Progress | Barbara, 64   47
7: Blind Date | Joan, 71   53
8: Summer Camp and the Walk of Shame | Kate, 60   57
9: Two Brides | Suzanne, 63   63
10: Wising Up | Peggy, 66   67
11: Forgive, Not Forget | Maureen, 67   77
12: A Mother's Journey | Bonnie, 68   85
13: Pushing the Envelope | Suzanne, 60   93
14: Step-Motherhood | Mary, 60   107
15: Proving Mother Wrong | Ingrid, 74   117
16: The Man in the Family | Jill, 66   129
17: Getting to Know My Father | Jennifer, 63   135
18: Famous Cousins | Brenda, 63   155
19: Buying the Farm | Cheryl, 65   163
20: Dog Lessons | Karene, 61   183
21: Being Bipolar | Jan, 63   195
22: A Spiritual Journey | Kathryn, 63   211
23: A Day in the Life of a Psychic | Deborah, 62   223
24: Cougar on the Prowl | Louise, 69   233
25: Sex? | Ruby, 73   239
26: Getting a Facelift | Norma, 65   243
27: The Body | Lottie, 84   251
28: Reality | Linda, 65   263
29: Erin Go Bragh | Nancy, 77   277
30: El Amor Cura Todo | Susan, 72   285

Afterword   293
About the Authors   295

FOREWORD

LINDA AND I WERE COLLEGE ROOMMATES IN MICHIGAN BACK WHEN dinosaurs roamed the earth. I always was just a little jealous of her, but liked her too much to be bratty about it. It didn't help that she got to be homecoming queen, but I was gone by then, living in New York City.

We followed each other's careers, marriages, disappointments, achievements—all of it—occasionally meeting for roommate reunions. We were both writers. We both had published books. And so when she approached me to co-edit a book of women's writing, I couldn't say no.

But I had one stipulation: it had to be writing from women over 60.

And the title? I stole it from Raymond Carver's iconic short story *What We Talk About When We Talk About Love*. In it, two couples sit around a kitchen table on a summer afternoon, drinking gin & tonic and talking until the sun goes down. Although their conversation is ostensibly about love, they drift around the topic, revealing more about their lives as the afternoon wanes.

At the end of the story, one of the wives asks, "Now what?"

And the narrator writes, "I could hear my heart beating. I could hear everyone's heart. I could hear the human noise we sat there making, not one of us moving, not even when the room went dark."

I loved the idea of human noise, and that is what spurred me to suggest the title to Linda who liked it, too. That's what this book is: a collection of human noise and heartbeats from women who have been around—not quite as long as the dinosaurs, but long enough to have something intelligent, funny, bawdy, or deeply moving to say.

This, then, is *What We Talk About.*

- **Sherri Daley, 66**

1 : MEN ARE LIKE HANDBAGS
LESLIE, 60

EVERY FRIDAY NIGHT, I GO TO THE DUCK. IT'S REALLY THE BLACK Duck, named after a legendary rum-running boat, but nobody calls it that. It's a bar in Westport, CT, which was once a sea-going refrigeration and ice storage barge built around 1840, refurbished in the 1900's, and anchored in the Saugatuck River since 1961.

In 1978, it opened as a restaurant and bar which has been going strong ever since.

One Friday, about a year ago, I was engaged in conversation with my friend, Brian, who claimed that everyone had an obsession. "What's yours?" he asked.

First I said I didn't have one. I think of myself as a practical woman, not consumed with material possessions, but he called me on that. After a little pressure, I came up with one: Italian leather.

I'd always been a bargain hunter and an avid fan of estate sales. Fairfield County is one of the country's most moneyed areas, a great place to find people who tire easily of their possessions and are anxious to buy new stuff. Their discards, in garage sales and thrift shops, always look good to me.

After I retired, after 33 years of teaching art in a public school, it came to me that I could subsidize my pension by selling off some of the beautiful leather goods I stumbled on in my search, every Saturday morning over the years, for treasures.

I began to put some of my precious finds on eBay, telling myself that I would keep this Gucci bag or that Prada or the rare Bottega Veneta woven cross-body if it didn't sell.

They always sold.

My obsession escalated to boots and shoes and other elegant leather goods. The Italian labels seemed to jump out at me. I didn't put up much resistance.

I retired from education when my daughter was just starting college. My financial advisor said that nobody retires right when their kid starts college, but I have never been one to follow the crowd. I retired, but with a computer screen full of photographs of Italian leather purses, boots, wallets, and bags.

I soon discovered that my eBay business would be a great help in financing my daughter's four years at Boston University.

It was hard work. It still is. The shopping, the research, the posting, the emails. The fun part is the shopping—or "searching" as I like to call it—although my getting up at the crack of dawn to beat the crowds to estate sales is not popular with my husband.

Soon the closets in our house, which was short on storage in the first place, were filled with my "finds". In my dreams, I had a basement. In reality, I had none. I begged my very generous friends to store things in their basements. Thank you, Betty, Shirley, and Sherri.

Still I continued to buy until I realized that it was my love of these leather goods that was driving me, not the intent to sell. In some subliminal way, I was satisfying my need to fondle these bags by buying and selling them.

With eBay, I had the opportunity to buy as many as I could find. I had given myself permission to purchase these beautiful items with only one catch: I had to sell them. Inventory was flowing, and baby needed a new pair of shoes.

I escalated my eBay listings and sailed full speed ahead.

And they sold…and sold.

Yes, a little piece of my heart went with each package to the lucky buyer, but there was, and is, always the option to go out and buy more. Even so, I would still clutch the bag to my chest and feel its "ultra-soft leather, made in Italy from a quality label," as I stated in my auctions. I could still carry that bag one more time before letting it go to another who shared my obsession.

My plans for retirement had taken a radical turn from turning my daughter's room into a studio where I could spend hours painting watercolors and designing jewelry. It was now a storage room, growing more cluttered by the day.

I cleared out a space for my daughter's bed so she would always have a place to sleep when she came home.

I was hooked. Hooked on soft supple leather. Hooked on the smell, the feel. I was done for.

Soon I was able to identify within a ten-foot radius the label on any bag that any woman was carrying on any street, airport, train station, or department store register.

I had a plethora of information, useless in everyday life, but so important to me. My friends made fun of me… until they wanted a bag. *And I knew exactly what they wanted.*

I began to discover how the purchase of a bag reflects the woman who buys it. I knew who wanted a Burberry Nova check bag. Who must have an Isabella Fiore bag, a bag with bling. Who will die if she doesn't have a Bottega Veneta. Which woman does not want any hardware on her bag at all. And who buys a bag made in China. (Oh no!) Large bags, small bags, cross-body bags, totes, messenger bags, clutches …

Then my minutia-stuffed brain made a connection: A woman chooses the man on her arm the same way she chooses the bag she carried.

There was a correlation. Does she prefer tall men, short men, stocky? Casually dressed? Suits or jeans & T-shirts? Rich men, poor men, bald men, big men, small men. Simple guys, complicated personalities?

I conducted an informal scientific survey. First, I asked my 25-year-old daughter. Did her friends choose a handbag like they chose a man?

Quick answer: yes. Her friend who carried a bag with many pockets and compartments was attracted to complicated and versatile men. Another friend wanted a man she could count on and she carried a bag with a sturdy base that could stand by itself.

An efficient overnight bag certainly speaks for itself. A clutch? The word itself calls up a vision of a man and woman embracing. A satchel, made to keep all your worldly possessions with you—sounds like a man you can trust to hold your deepest desires close to his heart. A cross-body bag is secure against purse-snatchers, like a strong man with his arm around you to protect you.

And what of the organizer bag? A man who keeps you orderly, steady, and safe. Rescues you from the precipice when you are about to fall.

Me, too. There's a correlation between my handbag and my man: It's my handbag I go to when I need money to buy things. It's my husband I go to when my checkbook is overdrawn and he comes through. My precious possessions are stashed in my handbag. So are my dreams and hopes stashed in my man.

And what of the beautifully worn vintage bag? I think about the woman who carried it. Where did she carry it? What dreams did that handbag hold? What man walked beside her, holding the same dreams? She may have wondered who that man loved before he loved her, who had the privilege of clutching his arm. What stories do our men have, unknown to us? What "baggage" has my man brought with him, now that he belongs to me? We women carry our handbags, but men have their baggage, too.

I once read a book about the making of a Louis Vuitton bag. It was very technical. I didn't like it. I prefer to fondle the finished product. I never tire of that. There are some women who do not fondle, smell, or love Italian leather. They carry the same piece for years. They are as faithful to their handbag as they are to their men.

... But then there is me, faithful to my man, yet always drawn to that sweet Kate Spade clutch, sitting on a shelf like a kitten in a pet shop. "Take me home," it whispers, and my knees go weak.

A SELECTION OF COMMENTS FROM LESLIE'S EBAY BUYERS:

"What will you take to end this auction early? The bag is already in my heart."

"I am sorry for the delay in bidding. I had a baby last week and have been out of touch."

"I won the Gucci bag. You were kind enough to send it to my girlfriend. She dresses up every day and is a busy gal. It opened her eyes to the fact that you can get things gently used. I thank you so very much and will be looking forward to size 12 men's shoes. You opened a new can of ideas in my office. From your new friend, Kenneth."

"You have a lovely selection of items. You live a charmed life if in fact these splendid things were culled from various family closets."

"I am glad I won this bag with the horses on it. These are not just horses. If you look closer, you will see how happy they are. Maybe they are male and female or just good friends. Look at the eyes and you can see how excited they are. I wish I was them, to have that moment."

"Can you tell me if this bag can hold everything a woman can hold?"

"My beautiful bag arrived today and I love it. I know it was hard for you to sell this wonderful bag, but take comfort in knowing it has a wonderful, appreciative home."

"Please hold the mauve bag until I win the black boots. They need me."

"You are helping put together a wardrobe for a successful comedian on the brink of really making it big. Not me, by the way. I am only kind of funny."

"I like this bag a lot. Would you be kind enough to wait for payment for three weeks when I get my social security check?"

"I was wondering if I bought more than one item you could combine shipping? I am trying to justify shopping. I need nothing, but want much."

WHO'S TALKING … Leslie Beatus is a retired art teacher. She presently has an eBay business selling high-end and designer accessories and clothing. She is devoted to reading, Pilates, and chocolate.

2: LOST LOVE FOUND
MARJ, 64

I ALWAYS IMAGINED MY LIFE IN A CERTAIN WAY. FINDING A SPECIAL someone to share my life with, having children, and settling down in a comfortable environment to raise my family.

But it didn't work out that way.

I got married when I was 34, after dating for a few years. I wanted to be a mother and this was the time to get married and have children. It was not the happiest of marriages, but being a mother was by far the happiest time of my life.

My children were born when I was 35, 38, and 40, respectively, and because of my age, I had to undergo an amniocentesis which would show any abnormalities and also reveal the gender. Thank goodness they were all healthy. I decided to let the doctor tell me whether I was carrying a boy or girl but kept that knowledge to myself. It was my special time and I reveled in 'my' mommy quiet time, talking to my future sons and daughter.

My marriage disintegrated going into its sixth year. I was nursing a six-month-old son, my daughter was two years old, and my oldest son was five when my husband decided it was time to have a girlfriend.

I didn't know at the time that it started, but things were not adding up and after some investigating, I found out what was going on. I told him that if he didn't end his relationship with his girlfriend, he would be a divorced man.....he didn't.....and he is! Honestly, he wasn't around very much and not involved in our children's lives, so although it was difficult financially, life went on with little disruption.

By the time my children were ready to be in school, I needed to find a job. I began working in the public school system which enabled me to be with my own children after school and not enroll them in a daycare facility.

Being surrounded with children has been both gratifying and challenging. It certainly keeps me young at heart. I am still employed in the same school system and can't imagine a better place to be than to be interacting with young people.

I got divorced when the children were young, and I take pride in having raised these wonderful young people all by myself. It wasn't easy, but we all got through it, with a lot of humor thrown in! I have always had a great sense of humor. I enjoy life, even when thrown into not too pleasant circumstances. Having children does that for you.

I remember the weekend that the court told us that we had to vacate our home. My ex-husband hadn't paid the mortgage. We had a large house and, as you can imagine, lots and lots of rooms to pack up. Our belongings were to be stored by friends and family and in a local storage facility. We borrowed a truck from a friend who owned an ice company to haul our belongings. A rickety, dilapidated, open-backed truck. I gladly accepted the help.

We had to drive the truck on the back roads as it wasn't fit to travel on the highway! After loading the truck, as we did many times over the weekend, we all piled into the cab. We made up lyrics to familiar tunes and laughed 'til our bellies hurt!

My children and I have developed a close bond and enjoy open communication. We have family meetings, sitting around discussing any concerns. I usually ask them for solutions to any family problems so that they all feel involved. I was so very proud of them, the way they handled themselves and were so considerate of one another's feelings.

They are all so very special to me in their own ways. Once in a while one of them will ask me, "Who is your favorite?" and I'll say," Stephen, you are my favorite as my first born; Elizabeth, you are my favorite as my only girl; Andrew, you are my favorite as my last born." That works.

I put my personal life on hold. I did see that other divorced friends had moved on and thought nothing of introducing their children to their 'dates'. This prompted my oldest son to comment, "How could So-and-so see another man when she has kids?!"

My children did not encourage me to see anyone new because I truly feel that I gave the impression that I was happy just the way things were.

My life was full, but at times I felt lonely for male companionship. There were occasions when I was "fixed up" with a friend's friend or tried a dating service. My children never knew of this as I felt that only if someone were to be worthy of a real relationship would I introduce him to them. They did meet two men I dated.

The last one was a result of Match.com. I had visited the site every so often, but didn't find anyone of interest until I was contacted by a former teacher of mine from high school.

I remembered him as a great teacher and a soft-spoken man. I responded to him and we agreed to meet. He was still a handsome man and a gentleman. We enjoyed each other's company. He traveled a great deal and asked if I had somewhere I would like to visit. I did.

He made an offer to take me to Italy which had been a dream of mine. He insisted on paying our way using his mileage and time-share options, so the cost would be minimal. I was excited at the prospect, but intended to pay my share. Time went by and he seemed to remember things differently and I began to realize that although he had good intentions, he was a bit cloudy on conversations that had recently taken place. He was a kind man, but not one that I could depend on. I relied on my judgment and survivor impulses, and the relationship ended.

As the years came and went, I began to be resolved that this was the way it would be. I didn't have any expectations for myself; I accepted my fate. Who exactly was I kidding? I do enjoy good relationships with my children and a few close friends. I am not at a loss to have something to do. I am content with myself and can find a million and one things to do with my time.

That being said, I did feel that there was someone out there for me. I needed someone who could share the good and bad, the ups and downs. Those close to me have heard me say through the years that I felt as though there was a piece missing. Like a jigsaw puzzle … not complete with a piece missing. I could never shake the feeling. Would I ever find true love, or I should say love lost? However, I quit looking at the dating sites, believing if it was going to be, it would be.

Approaching 63, I was a little apprehensive as I had lost my dad at 63. He was a wonderful man and my hero. He had been my rock. I had only seen him ill one time—when he had an operation to unblock his carotid artery. That was a very scary time for my family. But then he was diagnosed with cancer and three weeks before he died, he suffered a stroke. Unlike me, he smoked all of his life and enjoyed a scotch each evening after work. But he bowled and played golf and worked tirelessly each weekend taking care of chores and yard work. I had always thought of him as a healthy man, but a long life was not in store for him.

My hope is to be around for a long, long time. My life is good, I exercise and keep active. I take care of myself. I dream of my children having children and me being around to enjoy them. I didn't want to die at 63.

Little did I know what my 63rd year had in store for me and that it would be my happiest by far. In June, I received a card in the mail. I was perplexed as there was no occasion for me to expect a greeting card, and I didn't recognize the handwriting. I opened it, not thinking anything about it.

A picture was enclosed.

The picture was of an old boyfriend and me from one of our many trips to Cape Cod—and one of my favorite photos. He said that he had thought about me over the years and wanted to get together. He hoped that I was well. He hoped that I would consider seeing him, and he left his telephone number.

My son, Andrew, said I reacted like a giddy schoolgirl. I was so excited. My heart was pounding in my chest at the mere thought of him. What would this bring? Racing through my head were so many questions and scenarios. Why in the world, after all these years, did he want to contact me? I couldn't begin to imagine that it would be anything other than a hello, although my imagination was running wild.

My thoughts went back to another time, a lifetime ago …

We fell in love when we were both in our 20's, almost 40 years ago. His sister, Ann, and I were friends, which was how we initially met. I would visit Ann and she introduced me to her younger brother, John. Here was a gorgeous Italian with dark hair and soulful dark eyes. Eyes that I seemed to get lost in. I loved his mustache. He was a proper gentleman. I was smitten right from the start. He was so kind and wanted to please me at every turn. We were together for over two years and were very serious about each other. We had a great relationship and I can't think of one thing that I didn't like/love about him. We were compatible in so many ways and comfortable with each other.

We spent a great deal of time together. We enjoyed going out to restaurants and spending time either at his parents' home or mine. We also took trips to Cape Cod and Rhode Island; we loved the beach. We were getting closer and closer to making a commitment but I made a fateful decision that haunted me for years. Because he was four and a half years younger, I thought he wasn't ready to settle down for a long-term relationship. Perhaps it was me, but I wanted to be absolutely sure that this relationship would always be.

He remembers coming to my parents' home to see me. I was sick in bed. During that visit I explained to him that I wanted to break up. I actually told him to "sow his wild oats!" I was so in love with this guy, but had to let him go.

I was devastated, but I had convinced myself that I had done the right thing. I gave him my heart.

Many, many times I thought about him, hoping he would return. Unfortunately, my plan had backfired. And I waited. My "plan" backfired.

As time went on, life went on. I received a Christmas card from him the next year and foolishly I didn't respond. I can't for the life of me understand why I didn't. Perhaps being stubborn and thinking, 'Why didn't he call?' 'Why didn't he come to see me?' 'Why did it take him so long?'

I eventually married, seven years later, and then divorced. I still had a gnawing feeling about John, but my children were my life and I poured all my love and devotion into them.

Then I got that card.

I texted him saying that I had thought about him, too, from time to time, and that I hoped life had been good to him.

If 10:00 was not too late, he texted, he would call me that night. He worked the third shift, which explained the lateness of the call.

I waited for his call with such excitement, and it was wonderful to hear the familiar voice on the other end. When asked, I told him that I was divorced and that I wasn't seeing anyone. He told me that he was single again, too. And he had three children, two girls and a boy.

Would I like to meet? With absolutely no hesitation, I said yes!

We sent each other current pictures of ourselves and my heart jumped when I saw his. His eyes melted my heart, the same eyes that saw my soul all those years ago. He had grayed, but was still very handsome. I am a redhead and my hair is still its natural color, so except for the added laugh-lines here and there, I hadn't changed all that much.

The anticipation of seeing each other again, wondering if he would like what he saw when he looked at me, was excruciating. I have never been known to be patient, so I was very edgy waiting for the time to go by. I could hardly wait to see him again.

Looking through old boxes in the attic, I came across a photo album with so many pictures of us. Meant to be?! There was a reason that I held onto those photos after all these years. And I was about to find out what that reason was.

We arrived at the diner at just the same time, and as I got out of my car, I glanced in his direction and my heart jumped. We greeted each other with a kiss and then another. There was instant chemistry. I could feel my heart pumping as if it was going to jump out of my chest.

He told me over breakfast that he had never stopped loving me. I broke his heart all those years ago. Although I thought we communicated well then, so much was misunderstood.

We discussed why I felt it necessary for him to go off on his own. I explained that I had wanted him to be sure that he truly wanted our relationship. I listened to him tell me about his life since we had last seen each other. He had married shortly after sending me the Christmas card, thinking I wanted nothing to do with him. I quickly realized that we both really didn't lead happy lives.

Although I was excited about the feelings that were resurfacing, I held back. After breakfast, we went to a local nature museum and walked around holding hands and talking about our lives. Every so often, we would stop and kiss and I would melt. I felt as though I was in a dream and didn't want anyone to pinch me.

Our relationship is growing stronger and stronger. My children have all taken to him and are all so pleased that I am in a loving relationship. They gravitate toward John. If they have questions or issues in their lives, they talk to him. It's a confirmation of what a welcome presence he has become in our family.

We are talking about marriage and spending the rest of our lives together and I can't imagine my life any other way than spending it with him. We have discussed our retirement and where we would like to live. It is so exciting to contemplate sharing the rest of my life with him. I am a very independent woman as he is a self-sufficient man, and it works wonderfully for us. We complement each other. My life is richer because of him. I have a man who listens to me and pays attention. We have a history together and getting to know each other all over again is so easy and comfortable because the basic "us" is still there.

I am head over heels in love; and for the first time since we were together all those years ago, I feel love and loved. Each and every time I hear his voice or see his face, I am thrilled beyond anything I could have imagined.

This is a dream come true for both of us.

WHO'S TALKING … *Marj Lazzaro is employed in the public school system. When she's not putting out fires and holding down the fort, she enjoys hiking and running. Besides building a life with the love of her life, she spends her time with her best friends: her children.*

3: ROCK-AND-ROLL ROMANCE
MYRA, 68

IT'S HEARTBREAKING TO SEE PARENTS SLOWLY AGE AND BECOME sick and helpless, unable to care for themselves. They must be cared for as if they are children. It's a time when parents and their children switch places. It's only reasonable that we care for them as they cared for us when we were helpless.

But this is not something I have ever experienced. At 86 years old, my Mom and Daddy are still in the prime of their lives. We travel together just as we did when I was six years old. The backseat belonged to me. Just give me a coloring book and a new box of crayons and I was happy; except now, I bring a novel and read myself sleepy. Mom always tosses in a pillow and a quilt for me. With Daddy at the wheel, I feel as safe as a baby wrapped in her momma's warm, cuddly arms.

The story of J.W. (Jay) Brown and Lois Neal and how they met and fell in love reads like a Hollywood love story. It goes beyond love at first sight; it is two souls whose destiny was to be together. Little did they know, and little did they care, where life would take them as long as they were together. Nothing would ever be more important than their love for each other. It almost makes you believe they had been together in another lifetime; they were so made for each other.

As their first-born child, I've heard the story so many times I can recite it in my sleep.

It was a chance meeting. J.W. played stand-up bass in his

family band, "The Mississippi Hotshots." The band was comprised of his mother, Jane, who played the piano, one brother, Otis, who played fiddle and sang, the other brother, Charles, who played mandolin, and a family friend, Claudie, who played steel guitar. That night they were appearing at the American Legion Hall in the small country town of Winnsboro, Louisiana, which wasn't too far from the Brown's hometown. The price of admission: 50 cents. While on stage, J.W. spotted a dark-eyed beauty as she was swept across the dance floor by her dancing partner.

J.W. swears that at the very moment he saw Lois, he said to himself, "Now there's the girl for me." Later on that week, while driving, J.W. saw the guy that was dancing with "his girl" and tried his best to run him off the road. I am certain this poor guy had no idea why somebody was acting like a deranged madman trying to run him into the ditch!

"After all," I said to Daddy years later, "that was his girl, *not* yours. He should have run *you* off the road." Daddy would just laugh and snicker at me. He had found his "true love" and "it was just a matter of time." He had a lot of tricks up his sleeve and was quite willing to use them all.

Lois' Papa wasn't as fond of J.W. as J.W. would have liked. However, Jay didn't think running him off the road would be the best way to handle him. He quickly learned that everybody in town knew that if you were going to be anywhere near Lois, first you were going to have to be approved by her Papa Neal.

But J.W. was an entertainer, so he figured he'd "entertain Papa" with no problem.

Jay decided a phone call would be a good way to start. He reached for the phone and confidently dialed the number.

Lois answered, with Papa in hearing distance, watching her every move over the rim of his glasses. J.W.'s first comment was, "Ask your Papa, would he like to go fishing?"

Lois repeated it word-for-word: "Papa, J.W. said, 'Would you like to go fishing?'"

"Hell no," Papa replied. "I don't want to go fishing."

"'Hell no,'" Lois repeats from her Papa back to J.W. "He doesn't want to go fishing."

Jay comes back with, "Well, ask him if he would like to go huntin'."

Once again Lois repeats the message. "Papa, J.W. said, 'Would you like to go huntin'?'"

Once again, her Papa said, "Hell no! I don't want to go huntin'."

Not to be defeated, J.W. gives it one more shot. "Lois," he says, "ask your Papa what he likes to do."

"Papa," said Lois, in a little sing-song voice. "J.W. said for me to ask you, 'What do you like to do?'"

Papa pushed his glasses back on to his nose, looked straight at his daughter, and said, "Tell him I like to stay home and mind my own damn business."

This wasn't going exactly as J.W. had planned and he was caught a little off guard. Without hesitating, he said, "Well, tell your Papa I said 'go to hell.'"

Lois did as she was told. "Papa, J.W. said, 'Go to hell.'"

The next sound J.W. heard was a long-winded dial tone.

J.W. thought to himself, "There's more than one way to skin a cat."

The next day Lois came home from school, and turning the corner she spotted her Papa and J.W. Brown sitting on the front porch laughing, talking, and drinking beer. For fear of "what was going on" she sprinted up the porch steps two at the time and flew into the house, letting the screen door slam behind her.

J.W. had figured that if hunting and fishing don't appeal to a man, he's got to have something he enjoys. Turned out half a dozen cold bottles of beer did it. Especially if a man's wife won't let him drink in the house. "Porch beer" has got to hit the spot. Just how J.W. was able to hit the nail on the head is anybody's guess.

"Young lady," Papa called out, "where's your manners? Don't you see you've got company?"

Lois had visions of her mother, Roxie, marching onto the porch and confiscating their beer, so Lois approached her mother cautiously. Roxie looked up at her daughter and said, "Sweetie, your daddy and J.W. are on the porch. Why don't you go out and join them?"

Confused, Lois thought to herself, "There's something going on around here!!"

What was going on was that J.W. Brown had been welcomed with open arms from that first night on the porch with Papa. And Roxie loved J.W. almost as much as she loved her own kids. Instead of losing a daughter they had gained a son. As long as Oscar and Roxie Neal lived, there was never a cross word between them and their son-in-law.

It was a beautiful September day in 1943 when Papa proudly gave the bride away. Lois wore a beautiful blue dress bought by her Papa for this special occasion. The groom wore a white dress shirt and a pair of dress pants, his tie in his pocket.

They were both 16 years old. They were considered to be "kids," and maybe they were, but they were also certain, absolutely certain, of what they wanted from life. They each knew this was the love of their life and they reached out with both hands and embraced it with everything they had and gave it their all. They were in love with each other, and still are.

Now wouldn't you think that when their daughter got married a little young that they would have remembered this? ... but nooooo. For their daughter to marry at 13 to a man 22 didn't set too well with either one of them. There were no warm fuzzy feelings here. I was their only daughter and too young. It made my Daddy fighting mad that his own cousin had talked me into running away with him to get married, and we had to keep distance between the two men. My new husband's way of resolving this was to get to the airport and catch the first plane leaving town, no matter where it was going.

Somehow, I believe it was meant to be. It was the right thing for me and for my family. It gave my parents two beautiful grandchildren. None of us can see the future. It's unseen; it's unknown.

You will never know where the path "not" taken would have led you. You make a judgment call with your gut, your heart, and your head, and then pray to God it's the right decision. Give it your all, give it your best, and see it through.

For those of you who may not know, I was the 13-year-old child bride that was married to Jerry Lee Lewis in 1957. It created a huge scandal in the show business world. But lots of girls got married young in the South at that time. What can I say? We just grow up faster.

Jerry and I were married for thirteen years and were happy for the biggest part of the time. We had two precious children, a son, Steve, and a daughter, Phoebe. We lost our three-year-old son in 1962. Today Phoebe is a happily married businesswoman in Virginia.

So much happened during those years that I could write a book about it. Oh wait ... I did, almost 30 years ago. It was entitled *Great Balls of Fire*. Hollywood turned it into a movie with Dennis Quaid and Wynona Rider.

But now I'm writing about my parents' story, not mine. I wish every kid could have parents who love each other as much as mine. That love brushed off on my younger brother, Rusty, and me. There was never any doubt in our house that we were safe and secure and adored.

However, I did have a hard time with one decision that Daddy made.

In 1950, a Memphis newspaper was inadvertently tossed on my grandmother's porch. She asked J.W. if he would like to see it. He immediately went to the want ads and saw where Memphis Light Gas and Water was hiring linemen.

The very next day he made the five-hour drive to Memphis, parked in front of the building of MLG&W, walked in, and applied for the job. He was hired on the spot after they learned he had six years of experience. We have yet to find out who left the newspaper on my grandmother's porch, but it changed everything.

After working a week, J.W. returned to Winnsboro, where we lived, and packed up his little family, my mom and me. Everybody said their goodbyes and we headed north on Highway 61 to Memphis. But at five years old, all I knew was that Memphis was 250 miles away from MaMaw. I cried the entire 250 miles. I wanted to stay with my MaMaw. "I hate Memphis," I said, "and I don't want to go!" I cried to no avail.

My daddy loves to tell about how after being hired he walked to his car, paused, and looked west down the street thinking to himself, "This is home now, this is home." He was looking forward to a new start, a new job, and working for a company where he could someday retire. Yes, this will be a good move, he thought.

Fate had another plan. Memphis Light Gas &Water put him to work, then put him in the hospital, and then put him in show business.

You see, the offices of MLG&W were located on Union Avenue. A block down across the street was a small recording studio owned by Sam C. Phillips. It had opened January, 1950, and was known as "Memphis Recording Services." One day that sign would come down and in its place would be a round yellow sign that read "Sun Records."

My daddy had no idea how important that sign would become in his life.

It all started on a day like any other work day working the lines with MLG&W. By then he'd lost friends on the job, either because their luck ran out or they were careless. He was never careless, but his luck was about to run out anyway. The crew was replacing worn-out wires on a 60-foot pole when a wire slipped out of its cover, and like an angered serpent, it struck. First it set Daddy's shirt on fire; on the second strike it hit his left arm as he tried to fight it off, with the voltage coming out of the palm of his left hand and left foot. Unbelievably, the current never crossed his body. If it had, he would have been killed instantly.

J.W. remembers passing out from the pain and the next sound he heard was Lois screaming as she entered the ER. She saw his boots outside the door and thought that meant he had died, seeing that a dead man's boots are always removed.

The company gave J.W. a year to heal, with full pay, with an offer of a desk job as well. But he knew he was done. At age 30, he had climbed his last pole.

So he had to find work! The only other thing he knew how to do was play bass in a band. In fact, musical talent runs in his family. Jerry Lee Lewis is my daddy's first cousin, along with half the state of Louisiana. There's Jimmy Lee Swaggart and Mickey Gilley and so many other cousins you will never hear of. They are plain folks, but most are talented, good people, and many are preachers. The Lewis' are either real good or real bad.

Daddy knew that Jerry Lee had a reputation for being bad at some things, but he was real good at music. So in 1956, Daddy made a trip to Natchez in order to find Jerry. He knew Jerry was working at a club called The Hilltop. J.W. wanted Jerry to come to Memphis so J.W. could take him to meet with that Sam Phillips who owned that recording studio down the street from MLG&W. Regardless of how long it took, Jerry would be our house guest. Daddy thought that if only he could audition one time, just once, the rest would be history.

So it's really my own Daddy's fault that I even met Jerry. Of course he had no idea his cousin, already divorced once and presently married for the second time at age twenty-two, would woo a kid like me.

You might be wondering what my mom thought of this flamboyant houseguest and the desire to make a record and the dream of becoming a famous band. Well, my mom, as I've mentioned, was in love with J.W. Brown. Whatever made him happy made her happy, too. She trusts his judgment and has always supported anything he does.

Daddy arranged an audition with Sam Phillips and the rest is history. Jerry Lee, along with his new band, which included my dad, became an international sensation. My daddy also served as the group's business manager and driver.

Their new celebrity meant that Daddy had to travel all the time and we missed him terribly at home. But it was thrilling to see him on the Steve Allen Show on TV!

I've always believed that my mom could easily have been a celebrity, too. In 1959 my parents took Daddy's cousin, Mickey Gilley, to California to introduce him to the powers that be, like record producers, booking agents, and talent scouts. Funny now, but not necessarily funny then to the men, was that my mom got more attention than either of the guys. At age 29, Lois Brown was a beautiful woman in the prime of her life. She had dark brown eyes, an olive complexion, jet black hair, and a figure that reminded people of Marilyn Monroe. When she opened her mouth to speak, her Southern drawl was like sweet honey dripping all over the place. The booking agents offered her a contract on the spot—to work in movies. They would create an image for her as a female "Andy Griffin." Andy had a joke record out called, "What it was, was football," which was a big hit. They wanted a female version of that for her.

Her response was, "Gentlemen, I thank you but I have a five-year-old son at home. Actually, I have two children at home, including that big one over there," she said, pointing to my dad. She had no interest in the possibility of being a movie star.

I was out of the house by then, already married, so she didn't include me. At that very time I was living with Jerry Lee's parents while he toured, waiting for our first child to be born. I would always put on a brave face when I talked to my parents on the phone, not wanting them to know that I was terrified of giving birth. I figured I would probably die. If Mom and Daddy would have known how scared I was, I knew they would never have gone on their business trip. So I never told them until years later. After I'd survived.

Another interesting story about my mom in California is that once they were stopped at a red light and a man in the car beside them hollered at her that she should be in movies. Even strangers saw it! But she didn't want to do that. She liked her family life just as it was.

J.W. played bass in Jerry Lee's band for years, so long that eventually my brother, Rusty, grew up and played drums for him, too, from the time he was about 10 years old. When the band was no longer popular and Daddy and Rusty retired from that, Daddy started his own business as an independent contractor building roads and highways. He loved this work so much that he brought in Rusty as a partner and they have worked side-by-side for the last twenty-five years.

Recently Mom and Daddy wanted Rusty and me to take a road trip with them to visit family all throughout Louisiana, Mississippi, and Tennessee. Neither Rusty nor I relished the idea of traveling 1,600 miles like that, but how could we say no? We know that at their age it could be our last such adventure together and the last time they would see some of those relatives. But my brother and I laugh at that idea, seeing that we can hardly keep up with our parents. They're always doing something and going somewhere, mostly to the casinos in Biloxi. We made the trip, and Rusty and I didn't even fight once like kids do on vacation with their parents.

One thing that trip did was remind us of the love our parents still have for each other. That really is miraculous. Rusty is recently divorced—that's a whole story in and of itself—and I've been happily married to my husband, Richard, for twenty-eight years. But my brother and I can't live long enough to make it to seventy years with a spouse like our parents have done.

To this day my mom still combs her hair and puts on lipstick every time her husband is about to come home. And to this day, his eyes light up every time he walks in that door and sees his wife.

I suspect that in their minds they are still sixteen years old. She's still that beautiful, dark-haired girl, and he's that tall, handsome boy. They love each other today every bit as much as they did back then, and more.

Theirs is a rare rock-and-roll romance.

WHO'S TALKING ... *Myra Lewis Williams holds the distinction of having been kicked out of England when she was 14, because the Brits objected to her marriage to her second-cousin, Jerry Lee Lewis. Now she likes quiet evenings at home with her husband, Richard, and their dogs.*

4: A SNITCH FALLS IN LOVE
GILDA, 97

I WORKED FOR A COMPANY CALLED AMERICAN CHAIN IN BRIDGE-port, CT, before World War II, making $26 a week, which was pretty good money in those days. And I could walk to work.

Those were the days of tire chains, before snow tires. The work was steady.

The boss saw that I was pretty small to be working on the machine I was assigned to, and so he put me to work on an assembly line, putting labels on razor blades. It wasn't hard work; it was a nice clean job.

I worked on a bench with five other girls, and we all got along pretty good. I liked my job, but one day, the boss came to me and said he wanted to talk to me after work. He wanted to talk to me privately.

"I like the way you work," he told me. "You can watch the other girls." He wanted to be sure that each girl was doing the same amount of work, producing the same number of trays at the end of the workday.

I didn't want to be a boss. But I didn't have a choice in the matter, so I became a sort of supervisor—with no extra pay, of course.

As a matter of course, there was a discrepancy in the number of trays the girls produced: a girl named Viola used to hide a prepared tray at the end of the day so that she could be ahead of the other girls every morning. That way, she turned in one more tray of razor blades at the end of every workday.

I had to tell on her.

I felt bad having to get anybody in trouble, but she had done something which made the rest of us look bad. She was wrong.

But I still felt like a snitch.

I liked my job, and I had a good social life, too. I got a lot of reward and satisfaction from a young people's group that produced minstrels. I loved singing.

It's no coincidence that I loved the song by Fats Waller *Who's Afraid of Love?* When I sang it onstage, my friend, Eddie Watts, played the piano. When I finished, he just shook his head and said, "You're the best." That meant a lot to me, because you know you've done your best when it sounds good to you and it sounds good to your piano player.

And I was certainly not afraid of love. I met a handsome young man, and right away he said, "I like you very much. Maybe one day I could ask you to be my wife."

It didn't take long. We fell in love. He was handsome and charming; I was smitten, and I said yes.

A group of us got together at a friend's house to celebrate my engagement. One of my girlfriends brought out drinks for us all, a kind of fizzy, lemony thing, and I remember saying, "That's very tasty." So I had another one—and another. That was my first introduction to a Tom Collins. And my first hangover.

As was normal back then, I quit my job to be a wife. I quit just a week before the wedding. Our first daughter was born that year. Looking back, I kind of wish we had waited. I don't think we'd had enough fun with each other by ourselves yet. We waited eight years before our second daughter was born. And ten years before our third daughter came along.

We had a good marriage and a fine family with our three girls. Now more than ever I am grateful for them, especially now that David is gone. I don't mind so much getting older. I am happy thinking about my grandchildren and their achievements. I wonder how the rest of their lives are going to turn out.

If I had any advice for them—well, for anyone, actually—it would be to think things through before you say no. Do what you like; don't say no so quickly.

I have always tried to do that, but if I had thought things through a little more carefully, I probably would have pursued a career in singing. Neither my parents nor my husband encouraged that. They saw no harm in my singing for my own enjoyment, but not as a profession.

I started to study to become a nurse, but at that time, it was felt that a woman's purpose was to be wife and mother. Since David earned enough to support our little family, we really didn't need for me to go back to work. Motherhood would be my new career.

It's different for women today. They have a lot more say about their own lives, so they have the freedom to make their own choices. So I say, don't say no without thinking the situation through carefully.

And don't be afraid of love.

WHO'S TALKING ... *Gilda Edith Soderholm is spending her golden years in a small town in Connecticut where she reads avidly and keeps up with news of her grandchildren. Gilda likes to wear silly hats.*

5: THE OLD BOYFRIEND TOUR
SHERRI, 66

MOM ALWAYS WANTED ME TO MARRY DAVID MONTROSS. I NEVER had the heart to tell her that David never asked me to marry him, so she believed—for 30 years—that I didn't marry him out of spite because she liked him. Just like now, she believes that I am single because I am deliberately dating the wrong men.

I live in New York now, and Mom lives in Michigan, but I was home on a visit recently and ran into David on the street. He's grey and thinner, but he's the same lanky, earnest jokester with a high-pitched laugh; and as far as I know, he still doesn't want to marry me. When I told mom I saw him, she gave me the same old speech. This made me fall into a funk, thinking I will probably grow old alone and get eccentric and eat nothing but cereal and cold soup out of the can while waiting for the mailman to show up because he will be the highlight of my day.

On the plane ride back to New York, I got to thinking about the guys I almost married, and the guys I should have married (according to mother), and the guys I wished I had married, and the one I did marry, and by the time I landed at LaGuardia, I had successfully thrown myself into a black hole of nostalgia. I had singled out a few very special guys, and the more I thought about them, the more poignant their memories became. My eyes glassed over and I felt all gooey inside, and I wondered what had become of them.

Days later, I had my teeth cleaned.

I asked my dental hygienist, who is about my age, if she had any old boyfriends she gets all gooey thinking about. She got glassy-eyed, holding her weapons just above my upper lip for a minute. "Oh yeah," she said after a while. "One that really broke my heart." She seemed to go away on a little mind-vacation. "I wonder where he is now."

We shared that little moment, the suction tube in my mouth making its slurping sound and her heart thumping, before she snapped back into action and jabbed a little silver tool into my gums. "I could look him up on the Internet, I suppose."

That catapulted me into action. I raced home and fired up the computer and, within seconds, I had found George.

GEORGE

I developed a crush on George when I was 12. He was 15, the dishwasher at sleep-away camp. He was tan and wiry, with big white teeth and screwy-looking blond hair that was unmanageably curly. The camp was on the lake, and all the buildings never got quite dry so they smelled like wet sand and tree sap all summer. My girlfriends and I used to hide out behind the mess hall in a little stand of evergreens, waiting for the screen door to slam open so I could get a peek at George. I was smitten.

I saw him two years later at a YMCA dance, but he was with another girl, and besides I was in junior high, and he was in high school—too big a gap at that age. I grew up, though, and when we both ended up working at the same store on main street three years later, I was old enough to flirt with. He didn't take me seriously until the summer after my senior year.

That year was a dreadful year. My high school boyfriend, Burt, whom I intended to marry, was drafted. My dad lost his job. Then his father died of emphysema, and my uncle, his brother, drowned. My mother, in a desperate attempt to make the family normal, came into the store one Saturday afternoon and asked George if he would please take me to my senior prom. She didn't want me to miss it. She didn't want to miss it.

This was to be my undoing, because I fell in love with George—and he with me, I'd like to think—so by the time Burt came back from his tour in Germany, I had given my heart away. George went off to college in Iowa. I went to college in Michigan, and Burt volunteered for duty in Vietnam. It was a year of dread and guilt.

George may have loved me, but when I called him long-distance from a payphone in my dorm and asked him if he did, he said, "I keep running from you, don't I?" That wasn't the same as loving me back, but I kept chasing him and sometimes he let me catch him for the next five or six years until I finally lost track of him.

The Internet found him in California. He was thrilled to hear from me. He recognized my voice after 30 years. He didn't seem at all surprised to hear from me, and said of course I should come visit, if I was out his way. How long could I stay? He tumbled over his own sentences like an excited puppy. Couldn't wait to see me. He was single again; I could stay with him. When was I coming? He'd pick me up at the airport.

When I hung up, I only had a fleeting thought of what he might look like, or what he was doing, or anything that smacked of reality. The Internet was like a time capsule for me. I looked up a couple of girls I hated back in grade school, then I looked up myself, and then I searched for the handsome, bearded screen-writer/waiter I fell in love with when I moved to New York City after college.

HAIM

Haim was my idol. When I met him, we were both in our 20's and he lived in a tiny apartment on Manhattan's upper west side with a ratty old manual typewriter and a stack of books and a refrigerator filled with wonderful things like French cheeses and marmalades and cauliflower. He'd read everything I'd read and more. He quoted philosophers and songwriters and current films, and he strode through rooms like a bear.

I was in awe of him. I shrank in his presence. When he criticized my writing, I went back and edited and rewrote and wrote all over from scratch. When he told me I wasn't living honestly—that what I was doing didn't match with what I was—I went home and examined my life.

I was teaching school in the suburbs and shopping at department stores and eating at fancy restaurants. I wore little black dresses and pearls and sensible heels and voted Republican, absolutely forgetting I used to be a hippie. He said I should quit my job and refuse to subjugate myself to a government that sent young men to senseless wars and didn't support the arts. I should be writing. There wasn't any war to protest anymore, I told him, and I don't have anything to write about. But I knew he was right. When he left for California, I didn't blame him.

My computer told me that he still lived there.

Wow.

I could go on a tour, like a rock band. I'd start in Los Angeles and see George, and then I'd motor up to Pacific Palisades and see Haim, then I'd fly back to my hometown.

That's when reality poked its ugly head up.

BURT

In a small town, you marry early. I was 16 when I met Burt and 17 when I agreed to marry him. I was starting to put together a hope chest when the Vietnam War broke out.

It's funny, but I don't remember much about loving Burt. I know we were happy and I was content. I was ready to spend the rest of my life with him, happily ricocheting off the in-laws and raising babies. We were very much in love, but we were church-going kids from church-going families, and we were waiting until we were married to make love to each other.

Then our friends started to get drafted. One by one, we saw them off at the bus station with their duffel bags and brave faces until I couldn't go anymore. It ripped me up. I wrote an anti-war article for the high school newspaper, but our advisor wouldn't print it. That was before Burt got his notice.

Although I pleaded with him to marry me before he went, or run off with me and live in Canada, he asked me to wait for him. The night before he left, I threw myself into my dad's arms and sobbed. I was heartbroken, and I was ashamed because Burt was the one going to war, and I was the coward.

That was the year George took me to my senior prom, and dad lost his job and his father, both in the same month. That was also the summer that Daddy's brother drowned and George's friend, Chris, brought the body in with a long, metal hook. George came to the funeral and sat next to my father. They were both sitting with their elbows on their knees and their hands dangling empty when I walked in. I remember thinking that love was the strongest emotion I had ever known. I remember, too, that it was the first time I realized you could love more than one man and that there was more than one kind of grief.

I went off to college. I majored in theatre and pranced around on stage, and fell in love with several boys. I made love to them, and eventually to George while Burt was away in Germany, and finally, when he came home on leave, I told him that I couldn't see him anymore. I didn't tell him that the reason was because I was ashamed that I wasn't the same sweet hometown girl that he had left behind. I just told him, "You don't know me anymore."

The next night, the night after I told him, he brought a box and left it on my porch. Inside the box was every letter I had written him, every Valentine, Christmas card, every photograph. I suppose he meant for me to look at them and remember my promise, but instead, I took them out in back of the house and burned them before I went back to college. Burt volunteered for duty in Vietnam.

This is what I remember a whole lot more vividly than loving him. That awful memory wiped just about everything else out.

I knew that Burt came home from Vietnam intact, physically anyway. He married another hometown girl, moved away, came back, and moved away again. Perhaps they've come back by now, I thought, and the computer told me they had, but I didn't call. I had one more I wanted to find—the man I actually did marry.

RICHARD

I met Richard in college and talked him into moving to New York right after graduation. I don't quite know why, but I was very unhappy after we got married. Richard seemed to settle right in, while I seemed to fall apart. I rocketed around trying everything to see if I could make the pieces inside me fit. I learned to play tennis because he played tennis, I went back to college and studied history because he had been a history major, I learned to cook, I lost weight, I gained weight, I painted murals on the basement wall, planted gardens, and learned to crochet. But no matter what I did, I felt more and more alone, like I was locked inside a bell jar. I was invisible, too. I thought I was screaming, but nobody could hear me or see me. I guess I wasn't screaming loud enough, until I had an affair. That, everyone could hear.

I left him for the other man, who left his wife for me—and then, just desserts, I guess, the other man went back to his wife.

I didn't need the computer for this one. I hadn't seen him in more than 20 years, but I knew that he lived with his wife and daughter in a town only a few miles away. I looked him up in the phone book; way too close. Too easy. Too real. I decided I'd call him when I got back from California.

THE TOUR

Planning my trip meant I had to call Haim and Burt. George was a done deal, but last I knew, Haim and Burt were both married and their wives might not be too agreeable to an old girlfriend turning up after 20-30 years.

So I included them. "Hi. I'm going to be in town and I'd like to see you. Your wife, too, of course. I'd like to meet her."

Worked, too. Probably some cardiac arrest involved, but the women were smooth. I was ready to rock and roll by mid-summer.

This wasn't quite as easy as I make it sound. I was terrified. What would I wear? Could I lose 15 pounds in three weeks? I know I didn't have these jowls when I was in tenth grade.

I told my friends about my trip, and they got all glassy-eyed and stupid, drifted away in their minds, and went off humming old Jimi Hendrix tunes.

Everyone was jealous, and I had convinced myself that I was off on a holiday. I didn't imagine that time had stood still and no one had aged, but I still had the feeling that I was stepping off the planet where I would be dropped back into time. Old emotions and details would wash up like beach debris.

GEORGE

The gate area at LAX had its usual mess of people coming and going and waiting, and I picked out a man who looked about the age George would be. He didn't look like George, but then, none of us look the way we did 30 years ago, so I went right up to him and squinted into his face and said, "George?"

Nope. Not George.

Perhaps this wasn't such a hot idea, I thought. What if he wasn't there? What if he didn't recognize me? We could wander around LAX for hours, answering each other's pages and reporting to gate areas and walking right past each other, me dragging my luggage and George tapping middle-aged women on the shoulders and grinning at them like an idiot. Sooner or later, somebody was sure to get arrested.

But he did recognize me. He stood with his hands shoved in his pockets and rocked back a little on his heels, smiling so big, his face must have hurt. I would never have known him if he hadn't been smiling right at me. He wasn't George at all. I put my arms out for the George I loved when I was 12, and he put his arms around me. He said, "I feel like I'm hugging home."

It didn't feel that way to me. George felt different; his skin didn't smell the same. I kept staring at him because it was like George's voice coming out of a stranger's face, and I had the unsettling feeling that instead of being reunited with him, I was being unfaithful to him, as though the George I knew when I was 12 was a completely different person from the man who was taking me home with him now.

This man was solid. He worked as a sales rep for a small aeronautical engineering company. He drove a new car with a briefcase in the back seat. I tried to make conversation with this man, but I was floundering. We talked about the years that went by and what we were doing now; and we talked about common friends and our children. We even talked about his new car and how he came to buy it.

But we didn't talk about anything that mattered, really. We didn't talk about the afternoon our friend, Chris Benedict, found my uncle's body floating in the lake, or the night I called him long distance in the middle of the night. We did not talk about Vietnam, because if it hadn't been for the war, I would have married Burt, and he would never have taken me to my senior prom and we would never have fallen in love. I never, ever asked him why he kept running from me, and why, after all these years, he'd quit— and here he was, not running at all, long after it was too late.

He was proud of California. He pointed out things and explained the terrain, but he didn't look right in his car or in California. He was supposed to be blonder and tanner and have the smell of the lake in his hair. He used to have a little red TR-3 whose sides swooped down so low that if you hung your arm over the door you could touch the ground with your fingers. Now he had a black Honda Accord, smart buy, four-door. "Currant," he said, "Not black." Like a raisin.

I hated it.

He lived in a condominium complex with 16 species of tropical trees and a liver-shaped pool and a recreation area and huge parking garage that felt like it was air-conditioned. The cobblestone roads and paths sneaked in and around the gardens, and the sun was like a gold paste on everything, but I missed the wet smell of beach sand and evergreens. Seeing George in these surroundings made me homesick.

We never talked about where I would sleep. It was natural that I would sleep with George, but even making love had that lost homesickness about it, and I still felt like I was being unfaithful. He even said something about it. The second night, after we had made love, he said, "It's like you're not here." I didn't say anything, thinking maybe he would think I was asleep.

The rest of the time, we were like old married people. We read books at the pool and ate our dinner while watching a video rental. We talked about our jobs and our parents; and at the end of the three days, George said, "I had almost convinced myself that it was okay living alone." Then he took me in his arms and tucked my head under his chin where I could smell that other-man smell of him, and he said, "Why don't you just cancel your plans and stay here for the rest of your life?"

I didn't answer him, because it just wasn't the same George talking. If he had said that 28 years ago, I would have. If he was so dead set on running, we could have done it together; we could have run away in the same direction, but we missed that chance. Instead, he ran away to someplace I didn't want to live and he knew I wouldn't follow. There was nothing in the life that he had built that fit who I was now. I think he knew that, even when he said what he said. He never expected me to answer, and he didn't ask again.

HAIM

I rented a car to drive up to Pacific Palisades. Some mountains showed up about a half-hour into my ride, and the ocean rolled into view. It was late afternoon on a weekday, so the beach was nearly deserted and the sun lit up the patches of mist like runaway clouds. This was Haim's daily commute. He was a lawyer now. When I knew him, he was waiting tables and writing screenplays or hunched over his journal, wearing jeans and leather flip-flops, and drinking good wine out of jelly glasses. It was difficult to imagine him in a suit and tie.

I was early. I stopped at a florist and bought a dozen purple roses. Then I walked along the main street of the little town, looking in the windows of the shops and restaurants. I bought a book for George at a tiny bookstore that had piles of books on the floor and books in bins and magazines stacked on chairs and oversized atlases sideways on shelves. Pacific Palisades reminded me of San Francisco in the '60's. City Lights Bookstore. Golden Gate Park. Jefferson Airplane. But Pacific Palisades had the air of money about it. "Designer air," Haim used to call it when we walked past a ritzy store on Fifth Avenue. The smell of freshly folded shirts and air conditioning.

His wife met me at the door, a tiny wiry woman, a powerhouse of energy in control. I liked her right away, on top of respecting her for being so cool about my intruding. The house was bright and sparsely furnished, polished bare wood floors and straight-backed chairs. The back room opened into a garden. She put the roses on a table in the last of the afternoon sun.

When Haim rounded the corner, looking every bit the same as he did 20-some years ago, she looked over at me. "Doesn't he look great?"

He did. Beard grey at the jowls. Still striding purposefully (like a bear), but now followed by two rangy little boys who peered at me critically, and a grown daughter who shook my hand. The family was rowdy and smart.

We had a drink in the garden. The younger children came by and stared politely. The older daughter was calmly curious. But they took me in like I was family, perhaps thinking that I was, practically, because we all loved the same man.

They had made reservations at a local restaurant, and we had to get ourselves into their van. Who was going to sit where? Oh, shouldn't Sherri sit in the front, and who was going to drive? Haim opened the back door and began to scold his wife or daughter, or whoever was closest, about the trash on the floor.

He threw everything on the lawn behind him, cross with his family for messing up the car, his back to me, his voice deep with irritation. The old urge to please him burned up hot from some-place I thought was long dead, and I hurried around behind him, picking up trash, making things right, until I noticed his daughter smiling at me. She knew what I was doing, probably because she herself had done it, but she had long since learned how to handle his little tempers.

I realized that I was still unnerved by his energy. He was still my idol, and I was still abashed by his criticism, no matter how indirect. I stood up and handed a wad of crumpled tissues to his daughter who rolled her eyes, and I knew that she had decided she liked me. She knew right then, from that act of trying to please, that I had loved her father very much.

Haim told me later that the best time of our visit was after dinner at a local Starbuck's, where the boys crawled onto his lap and his wife and daughter chatted with neighborhood passers-by, and the traffic made colored light patterns in the dark. Everything smelled like flowers and coffee.

He called me after I got back home and said that the roses opened and looked more beautiful than the night I brought them; did I remember how their petals were all tight like a fist? I did remember, and I also remember that when Haim looked at me, I had to look away. I was afraid that he would see that I still felt the same, and I was afraid that I would see he didn't.

BURT

I flew to Michigan feeling a lot less like I was on holiday than I did when I left New York. This wasn't anywhere near as much fun as I thought it would be. It was more like an exercise than a vacation, and I was almost sorry I had come. I'd stirred up feelings I thought were properly settled, and I missed them. I wanted to feel like that again even if it hurt, even if I knew how it was going to turn out.

Going home wasn't going to help. It's always a shock to come home and see how things have changed. There are wide boulevards where there were tree-lined streets, the old clapboard houses with their sagging porches left naked to traffic. Shopping malls have stolen the activity from downtown merchants, and years ago, they razed the drive-in movie theatre and just left the lot empty.

No matter where you are in town, you can smell the lake. It's moody and imposing. It sends a cool breeze inland under the miserable summer heat and grinds huge blocks of river ice along the shore in the winter. The water is clear and fresh, no industrial sewage or saltwater muck. It is ice-blue or aquamarine, or sometimes navy blue or an odd shade of green just before a storm, but a Great Lake is completely different from an ocean. Just as mysterious and commanding, but sweeter. It's the only thing I really miss about my hometown, the only constant.

As kids we swam until our lips were blue and our fingers wrinkled up. It's fresh water, so we could open our eyes under water and swim around like fish or submarines. We clacked rocks together and scoured the bottom for beach glass. In the early evening, we skipped stones.

When we grew a little older, we went to the lake to meet guys or girls. Back then, there was a road that went by the beach and we staked out the best parking places so we could hang out by our cars and listen to the radio. We played cards. I learned to cheat by reading my opponent's hand reflected in his sunglasses. My first bikini came up over my belly button.

The water was ice cold, even in August. There was only one way to go in: run as fast as you could and throw yourself in before you could change your mind. It would take your breath away, but afterwards, you felt scrubbed clean and refreshed clear through to your bone marrow. The water was so clean, you could go swimming and afterwards, your hair would still smell like shampoo

We used to park there at night so we could kiss and go as far as we felt we could. Sometimes we would drag a blanket out to the sand and lie there together and make ourselves blind with "almost" doing it. In the winter, the moon lit up the huge slabs of ice that drifted in close to the shore and jammed together in huge, sharp, jagged peaks. The ice looked solid, but we all knew the lake was dangerous and nobody ever tried to walk on it.

The lake was so much a part of our lives that I specifically asked Burt and his wife Carol to meet me at a restaurant that overlooked the river at the mouth of the lake.

Burt showed up alone. He appeared as if conjured up; I didn't see him coming. Like George, I wouldn't have recognized him if he hadn't presented himself directly in front of me. He was older, of course, but so was I. I hadn't seen him since I was 19. Thirty-four years. He had a full beard, too. I remembered that his older brother had one the year Burt went off to war.

He wouldn't order, and I felt odd eating in front of him, so I didn't, either. He didn't even order a glass of water or a drink or a cup of coffee. I let my glass of wine sit.

We talked about his kids and mine, and where we'd lived, and what we'd done, and then we had to talk about those last few weeks before he went into the army. His younger brother had tangled a toy in my hair the night before he left. His mother had bought me silverware for my hope chest, and I still use them.

Out of nowhere, when we were talking about something else, he asked me if I still had the music box he sent me from Germany. I said I did, and I told him I still had a little toy mouse he gave me, too. He followed with a *non-sequitur* that unbalanced me. "I always wondered how you felt," he said. He wasn't asking me, just stating that he always wondered.

His mouth trembled, and I thought it was a nervous shiver. Then tears slid out of the corners of his eyes and I realized that he was crying. It was the last thing I expected and I was totally unprepared for my own reaction. I was filled with shame. "I felt horrible," I told him. I started to cry, too, but I was much less in control than he was. I was afraid that I would start to weep out loud. "You went to war," I said. I could hardly get the words out. "And I didn't wait for you."

Here I was, 34 years later, the shame practically gagging me. "Three hundred and sixty-six days," he said.

This kind of grief, stored-up stuff, was amazingly strong. I felt unbearably sad for the two teenaged kids we used to be. They were both lost, and I missed them. I wanted them both back.

The waitress tactfully left us alone. I wanted to touch him, but I knew it wasn't right to hold his hand. It was too trite, not enough. I took hold of his wrist and held it while I tried to catch my breath. Then we talked for a little while longer, until I ran out of things to say.

"I don't know what to say anymore," I concluded lamely.

Burt said, "I could sit here with you and talk about nothing for hours."

Nothing was exactly what we had been saying to each other for 34 years, and I didn't want to go on talking about nothing. I wondered what kind of a life we would have had together. Would I have made him as happy as Carol did? Why didn't he hate me? He had every right to.

But I didn't ask him any of those things. In fact, I don't remember anything we said after we started crying. Driving home, I wished I had said, "If it were now, I would wait." If it were now, I could wait. I know now how wonderful young love is. It's pure, and you just don't get it twice.

RICHARD

I came home feeling like I needed one those decompression chambers deep-sea divers use, but I needed to finish the job before I got a chance to get back to normal. I was ready to call my ex-husband. He couldn't possibly make me feel any worse than I did.

His wife answered the phone, and I told her I had just discovered the Internet, and, wow, there they were only 10 miles away, and would they like to get together for a drink or something. Brisk and cheerful and secure in her marriage, she said, "Sure!"

But my ex said he didn't see what purpose it would serve, and besides, he was old and bald and an old fuddy-duddy who just loved his daughter.

He was an old fuddy-duddy when we were married, but I didn't bring that up; and I liked that he loved his daughter, but he was adamant. He said that it would be a conversation gummy with old gripes.

I didn't have any gripes, and I told him so. If anybody had any gripes, it would be him, because I was the one who was unfaithful, and I have never had a chance to say I was sorry.

I realized right then that I hadn't told Burt I was sorry. Sorry is an awful small word sometimes.

Even so, I had my ex-husband on the phone, and I could tell <u>him</u> that I was sorry. When my marriage fell apart, I didn't know how to fix it, and I did all the wrong things. "I am sorry about the ways things happened," I said. "I really am."

"Don't be," he said. "You don't have to be. I was irresponsible. If I'd paid more attention to you, you wouldn't have to be sorry." This was the most personal thing he'd ever said to me, even while our marriage was falling apart and while I was falling apart. I took all the blame, all these years, and now he said, "You don't have to be sorry."

What an incredible relief. I felt closer to him than I had during all the years we were married. He understood at last. He *had* heard me screaming.

* * *

My grandfather said that the more you stir up cow manure, the more it smells. But he also said that it was the only thing that made his roses grow tall and sweet and thick with leaves. Thomas Wolf said you can never go home again, but what does he know?

I say that love never, ever goes completely away, that it is part of what makes us who we are. We can get old and fat and grey and nearsighted and forgetful, but there'll always be that sweet smell of the lake and all the other stuff that goes along with growing up and growing old. There'll always be the things you figured out too late or wished you'd said after someone has left the room.

Not only was I able to say some real important stuff to the men who played such a big part in actually creating me, but I was forced to look at myself—as I was then, and as I am now. I think I liked the girl who was engaged to Burt the best. Before the war, before my uncle died. She was the most honest and least confused. Maybe that was the girl that Haim and Richard and George all loved, too, even though it got harder and harder to get to her as I got older. Perhaps I created that bell jar to keep the confusion out, but by mistake I bottled some up with me.

Maybe Mom's right. Maybe David Montross had asked me to marry him, but I didn't hear him. Like my husband didn't hear me screaming.

Maybe I should have listened to my mother. Radical concept.

WHO'S TALKING … *Sherri Daley, a public schoolteacher and freelance writer, wants to retire, but first she must hunt down the creators of the Common Core curriculum. www.sherridaley.com*

6: A WORK IN PROGRESS
BARBARA, 64

TURNING 60 WAS NOTHING LIKE TURNING 50. FIFTY WAS AN INTER-esting celebration; I felt a powerful sense of personal freedom and joy. I recall saying to myself and others, "This feels great ... what a sense of accomplishment and personal satisfaction I feel." I was happy with my career and still in love with my husband of 30 years.

He was a born talent—a gifted illustrator and fine artist. Throughout his career, he worked for IBM and numerous advertising agencies in New York; his work was displayed in several galleries and housed in private collections.

I had a marketing communications consultancy. I was the account person and operations manager; he was my creative department. Inseparable? You bet. In work and in love.

My office was located in one end of our home, his studio in the other. We were a dynamic team for 30 years. We had no children, but our little Yorkshire terrier, Guinness, filled the bill.

My 60th birthday offered me quite different thoughts and feelings ... more akin to shock and awe, as in "Holy mackerel, I'm freakin' what?" I suddenly recognized the truth in what my mom had always claimed, "Life is short, dear; make hay while the sun shines."

When she died, I think I finally realized exactly what she meant. Sixty was a new benchmark with new considerations, but I never really thought much about that "making hay" thing before, probably because I was busy enjoying life with my husband while caring for my elderly mother who lived with us then and our sweet little dog. I wasn't depressed about turning 60…just aware of being 60… and stunned.

Fast forward to one year later, September 14, 2011. My precious, beloved, sweet, honorable, and talented husband was diagnosed with stage 4a lung cancer. His chances of survival were 30% for five years. What the hell did that mean … for him … and for me?

We heard the diagnosis together. My stomach churned. My husband was 15 years my senior, and recently, I had sensed a bit of mental confusion at times, but I saw no reaction on his face from the diagnosis.

We barely discussed it. We were in shock.

We were expected at my uncle's farm in Vermont that day. Other family members had flown in from California. We had to go. So we drove the 200 miles in near silence, trying to wrap ourselves around our new reality. The vistas were lovely, midsummer in the Vermont countryside. We didn't say much. In fact, I don't recall much about the road trip, only that we decided not to share the news. We arrived, hugged and kissed, tried to behave normally, and did. It was our rotten secret.

It was not for weeks that we told any of them what had happened on that day. We told them much later after my husband began treatments; they were quite amazed that we had kept the news to ourselves throughout our visit with them. Naturally, they were saddened.

During the eight months that ensued, I was numb, moving on autopilot, only I didn't realize it until much later. Our new daily routine was focused. It included visits to the radiologist to map his treatment and consults for both of us with the oncologist to understand the chemotherapy drugs and the effects of it all. He started radiation treatments five days a week for six weeks. He never complained.

I accompanied him on all visits to all doctors and chemo treatments, which began in late November at the conclusion of radiation therapy.

What an awful drill. Every time he saw the oncologist, blood was drawn and we had to wait for results. He had negative reactions to two drugs. Not good. By Christmas he became increasingly fatigued and pale. But, still, he never complained. Never once.

January morphed into February, and he was now on a new test drug at a cost of $660 per pill. Fortunately, because the drug was in the experimental stage, the manufacturer picked up the tab.

But his decline continued. Walking on his own strength proved too much for him, so visits to all physicians required him being transported in a wheelchair. My man was not well.

Soon the pulmonologist prescribed prednisone and put him on oxygen to deliver the air he needed to breathe properly.

Within a month, even while inhaling six liters of oxygen, he was out of breath after walking ten feet. What a decline.

Now our routine included twice weekly x-rays. That meant filling the portable oxygen tanks for the car trip, loading and unloading him in and out of the wheelchair and in and out of the car.

Apparently, the radiation treatments created vast amounts of scar tissue surrounding the tumor. Though the tumor in his left lung decreased in size, the lung was not properly functioning. As a result, fluid was collecting in the lung, requiring twice weekly drainage, first at the medical center, then at home. Not good.

By March, he required drainage every other day. Life was becoming increasingly difficult for him. But he kept his feelings to himself.

On Friday, April 1, 2012, a girlfriend and I went out for a light dinner; her husband sat with my husband. The intention was to get me out and away from the caregiving and give me a break.

It also provided some male company for my husband since he wasn't spending time with his buddies outside the home. When our friends left for the evening, we went to bed.

In the middle of the night, he awoke with severe pain in his lower abdomen—excruciating pain. I called an ambulance. They sped him away. I closed up the house and followed in my car.

In the ER, I was asked if he had a DNR, a "do not resuscitate" directive. My jaw dropped; my eyes opened wide. He did not. We never even contemplated such a thing. That was for old people with serious conditions.

The directive? Yes, resuscitate. Diagnosis: perforated ulcer and life-threatening. Emergency surgery. Compliance mandatory.

Seven hours later I went home, scared, shaken, and exhausted.

He made it through and was home ten days later, but I was beginning to feel weary. I knew we were going downhill.

Days later, we returned to the medical center for x-rays and more draining of the damaged lung. The draining procedure was overwhelming for us both. Something had to be done.

In late April or early May, he underwent a procedure that glued the outer lung layer to the chest wall in an attempt to prevent fluid build-up. The procedure was successful, but stressed his already very weakened system. Following several days in the ICU and then ten days recuperating in the hospital, he was released.

He entered rehab. The physical demands were great. He'd spent so much time in bed with two surgeries, without walking, that he found it nearly impossible to tolerate the actual physical efforts required to ambulate unassisted, lift himself from the wheelchair, or even get in and out of bed by himself. He never complained. He wanted to come home.

It was then that I knew he was giving up.

I brought him home and attempted to return to some degree of normalcy. He slept in our bed; I maneuvered him into and out of bed using techniques I had learned in rehab. It was tough. On one occasion, while sitting in the wheelchair in the living room, he slid out of the wheelchair and onto the floor. Unable to lift himself, I tried with his assist, but to no avail. I phoned a neighbor to help and got him into bed.

Physical and occupational therapy began at home. It was early May. Within days, while trying to feed him his liquid meal, there was no reaction on his part. He was shutting down. Hospice care came to our home; friends and family came to visit. We knew what was happening.

On the morning of May 14, I awoke at 6:00 and went to his bedside. His chest showed no movement. I knew. His hand was cold, but when I placed my hand on his heart, it felt warm. He was just barely gone.

Numb. A surreal experience. The cremation people came, observed, and recorded. Dazed, I stepped outside to my patio and sat. I watched at a distance as they placed his lifeless body into a black bag. They're taking him, I said to myself. He's gone. Oh, God.

I phoned his nurse to let her know. When I asked her what I should do now, she offered, "Live your life." But he WAS my life.

For the eight months I cared for my husband's physical, mental, and spiritual needs, I operated on autopilot. I had few concerns for myself. Now I felt like I was on autopilot again. I went through the mechanics that a widow needs to perform. I focused on preparing his memorial service and those details: timing, location, the reception, travel, and lodging plans. It was held in July and was lovely.

Thank God for Guinness, my 10-year-old wonder-dog. He was my best buddy, at my side throughout, always with a lick, kiss, or snuggle. We needed each other and I could tell he missed my husband. They had been inseparable.

When Hurricane Sandy arrived at our home in late October, Guinness and I sat by the blazing fire for six nights as we tried to keep warm, read by flashlight, and listen to shortwave radio. I know he wondered what the heck was going on. No lights, television, telephone, internet, cooking ... nothing. And his daddy was gone. He and I bonded.

On December 21, I noticed Guinness was lethargic, as if his body was bothering him. He behaved as if he was experiencing a relapse of the Lyme disease he had years prior. I made an appointment with the veterinarian for the next day, but Guinness died two days later, on Christmas Eve, from pancreatitis.

I can't recall the number of nights I cried myself to sleep. It was many.

By September, I felt the need to talk with a professional to determine if my feelings and thoughts were normal. So I joined a bereavement group. That was wise. I discovered that what I was experiencing was quite normal.

Fast forward to today, one year and six months later. The nurse had said, "Live your life." And so four months after the second death of a loved one, I enrolled in courses at UConn to relieve my mind of the constancy of grief and to give myself a mission.

I completed those courses in September, 2013, and graduated in November. While they served a purpose, they're done, and I'm now confronted with a very large question which has been festering like a painful boil: What shall I do with the rest of my life?

I have no children and no immediate family lives nearby. I am now alone. Very alone.

Now what?

My life is a work in progress.

WHO'S TALKING ... *Barbara Smith is a marketing communications consultant. Passions include the culinary arts, gardening, dancing, reading, caring for loved ones, golf, chocolate, and kind and handsome single men.*

7: BLIND DATE
JOAN, 71

A LOVELY CUSTOMER OF MINE WHO OFTEN CAME TO MY SHOP IN-vited me to her family Christmas party. She was so insistent and convinced me it was the most festive and joyful party I would ever attend. I rifled through my closet to find something appropriate, all the while trying to ignore nagging doubts. I settled on some-thing with a tame shimmer, cast my doubts aside, and trotted off to the party.

There was no mistaking the house. It was shimmering with lights, windows glowing with candles, and the doorway festooned with holly and ribbon. The hostess, Rosa, bade me a warm wel-come. A Christmas tree normally attacks my central nervous sys-tem, but the gaily decorated spruce in the grand entrance imbued the room with a festive rhythm. At least a dozen children were being folded into their coats and mufflers to be shepherded into the night to the children's party at a nearby house.

I was ushered into the grand living room and introduced around. Lovely, friendly people all made me feel welcome. I smiled and thought this was going to be a lovely evening.

Until we got to Uncle Arthur and the pig.

After considering the offerings at the bar, the host recom-mended the eggnog spiked with cognac. I pondered the wisdom of this choice, calculated the caloric content, and could feel my hips begin to inflate like life rafts. I looked up from my eggnog and saw my hostess bearing down on me with an exceptionally generous grin. She had her Uncle Arthur in tow.

"This is Uncle Arthur" she announced. "He is a bachelor. ... and this is Joan," she added. "She, too, is a bachelor."

I was struck with a paralyzing awkwardness, clutched my eggnog, and looked with some chagrin at the trophy being presented. I extended my hand and engaged his, but all his energy was being drained into his toothy grin and determined focus of eyes on my breasts.

The evening began to show signs of deterioration. I judged the distance between where I stood and the front door and thought an easy sprint would deliver me from the net Uncle Arthur was about to cast over my head. These thoughts collided in my brain until I felt Arthur place his hand in the small of my back and pilot me to the buffet.

A banquet that would rival a Roman orgy was spread on the table. My eyes then came to rest on the object sprawled in the center of the feast—a baby pig with an orange stuffed in its mouth. To my way of thinking, a dead body is a dead body. I don't care how much it is disguised in curly tin foil or draped in parsley; this was a dead body with an orange in its mouth.

Uncle Arthur was beside himself with joy. He was squealing with delight at the anticipation of carving up the pig and expounding over its texture and taste. Even through his very heavy accent, I was able to decipher the meaning of his words. Rosa told me Uncle Arthur maintained a home in Portugal and he was gesturing wildly toward me. I quickly got the gist that he wanted to take me back to his homeland. There I was, standing before this pig and Uncle Arthur, with Rosa beaming across the table at us. I nervously scanned the room, fearing a preacher had been arranged to secure this union and turn the Yuletide banquet into a wedding feast.

I made an attempt at escape. But Uncle Arthur was at my side, prying my perspiring fingers from my eggnog glass. It was announced that it was not time for eggnog...it was time for wine! Homemade Portuguese wine! He extended a glass containing liquid the color of Draino. One sip confirmed my suspicion that this was how they killed the pig and I discretely made my way to the sink.

Several attempts to release myself from the bondage of Uncle Arthur ended in defeat. At one point, I was enjoying a conversation with a very interesting young man and turned to see Uncle Arthur, who was upon me in an instant, waving the jaw bone of the pig.

He had been victorious in capturing what he evidentially thought was the tastiest morsel from the platter and was intent on pressing his dowry on me, his reluctant lover. I can tell you right here, it would take considerably more than the jaw bone of a pig to entice me into anything past a handshake with this grinning, overbearing, fading Portuguese Romeo.

All attempts at diplomacy were abandoned and I informed Uncle Arthur that I hated meat. He stopped waving the jawbone long enough to make a careful appraisal of my body and then mumbled something unintelligible. I am certain it was fortunate for him that I was unable to understand the comments resulting from his appraisal. Planning my escape became my consuming ambition.

After some polite conversation with the hostess, I managed to extricate myself from the party and make my way to the hall, in spite of Rosa's emotional protests. Warm breath on my neck confirmed my fear that Uncle Arthur was closer at hand than I desired, but I was three yards from the goal line and felt I could afford to grace him with a charitable smile.

This proved to be a fatal error in judgment. My smile was tantamount to an invitation and Rosa asked Uncle Arthur to see me to my car. Yogi Berra once said, "It ain't over 'til it's over" and Uncle Arthur was going for extra innings, determined to continue his amorous pursuit up the driveway.

We reached my car and I extended my hand, which Uncle Arthur seized and pulled up to his face like an oxygen mask. Before I could react, he reached for the back of my head and his gaping mouth headed for my face. I don't know if anyone has ever tried to kiss you after consuming the jaw bone of a pig, but I can report to you that kissing the pig would have been infinitely more desirable. I yanked back my head just in the nick of time as his hot pig breath and anxious lips grazed my ear.

I am grateful for my aerobic training that enabled me to duck down, spin around and leap into the driver's seat of my car before Uncle Arthur realized he missed his target. Grinning with relief, I waved good night. I heard him exclaim as I drove out of sight...."I like you...very much, I like you."

As I drew a veil over another holiday, I berated myself for not knowing that nagging doubt is often intuition and needs to be minded. I tried to immerse myself in the beauty and wonder of the season, but the real wonder is why ladies interested in advancing my romantic life are never related to more appealing senior candidates–perhaps closer to the look and style of Pierce Brosnan.

WHO'S TALKING ... *Joan Ruggiero divorced long before it was fashionable and opened an antiques shop in Connecticut. Three antique shops later, she opened a silk flower shop. Currently single, she lives with her cat, Lily, and writes for her own amusement.*

8: SUMMER CAMP AND THE WALK OF SHAME
KATE, 60

FOR MANY "BRIDGE-AND-TUNNEL" NEW YORKERS, SUMMER CAMP IS a rite of passage, an escape from the heat, humidity, and hubbub of the city. We went to camp because our parents decided we needed some fresh air and to see more trees than stood feebly in our urban or suburban neighborhoods. And surely, they welcomed the break from their children, as much as they loved us.

To our parents, whether they grew up across the Atlantic like mine or in borough neighborhoods like others, summer camp was one luxury they could afford for their children. Many a Jewish geography session includes, "So, where did you go to camp?" This leads to, "(insert camp name)," which then leads to "Ohmigawd, my (insert sister, brother, cousin, best friend, self, etc.) went there!" "Do you know......?" *Ad infinitum* until you determine you are really second cousins once removed.

I have no idea why my parents sent me to camp. We spent summers at our cabana club on Atlantic Beach, or traveling to Europe, or national parks. I was completely occupied at age 12, whether on family outings, with friends, or by simply reading, a favorite pastime. My mother cannot remember why she sent me, either, other than that her best friend at the time had sent her daughter to the same camp and the daughter came back unscathed. Why not, then? It was a completely random decision to send me there for a three-week "trip".

So even though I already knew what trees looked like, I boarded a yellow, un-air-conditioned school bus, knowing not one other person there, at a parking lot in Flushing, Queens, one steamy summer morning. My big green army duffle bag was stowed in the back of the bus. I never felt anxious about going off to a place I'd never been with people I had never met. Looking back, I might have felt something closer to serenity.

I feel more anxiety today about camp than I did as a pre-teen. What if my parents hadn't sent me? What if they hadn't known the friends whose daughter went there? What if I had gone to a different camp? My entire life would have been different. Fate. It's a funny thing.

If I hadn't gone to camp I wouldn't have had my first chaste kiss atop a (rather short) mountain on a tent-less overnight (with a man whose Facebook profile tells me is gay—did our kiss have anything to do with that?), my first "kumbaya moment" while actually singing "Kumbaya," or learned how to pull off the legs of Daddy Longlegs or melt slugs (nowadays I would call PETA), or lost a few pounds of baby fat very quickly from schlepping up and down the hill to my bunk countless times per day.

Breakfast, cleanup, arts and crafts, change for swim lessons, change for lunch, rest hour, nature shack, hike, change, dinner, nighttime activity, schlep back up to bed. Even going to the bathroom was taxing as it was *all the way* across the little road instead of attached to my bedroom. And the sinks were outside, attracting all sorts of creepy crawly things, especially at night, when moths hovered around the lights. It was paradise. Who knew a spoiled only child from Queens would thrive in this environment?

The "summer camp without a theme" tradition is primarily an East Coast invention bred for families who could not afford true vacations to enlighten their children about nature. Indeed, in

1902, "my" camp was founded to provide a summer vacation for Jewish boys from the tenements of the Lower East Side of Manhattan; at one point its mission was even to care for malnourished boys. Over one hundred years later, the camp stands proudly and has expanded its offerings to off-season retreats, weddings, and conferences, out of financial necessity. But it continues its tradition during the summer and has fostered a lifetime of memories for the thousands of campers it has hosted.

This verdant green valley oasis with a large lake at its center continues to build on its legacy while sustaining its Jewish mission and focusing on scholarships. When I attended, I didn't know which of my friends were there on scholarship. Once ensconced in our rustic, electricity-free, smelling-of-years-gone-by cabins, we were all equals, to a point. The pretty girls, the cute boys, hovered at the top of the social pyramid. I never experienced or heard of bullying or mean girls (or mean boys) at camp. I saw more (and experienced it myself) at my public school in Queens. Something about this camp and its staff, year after year, promoted equality, fairness and fun. And the result: lifetimes of friendship, marriages, children, and memories.

At 16, I returned to camp for my first go-round as a staff member after being a camper for the previous four years. . We couldn't become counselors directly after being campers; we had to do some menial work in the kitchen to earn our stripes and the privilege to move on to counsel groups of a dozen snot-nosed, sometimes bed-wetting children in cluttered bunks without indoor plumbing. Again, paradise. No sarcasm intended.

For those of us who aspired to be princesses, it was liberating to pack our Huckapoo and Nik Nik shirts into our camp trunks and work in the trenches with the rest of our friends. It was hard to keep pretenses alive in the Hudson Valley humidity, especially without portable blow-dryers, flatirons, and hair product. Frizz prevailed. Clothes were wrinkled. Makeup was minimal. We became our true selves. The one counselor who carried a purse was seen as an oddity.

Camp was a more important social sphere than our junior or senior high schools were. It was always a fresh start. Living lakeside, surrounded by the shadows of the hills, sharing bad camp food, "bug juice," good camp songs, overnights with the stars as our canopy, and sleeping on creaky cots in bunks whose walls were time-stamped with toothpaste graffiti going back decades. It was all magical.

Our teenaged hormones were certainly looking to be put to good use, but most of us were not focused on finding everlasting love. It was more about securing a nice lakeside make-out session—or ten lakeside make-out sessions. It was the 70s, so we were not as progressive as today's teenagers. Yet, despite our not being focused on our matrimonial futures, love happened. "I'm going out with Brian" became, years later, "I'm marrying Brian."

Last fall, a dozen of us gracefully-aging, upper-middle class career women/wives/ mothers arrived at a low-slung building for the twice-yearly reunion of our core group—fall at camp, spring at the spa. We bore bed linens, towels, electric toothbrushes, Patagonia vests, North Face jackets, Merrell hiking boots, and Prada sunglasses. Also along for the trip were memory foam pillows, custom orthotics, book club lists, and the occasional pair of progressive lenses. We made our beds in "J-Lodge," in its prime lakeside location, with a rainbow of warm blankets atop our thinly-mattressed cots. Not one complaint about the accommodations from this worldly group.

We were back to being teenagers, although with physical reminders of our true ages. No bosses, not even our camp supervisors, were there to approve or disapprove of our behavior. We didn't wear makeup. Some of the better-skilled built a roaring fire in a fireplace that has seen generations of campers enjoy bedtime milk and cookies.

That weekend, the fireplace observed us enjoying goat's milk brie and designer chocolates, rather than the coveted chocolate cream donuts we hitched to Dunkin' Donuts for when we were summer migrant workers without cars, or the oddly flavorless cookies served at "milk-and-cookies."

But I am sure the fireplace saw us as the teenagers we once were. We spoke like bridge-and-tunnel teenagers. There is nothing like letting your guard down and not being judged, just as we weren't judged stepping off the yellow bus in the sweltering summer.

Nine out of the twelve in our group met their husbands at this camp. Dozens—dare I say hundreds?—of others have done the same over the generations. There is such a sweetness to that history, to share it with others.

While I love being with these women, there were moments that weekend when I ventured away from the group to be alone with my memories. Standing on a grassy patch on the lakeside, I remembered the 5 a.m. "walk of shame" following the illegitimate sleepovers in my husband-to-be's bunk (with his bunkmates present. Hmmm).

On those early mornings, the steam rose from the cool lake into the warming air; the 500-acre camp was still, the hundreds of campers, counselors, and staff still deeply asleep in their cots, blankets in place against the cool mountain air. The day had not yet begun, memories of that day not yet forming their everlasting roots. The shouts of children who were once strangers had not risen to be heard across the lake during a game of Capture the Flag. The smells of breakfast cooking had not yet wafted across the road from the big stone building. It was only me, alone on the lakeside, remembering how that stuffy yellow school bus filled with strangers was the first leg in the journey to my future, filled with love and friendship.

WHO'S TALKING ... *Kate Fuerst is a marketing/communications professional. A workout enthusiast, she is also obsessed with good food. So the workouts are a necessity. She is still crazy about her camp boyfriend, still her husband, and is a devoted mother to two boys and her cats.*

BUY ONE, GET ONE FREE!

This holiday season, when you buy a 1-year (12-issue) gift subscription, you can give a second one for FREE! **That's 2 subscriptions for $24 — the same price as 1!**

From:

Name _____ (please print)

Address _____

City _____ State _____ Zip _____

Email _____

☐ Payment enclosed. ☐ Bill me later.

CookingLight

To order faster, go to

www.cookinglight.com/holidaygift

16ICKIAL   CKBG9A5

2 subscriptions for $24 (same price as for 1). Plus sales tax where applicable. Cooking Light publishes 1 double issue, which counts as 2 of 12 issues in an annual subscription. Delivery in U.S. only. The first issue will mail 4-8 weeks from receipt of order.

Gift Subscription #1:

Name _____ (please print)

Address _____

City _____ State _____ Zip _____

Gift Subscription #2:

Name _____ (please print)

Address _____

City _____ State _____ Zip _____

9: TWO BRIDES
SUZANNE, 63

AT OUR REHEARSAL DINNER, OUR PLAN WAS TO MARCH DOWN THE aisle to Eva Cassidy's "Songbird," a breathtakingly beautiful song. We had timed it so that we would arrive at the pulpit just at the end of that gorgeous song.

But the next day, October 29, 2005, at our civil union ceremony, the song ended before we even arrived. Rev. Frank Hall, who was officiating along with Rev. Barbara Fast, spoke first. "It took them so long to get here because it took them sooooo long to get here."

No truer words were ever spoken, and we have cherished his acknowledgement of our process and have never forgotten that moment—what it says about us, and about marriage equality.

I was born into a large Catholic-Irish-Sicilian family of eight (my parents and the six of us siblings). I guess you could say that the life I am living now is not what anyone in my family would have expected of me. Expectations being the sacred right of all parents, mine expected me to be a teacher with long summer vacations, and have several children running around the house.

I graduated from SUNY-New Paltz, and still my family expected me to know my place and not make too many waves. In their humble opinion, I was to serve my husband and raise his children. However, having already taken care of my two youngest sisters as they were growing up (my mother was too ill to do so), I felt like I had already been there, done that.

Our civil union marked a huge victory for Rozanne and me. It was a day to celebrate what had been a long political struggle to secure our right to equal protection under the law. We wanted only what other married couples in Connecticut have (or want to have)—a person who loves them, lives with them, with whom they share their lives, pay taxes, and basically share the fruits of their labors, a loving person to share their lives with and enjoy.

We had been taking trips to our state capital in Hartford to the judiciary hearings where people from all walks of life came to express their feelings about same-sex unions—some were fearful and anxious, others hopeful.

Some of the ministers in attendance were downright nasty and on the edge of being cruel about gay people. Our supporters, however, far outnumbered them. We had our State Representative, Joe Mioli, on our side. We had many meaningful discussions with him about why it was so important to us, and so many others, to have Civil Unions as at least a stopgap measure until we could have parity or equality with other married taxpaying couples. We wanted only our rightful place in society.

There had been a time when gay people feared losing their jobs if outed. I worked for myself so no one could fire me because I'm gay. Having personal freedom, including the freedom to marry the person I love, is as much a part of the American Dream as anything else.

We wanted our civil union day to be a magical day, full of joy and peace and love, filled with friends and music, well-wishers, and lots of drinking. As we kept adding to the guest list, we knew that this would be a large gathering.

Knowing that we would need help with the logistics of this affair, we called upon our most organized of friends, Karen Wright. She and Rozanne had masterminded First Night Westport/ Weston for five years so we knew they could master a measly 300 people for one event.

We had many design sessions at our kitchen table. The three of us would laugh out loud at some of the ideas we came up with. Karen found some awesome rainbow-colored candles online.

Since neither of us is a traditionalist, we felt that the typical white gown was not "us". Some of our lesbian friends chose to have one partner wear the tuxedo and the other wear the dress. Not going to happen! We felt it would be wasteful to wear a dress (or a tuxedo) once and then put it in mothballs. So our decision fell into the capable designing hands of Ulla Surland. We decided to buy and wear all-black pants outfits that she designed.

The outfits were super-comfortable, super-slimming black stretchy nylon scoop-neck tops with matching, comfortable stretchy pants. We wore these outfits for hundreds of occasions after the wedding—until the elastic wore out and they fell apart. How many brides can say that about their white wedding dress?

We also picked out beautiful hand-made silk scarves; Rozanne in beautiful deep red, and me in a rich blue-green sea color.

We knew that we wanted lots of music, so we thought first of our talented friends—Chris Coogan, the late Matt Nozzolio, Robin Batteau. And we wanted lots of food. Our friend, Bobby, helped with all the food logistics and was our bartender of choice. Our menu consisted of sushi, Italian everything, hot dogs and hamburgers from the grill. We had cake and champagne and just about anything anybody would ever want to eat.

We had bluegrass music as people entered the church. During the ceremony, I sang twice. One moment I will never forget—the day started out being overcast, but when I got up to sing "Beautiful in My Eyes," the sun broke through in all its golden glory. True story.

Friends in our wedding party told little stories about Rozanne and me and I will always remember the way I felt—but it is still indescribable. When the ceremony was over, all 300 of us danced out in a Conga line to Bob Marley's *One Love*.

My brother was the only one from my family who came. No one from Rozanne's family came. Lots of reasons, but the feeling was one of "you are on your own." That was OK with us. We did not expect our families to be overjoyed. We had been living together for nine years so we really did not need anything from them.

In the end, it was an amazing day. At the reception, we had a champagne toast. All raised their glasses to our happiness.

It took a whole village to bring this miracle day to reality and everyone danced with full hearts and full bellies. We danced and drank to the rock-n-roll band, The Key Ingredients, until close to midnight.

Except for me. I didn't dance because I was the lead singer in the band. It was as close to feeling like royalty as we will ever feel and we still hear people talking about that wedding as the best wedding they have ever attended.

Wow. How great is that?

WHO'S TALKING ... *Suzanne Sheridan has been married to her partner, Rozanne Gates, since 2005. Before she retired, Rozanne was an agent to many stars; Suzanne sings like a star, so it's a match made in heaven. They support each other in everything and have fun doing it.*

10: WISING UP
PEGGY, 66

CHILDHOOD, COLLEGE, VIETNAM WAR, MARRIAGE, DIVORCE, PEACE activist, marriage again, divorce again, Women's Rights activist, career, spirituality, family deaths, love with marriage.

As they say, the greatest of these is love with marriage. It's been a long time coming, but I finally got here.

Soon I will be 67 and marrying a man who is amazing. It has taken me a lifetime to open my heart and trust the universe when it comes to love. You see, I have been married before. In fact, I have either been married or living with a man for 37 years. Well, four men exactly. But I haven't been legally married for 32 years.

At 35, with two failed marriages under my belt, I brilliantly vowed never to do that again—marriage that is. I stopped trusting myself with marriage.

Let me tell you a little about the end of that last marriage. That marriage lasted two years. Actually, we were only living together for one year. After the first year, he disappeared and it took me another year to find him before I could get a divorce. That one year of living with him was the absolute worst year of my life. I always felt I had a vulture on my shoulder. But the disaster of the marriage magnified after the divorce. Too bad I didn't foresee what could still happen. Little did I know there was a 'gator hiding in the bog.

About a year after the divorce, I received a letter from the IRS. It said that in two weeks I had a meeting at their local office. I had no idea why. Two days before the meeting, I received a letter saying the IRS had placed a lien on my house. When I got to the meeting, the IRS agent said, "Your ex-husband owes us a lot of money. We have been looking for him for eight years." She showed me a two-foot tall pile of papers. Evidently, that was the paperwork they had on what he owed them and how they had tried to find him. "We know where you are. You have a job. You are stable. You will pay us the money." He owed the IRS what my salary was for an entire year. All of the pain and memories of that one year of my life came back to haunt me.

I immediately contacted a lawyer. The tax lawyer said, "You fit the profile of my typical client base. Female, white, educated, mid-thirties, blonde, great career, homeowner, and living in the same city your whole life. Your ex-husband was a con artist. They know what they are doing. They find women just like you to clear up their IRS debt." He informed me I was getting off easy. He told me horror stories of the financial ruin of other women. He talked about the ex-husbands who owned large companies and never paid their employees' Social Security. The men were missing, so the IRS came after the ex-wives.

The lawyer said before you marry anyone again ask him to sign the IRS form 8821, which will let you see his previous years' IRS returns so you can find out if he has paid the IRS all taxes that he owes.

Thankfully, I had done a pre-nup before the marriage, protecting my business, my house, my car, and some family land. At the time of the divorce, he got nothing that was mine prior to the marriage. Surely, there is some way to protect yourself even after you are divorced.

Evidently, there isn't. You have to protect yourself before marriage. I had no idea where he was. Until that week, I could not have cared less. I was just glad he was out of my life and I was divorced.

At this point, I had no choice but to agree to work with the IRS agent and I negotiated a payment with the IRS. The last time I met with the agent and she had gotten the money she wanted from me, she said, "Here is his address if you want to find him." She had lied about not knowing where he was.

I had never really known I was capable of such intense anger until that very moment. But it wasn't directed toward my ex-husband; it was directed at the IRS agent taking advantage of me and lying about not being able to find him. The reality was they knew they would never get a penny from him because he moved often, changed jobs frequently, and didn't have a penny to his name. Remember, he was a con artist.

The other strong suggestion I have for you is if you ever get a letter from the IRS, never, I mean absolutely never, go to their office yourself. Get a power of attorney for your lawyer or your accountant to go in your place. Someday, I will write a chapter on the nightmare of that one year. But to this day, it is still the most humiliating situation of my life.

I think you have a little insight into why I decided marriage was not for me. It took me three years to find my equilibrium after that ordeal. I concentrated on building the consulting firm I had founded when I was 32. I went to weekly therapy sessions and tons of self-help workshops. I read every spiritual book and self-help book at the bookstore. I decided I would never be that vulnerable again. I decided the way to do that was not to marry.

After three years of "working on myself," I thought I was smarter when it came to men. I was ready to date again. Obviously, I wanted to be really picky this time. Dating ads had just started. They were published on the back pages of the alternative magazines. I got a PO Box, naively thinking that no one would be able to find where I lived. I wrote my ad for prospective beaus and heard from 16 men. I started meeting each one of them for coffee. After meeting every single one of them, there was only one that I wanted to see again. He had a college degree, he had a great job, and he was funny.

He ran a department in city government. After about six months (way too soon, I want to add), he moved into my house with me. Obviously, I still wasn't paying attention to my past experiences, my gut, nor my inner voices. Within six months of us living together, the mayor changed. The new mayor closed the department where my partner worked and he was out of a job. My own company had taken off and my professional and financial life was soaring. For the next seventeen years, yes, *17 years*, my "spouse equivalent" looked for a job but never found one. For all of those years, I begged and pleaded with him to bring in some money so that at least he could take care of his own personal wants and needs. In reality, he was a stay-at-home partner and not a very good one. He didn't create menus, shop for groceries, cook the meals, wash the clothes, or clean the house.

I guess we would have continued on like this forever except the game changed on my part. Well into their eighties, both of my parents died within one year of each other. I was their sole caregiver while continuing to run my company and my own house. Being with my parents during their last years was one of the greatest gifts of my life. After their deaths, I was exhausted, both emotionally and physically.

Initially, I changed how I worked. I no longer felt the need to be an ambitiously driven entrepreneur. I let my employees and contractors go and started delivering all of the work myself. After two years, I was still mentally, emotionally, and physically exhausted, so I decided to shut my company down and take a one-year sabbatical.

We moved to a very small town northwest of Albuquerque, New Mexico. No one there was ambitious. No one wore fancy clothes. No one drove expensive cars. And no one wore much jewelry at all. It was fabulous to be off the fast track. It is one of the most beautiful places in the United States. I spent the year healing from the grief and exhaustion of my parents' deaths. I got involved in every aspect of the small village we lived in and enjoyed the spiritual energy of New Mexico.

When it was time for the winter solstice celebration, I found a group of people that included two Shaman, two Wicca, two Buddhists, a female Rabbi, as well as four other spiritually-diverse individuals. On one of my visits back to Dallas for appointments with my alternative healers, I went for a spiritual clearing. At the time, I didn't know much about the woman's process, but I felt a big shift of stress leave my body.

After one year in New Mexico, I was ready to get back to Big D and ready to get back to work. I started another consulting firm and changed the focus of my client base. I was the only employee and worked with universities to support graduating MBA students with their job searches. I loved my work and loved being an individual contributor. I was no longer driven to have a large company with employees and contractors. I no longer wanted to put out the energy to work for "big bucks." I did not want to travel 100% of my time for work. After being "off the grid," so to speak, while living in New Mexico, I no longer cared a thing about buying the newest foreign car, shopping for elegant clothes, or eating at the fanciest restaurants. I was ready to be more relaxed, enjoy my work, and enjoy my life. During this time, I continued my spiritual sessions to clear myself of a lifetime pattern of suffering when it came to men.

Even with all of the stresses placed on me over those years and the changes in our lives, my partner did not get a job. He was now a big strain on me mentally, emotionally, and financially. I was no longer willing to have a high-powered career just to take care of him. In the end, I finally realized if we stayed together, I would be taking care of him for the rest of his life and working myself into poverty and an early grave. After all of these years of supporting him and encouraging him, I was done. Having him around was killing me and I felt like I was going to lose myself. I felt like if I continued to have him around for even one more day, my body was going to disappear. I had to get him away from me. I told him he had to leave the next day.

"Why would anyone aspire to be long suffering? … Lies you are telling yourself that are keeping you stuck in your misery. If you can't trust yourself to tell you The Truth, your situation is indeed dire," writes Jill Conner Brown in *The Sweet Potato Queens' Book of Love*.

It was right before Thanksgiving. I think the universe was clapping and saying, "Thank God! Why did she take so long? We have been waiting for this moment for a really, really long time."

I started to relax and be able to breathe again. I thought how great the rest of my life would be now that I was alone. I never wanted another man in my life. But different plans had been made for me. Two weeks later, the universe brought me a miracle. I received an e-mail from a professional male client I had not talked with or seen in 12 years. The e-mail said, "My wife of 35 years and I are getting a divorce. I have moved to Mobile, Alabama. If you ever get by this way, I hope you will look me up. I would love to see you." He included his phone number.

I was so surprised and taken aback. I thought about the e-mail for a week. Then one night after work I gave him a call, and we talked for two hours that night and every night for the next three weeks. After a couple of months, we started talking about the possibility of seeing each other. I was 58. The last time we had seen each other I was 46. Lots of scary changes had happened to my body in those 12 years. I had gone through menopause and my previously thin body had totally changed. The new shape of my body went from wearing a junior size in clothes to wearing a misses size—meaning round and full-bodied.

We decided not to send any pictures of each other. For the next few months, I started walking and going to Curves. I bravely looked at my body naked in the mirror every morning and said, "You are beautiful." It worked. I went from a dowdy size 16 to a tiny size 10 in two and a half months. I know that grieving my parents' death and being unhappy in my relationship over an extended time showed in my body size. The excitement and anticipation of seeing Rick helped tremendously in feeling good about myself and dropping those pounds.

The time had come for us to meet. I decided to go visit him in Mobile. Of course, I wanted to be totally in control and take it very slowly so I booked a hotel room. When I arrived at the DFW Airport, I saw a turquoise cowgirl hat and bought it. I called him from the airport and told him what I was wearing so he would recognize me. When I arrived at the airport in Mobile, I rounded the corner to head out to security. I stopped in my tracks. At the end of a football-length hall, there were floor-to-ceiling glass walls. I couldn't see out, but the people on the other side could see in. I knew he was watching me walk the whole way. I was the only person walking down that long, never-ending hall. I was a nervous wreck and thought I would die before I got to the end.

Rick was waiting at security with a dozen red roses and a beautiful grin. It was Mardi Gras weekend, and on Saturday we went to one of the parades. In Mobile, the parades are a family affair. The people on the floats toss Moon Pies, beads, and stuffed animals. We had so much fun together. I stayed at my hotel on Friday and Saturday nights. We had both started to relax and started to enjoy getting to know each other.

Sunday came too quickly and we headed back to the airport in Mobile for my flight back to Dallas. As Rick dropped me off, I sensed that strange feeling that you get in an airport when you know "something is off." I discovered that Dallas was in the middle of a rare ice storm. As most people know, it is always hotter than hell in Texas. I called Rick on his cell phone and told him that the universe was working miracles. Hell had frozen over for us. We had one more day together.

Knowing that we had been given a special gift of a little more time together, we went off to explore the city and enjoy one of the many local songwriters. That extra time let us both know that we wanted to continue getting to know each other.

I was determined we were going to take this very slowly and I was not going to rush into living together. For the next year, we took turns going back and forth between Mobile and Dallas. Over that year the time between the visits got shorter and we were getting together every other week. After that first year, we had another miracle. Rick's company moved him to a job in Texas that was only an hour and a half east of Dallas.

For the next year we saw each other every weekend. We were definitely taking our time getting to know each other. Rick got a call from a recruiter asking if he would be interested in a job in Savannah, Georgia. He asked me if he applied for the job and got it, would I go with him. In a nanosecond I said, "Yes!" And then the adventures really began.

By this time I had completed the certification process for Spiritual Response Therapy and was asked by the Association to be a phone consultant for individuals calling in for clearing assistance from Europe, Canada, and the Eastern United States. My career totally changed and I became a full-time spiritual healer.

We have had an amazing life together. After living in Savannah for two years, we moved to Virginia where the Blue Ridge starts. We have decided the time to marry is now. I know we cannot know what the future will bring, but I know there is nowhere I would rather be than right by Rick's side.

Good things happen when you let go, trust your higher self, go into your heart, and ask for your highest good.

Of course, we will be getting a pre-nup and visiting an estate attorney before our marriage. I guess I have finally learned to listen from my knowledge and experience as well as from my heart.

WHO'S TALKING ... *Texas born and bred, Peggy Womack lived in her beloved Dallas all of her life—until she fell in love with Rick and moved away with him. A former busy business consultant, now she prefers to spend her time dancing with her man.*

II: FORGIVE, NOT FORGET
MAUREEN, 67

IT IS SAID THAT WE TEACH MOST WHAT WE NEED TO LEARN. I NEED-
ed to learn to forgive.

I went to a class and the instructor asked who had a resentment they would share. My hand was up quickly and I was chosen. I told about someone who had hurt one of my children seven
years before. The class loved it. They identified.

I was quite proud of myself until the instructor asked, "Why
haven't you forgiven her?"

I was speechless. What a dumb question. When I finally
thought of an answer, I said, "Because if I forgive her, she'll get
away with it." I could see everyone agreed.

The instructor just got worse and said, "She got away with it
seven years ago. You've been keeping that alive all by yourself." She
told me how my resentments affected everything I did, said, and
thought. I immediately decided to resent the instructor, too.

Her words gnawed at me. I knew she was right. I should let
the resentment go, but I had no idea how to do it.

I am Catholic. I am educated. I have gone to counseling.
One would think I would have learned to forgive somewhere

along this road. But no one ever told me how. They just said, "Do it."

I went back to the instructor and said, "I have decided I want to forgive her, but I don't know how. *What do I do with all these feelings?*"

What a wise woman she was. She prayed with me and then taught me three steps to forgiveness.

I have used them many times. I found I had a long list of resentments I needed to let go of, some since childhood, some more recent.

The three steps the instructor taught me have changed my life.

STEP ONE: THE ACT / DECISION

We decide intellectually that we want to forgive. It is a decision we make to ourselves and our God. It doesn't feel good yet. We are still in pain. Lao Tzu said, *"The journey of 1,000 miles begins with a single step."*

Mother Theresa said, "A true test of faith is whether or not we can forgive." It has also been said that asking God to help us forgive is the highest form of prayer.

When I was a young mother, my grandma sent me a poem by an unknown author.

Letting it go is difficult. When we make that decision, we don't have to like it, but we do have to be sincere.

STEP TWO: THE PROCESS

We need to feel / process all our feelings in this situation. We have to feel the hurt, anger, grief, betrayal, resentment, hate, or whatever emotions we have. We may need to write about them, to talk about them, to do whatever we can to work through them in positive ways. Once a counselor told me to walk and consciously think of my anger. It was a much more aggressive walk and a positive release.

When you see a man on the top of a mountain, you can bet he didn't fall there. Feeling our feelings takes time and can be very painful. In the film, *The Prince of Tides*, Barbara Streisand says, "Tears won't bring him back, but they might bring you back."

Sidney Simon says in his book, *Forgiveness*, "When we shove our feelings under the carpet, they just make ripples that we will trip on." Feeling our feelings is tough work, but it liberates us. Hopefully, our pain will ebb.

I have a physical scar where I was cut. In the beginning, it hurt and was tender. Now it has healed over. I still see it. I know it's there and where it came from, but the sting is gone. So it is with our emotional scars. They heal over. They no longer give us pain when we touch them.

They just become part of who we are and part of our life's journey.

A counselor once told me, "Everyone has a cross to carry in life. These are just part of your cross." Put in that perspective, the carrying of them doesn't seem so heavy.

STEP THREE: THE STATE OF FORGIVENESS

I believe that forgiveness is a God thing. I believe that if we do the first two steps, God will do his magic and bless us with the state of forgiveness. Often when we least expect it. Sometimes when we think it is impossible.

Inner peace is created by changing ourselves, not the person who hurt us. When we forgive we look at them through new eyes. We see them, we remember, but it doesn't hurt us anymore. We may even wish them well and go on our way.

We are imperfect people and we live in an imperfect world.

Pain is inevitable. Suffering is optional. Forgiveness is one of the hardest things we will ever be asked to do. Is it worth it?

You bet. Because we are worth it.

Marie Balter was locked in an insane asylum for years. She wasn't insane. Marlo Thomas portrayed her in a TV movie. When she was released she said, "I would not have grown one bit, if I had not learned to forgive."

Though forgiveness is a personal journey and a gift we give ourselves, the benefits radiate to our families, our friends, and our world. I love the short prayer, "Lord, give me the guidance to know when to hold on, when to let go and the grace to make the right decision with dignity." When we are able to do this, a grand miracle is performed.

Forgiveness is a choice. We can choose to harbor hurt and resentment or we can choose to heal and give ourselves the peace we deserve. Don Juan, in *Journey to Xtlan*, said, "We either make ourselves miserable or we make ourselves strong. The amount of work is the same."

Hurts come in all shapes and sizes. They come in different ways. Sometimes folks mean to hurt us. Sometimes they don't even know they have.

What do we need to forgive? Not irritations. What we need to forgive are deep personal hurts.

We need to forgive actions, what people have done, not who they are and what they are like.

When I began my journey of forgiveness, I really didn't want to forgive. I just wanted the pain to end. I wanted to feel healed. But to do so, I had to let it go and quit licking my wounds.

Sometimes, I think it is harder to give it up than to go through what happened in the first place. One woman shared that her counselor asked her, "How long do you want to bleed over this?" Is holding on worth the price we are paying? Would we rather be right than happy?

There are some people who are very difficult to forgive. Perhaps they're still mean and nasty.

They're never sorry. We want them to beg for forgiveness. They don't. We want them to pay, to

hurt as we have. They don't. Some of them even die and leave us with the whole burden.

A wonderful thing to learn is that we don't need their repentance to forgive. It is really not about them. It's about us, our healing, and our future.

Often we want two things. We want to keep our anger and we want to have peace. We can't have it both ways. The word forgive means to give up.

There are some important things that forgiveness is and is not. Forgiveness is not forgetting. We don't get amnesia when we forgive. Often we need to remember so we can protect ourselves.

Forgiveness is not trusting. We don't have to become a fool to forgive. Some people should never be trusted. Others we may be able to trust again. Each situation is unique.

Forgiveness is not understanding it all. I want to understand everything, to talk it through. That is usually a fantasy. We need to accept confusion as we forgive.

Forgiveness is not tolerating, excusing, or condoning. When we forgive we are not saying it was OK, nor are we saying we will allow it to happen again. Our forgiveness does not let them off the hook. It is not absolution. They remain responsible for what they did.

Forgiveness can't be forced or phony. We can't forgive because it's our duty or someone told us to do it.

Getting even doesn't work. It's a game no one wins. When we forgive, we quit playing the game. We walk away. We leave the score unbalanced. We surrender . . . our resentment. We

win . . . peace, joy and healing.

Forgiveness can't wait for the circumstances to be right. They may never be.

We need to limit our expectations of forgiveness. We must accept imperfect forgiving.

Perfection locks us up. We may not get a rosy ending. We may never be best friends again. We may not kiss and make up. We may not like them again. We may have to let them go out of our life. We can still get peace.

There is no one way to forgive. We can forgive in many ways: face to face, by letter; by actions, silently within ourselves. Every situation calls for a different approach.

Forgiveness occurs one step at a time and sometimes they are just baby steps. Be patient.

Forgiveness can't be rushed. The deeper the wound, the longer it takes. Forgiveness is not an event, it's a process. Even when you feel it's not coming, don't give up.

There is only one thing that can prevent you from forgiving and that is your will, simply refusing to do it. It is not "you would if you could". You can. It is in your hands.

Pray for the person you need to forgive, perhaps even out loud. You can do it through clenched teeth. You don't have to like doing it. You just have to mean it. It's like priming a pump. It opens you to God's power and allows Him to perform His miracle and free you of the hate, resentment, anger, and pain.

Most of us have hurts and resentments we need to heal. We have the power to choose healing or harboring. Lao Tse said, "If you do not change directions, you may end up where you are heading." Is that where you want to be?

I don't know about you. I don't know the journey of life you have been on. What I do know is that the act of forgiveness has changed my life for the better—way better. It has eased my pain and lightened my load. Did anything change that had happened to me? No. But I changed. They have lost their power over me.

The wrongs no longer hurt me. I have made it through the fire and I am free—free at last.

WHO'S TALKING ... *Maureen Burns is an international professional speaker, author of six books, and a newspaper columnist. She has been married for 46 years, has four grown children, two adorable grandsons, and a very gifted dog. www.maureenburns.com*

12: A MOTHER'S JOURNEY
BONNIE, 68

GLENN DAVID ROSS WAS TWO MONTHS SHY OF HIS 40TH BIRTHDAY. He was filled with excitement at having just finished his Master's Degree and looking forward to more freedom, a pay hike, spending more time with his long-standing girlfriend, and to receiving the official letter from the university acknowledging his accomplishment. It was the same day of the horrific Haiti earthquake, January 12, 2010, that I lost my son to a rare disease. While his struggle was over, mine was about to begin.

It's painful that my son, Glenn, is gone. Yet he added so much value, meaning, love, caring, laughter, and friendship to those whose lives were touched during his time with us.

Glenn led his life with dignity. In spite of an illness that was his constant companion, he never let that interfere with living his life at full throttle. I can remember times, after the fact, that he'd talk about jumping out of an airplane, whitewater rafting, competitive tennis, soccer, and rock climbing in Jamaica. Knowing I'd try to talk him out of it, I understood why he never told me ahead of time! Glenn let nothing stand in his way when it came to a great time!

As a former educator, when Glenn made the decision to enter the teaching profession, I was thrilled. All of us knew he'd make a great teacher. Unable to have children of his own, he loved kids. He was a joke teller and juggler and his classroom was the perfect setting for his authentic self. During student teaching, Glenn shared a required taping with us, and when I reviewed it again recently, I smiled just seeing him in action.

I had emailed Glenn back then that I was not prejudiced. Even if I wasn't his mom, I could honestly say his science lesson rocked. As soon as you saw kids clamoring to answer his questions, you recognized his impact on his students.

All parents raise their children to be honest, to care about others, and to contribute who they are to make the world a better place. Glenn was truly a gift to the world. Whatever his dad and I did, even with the inevitable mistakes along the way, Glenn grew up to be an exceptional man. In our lifetime, we all desire to make a difference in the world—to leave it a bit better than before and to know that our life mattered.

While Glenn's dash was cut short, who he was and what he accomplished in his 39+ years had a huge impact. He will forever live on in our hearts and in the lives of those he touched, including his beloved colleagues and students of Hull Middle School in Duluth, Georgia.

In their 2010 yearbook, a special page was included to memorialize Mr. Glenn Ross. With love and pride I share this acknowledgement.

Gone from our school that smiling face, the cheerful happy ways.
The heart that won so many friends, in bygone happy days.
Lonely is your class without you, science to them is not the same.
All the school would be like Heaven, if we could have you back again.
We miss him and mourn him in sorrow unseen.
And dwell on the memory of days that have been.

Dates have a way of reminding us of joys experienced and sorrows endured. At the beginning of every year, all of us imagine fresh possibilities, goals to be achieved and the promise of happiness. And, yet, on the 12th day of 2010 I went from excitement and anticipation to the depth of despair. A beautiful and loving son, a middle school teacher who was devoted to his students. All who admired and respected Glenn's carefree, easy going life were suddenly facing an unimaginable loss.

I never imagined that I'd join the sisterhood of mothers who've lost children prematurely. Our family was acutely aware of his condition, a unique genetic disorder called Ehlers-Danlos Syndrome (EDS for short). Yet, in spite of the odds, his outlook, activities, and zest for life never gave us any indicators that we'd lose Glenn so soon. It was both unimaginable and unthinkable.

This is a mother's journey of going from light to darkness and back to the light. It was a tough trip. Your mind is filled with regrets. You look back and wish you had handled certain situations differently. You recall the decisions that had lasting impact. Admittedly, Glenn and I weren't best friends. As hard as we both tried, and I really believe we did our best, there was a constant edge in our relationship, similar to a nagging ache or pain that doesn't go away.

Although Glenn's condition was diagnosed as genetic rather than hereditary, I guess deep inside of me existed a gnawing feeling that somehow, in some way, I was responsible for his shortened life. Each time we talked about it, he did his best to reassure me that he felt no anger or resentment toward me for what he had to endure—continuous hospital stays, operations, treatments, and on and off sickness. Because of the recurring challenges he faced over the years, I often avoided honest communication. Not wanting to cause any more discomfort than he was already enduring, to say, "I walked on egg shells" was in many ways the truth.

My journey began slowly and without direction. Sympathy cards and condolences kept coming, even from individuals with whom I had lost contact. Somehow they found out about my loss and wanted to express their sorrow. I felt and appreciated their need to offer support. It helped. It was really challenging to find a 'good day' or a 'pain-free day' when my life as it had been was torn apart. My faith was shaken and no one could really understand my broken heart.

In the beginning I found the most comfort in books. They were written by well-known authors who focused their writing on death and dying. In reading stories of near-death experiences or individuals who communicate to loved ones after dying, I slowly began to accept the possibility that Glenn would find a way to connect with me. I even had a few sessions with individuals who have the capacity to communicate with 'the other side'. During one particular instance, I was actually told that Glenn was present with me, loved me, and wanted me to know he is safe and happy. His reassurance through a third party was overwhelming and I held onto that experience for a long, long time. Since then, on my own, I have repeatedly asked Glenn to communicate—a light touch, a vision, a whisper. While it hasn't happened yet, it doesn't stop me from still asking.

Glenn's smile shines on me every day. There's a beautiful picture of him sitting at his school desk that I've placed beside my work area on my computer desk. It helps me to glance at him throughout the day and think that the smile is really here. I have placed other reminders throughout my home, so Glenn is never far from view. I suppose others do the same thing. All of us in our own ways do our best to hold onto memories and pictures to keep loved ones ever-present and close by.

Healing happens as time passes. You focus on all the good memories. You build your faith and trust and slowly accept those circumstances over which you have no control. You change what you can control—yourself.

I've done my share of asking, "Why?" Why did this happen to my son? Why did he have to endure so much suffering between times of joy and well-being? Why did God end his life when he was just beginning to *live*? It was almost easy for me to overlook Glenn's illness because everything around him was so positive. But he could never forget. He lived his reality. He dealt with it. He recognized he *had* to live with gusto when he felt at his best. He *knew* better than any of us his time was running out.

The journey that ultimately brings understanding and acceptance must be traveled individually. There is no answer to the 'why' that plagues all who suffer. It's taken me a long time to recognize that the question is not 'why' did something happen the way it did. The answer comes from finding the strength to believe in the invisible, trust in the way life unfolds and be grateful.

Glenn loved teaching. His enthusiasm for science, for the kids in his classroom, and for the staff and administration were fulfilling parts of his life. He'd share stories and brag about the progress his students were making. You could feel his energy and happiness in his calling as an educator. The classroom was a great diversion for what was going on in his personal life. No one ever knew of his health challenges. He never wanted anyone to treat him differently if they were aware of his fragileness.

As a family, we wanted to do something special in honor of Glenn's memory. We came up with the idea to provide an annual financial award to a deserving 7th grade science student. In some small way, this gesture would keep Glenn connected with the school he loved for years to come. A plaque currently hangs in the school's hallway with the names and years of three students voted by teachers as the outstanding student based on an essay contest. Returning to Hull Middle School for the annual awards assembly has been a great blessing, and part of our healing.

There's a saying that goes something like—*You can't possibly know what it feels like to walk in someone else's shoes.* It has more meaning to me now than it ever did before losing Glenn. People are suffering every day. Individuals everywhere are dealing with death and dying. No one can ever know how one will re-spond to life's toughest challenges until it happens. At the time of Glenn's death, I was often asked, "How will you ever get through the loss of your son?" I didn't have an answer. What could I say? For a while, I was dying inside. The expression—one day at a time—could never have been more real than it was three years ago.

Today, I love my son more than ever. I made a choice to remember the best of times. I know that he is without pain and that God did have a plan for Glenn when he was taken from us on the day of the Haiti earthquake. God chose Glenn because HE knew that my son was the perfect person to welcome, to embrace, and entertain the children of Haiti that lost their lives under horrific circumstances. I choose to believe this because Glenn loved children. And there is no doubt that that's what he's doing right now.

We can find hope. We can move on even when facing the challenges that feel like climbing Mt. Everest one step at a time. I have moved from darkness to light. If you are facing a difficult time, I know you can get through to the light as well. Give your-self time. Trust that if you are willing to be patient, answers will come. Know that what we *see* is not necessarily what *is*. We can only do our best, be our best, and have faith that our journey has purpose. Seek meaning for yourself. Don't ask *why.* Ask yourself, how can I grow from what I am experiencing? How can I become a better person? What can I do to strengthen my faith and be a light to others? Light overcomes darkness. All you have to do is light a candle to know this is true. May my story inspire you to meet your challenges with courage, faith, and trust. You are never alone.

WHO'S TALKING … *Known as "the boot girl," Bonnie Ross-Parker is founder of The Joy of Connecting and Xperience*

Connections, organizations that support women in reaching their professional goals. She also writes books on success. www.xperienceconnections.com

13: PUSHING THE ENVELOPE
SUZANNE, 60

TURNING SIXTY IS ONE OF THOSE MILESTONES THAT FORCES ONE to look back and take stock. My life has been complicated and challenging, mostly through my own choices. I was not one to follow a prescribed path, and I think about things I might have done differently, and things I would not have changed.

One thing I would not have changed is having my now 37-year-old son whom I raised as a single mother. He is an accomplished attorney, married now, with a child of his own. I feel like, "We did it!" We beat the odds, we beat the skeptics, and we beat the statistics. Now, I can finally look back with a better understanding of how we traveled the difficult road to get here.

I grew up in a middle-class Jewish home in Queens. I had loving parents: my father was a self-employed builder and my mother a homemaker. They were stymied by their youngest child (me), growing up in the 1960's, immersed in exploring all the alternative choices the world had to offer. My brother, nine years older, and my sister, two and a half years older, grew up with a much stricter set of rules.

My parents had tried unsuccessfully to have a third child, and when I arrived, I was like a self-propelled prediction of the future. I was born at home. After they had impatiently waited and tried to hurry along my arrival by such old-fashioned methods as a ride in the car on a bumpy road, I surprised my expectant parents, leaving no time for doctor or hospital. Their terror at my unexpected arrival turned to joy (my mother has told me about my brother and sister peeking from their bedroom doorways at 2:00 AM to see what the commotion was).

They treated me like a wonderful toy that they had been waiting for, allowing me tremendous freedom to discover myself, and then later couldn't relate to any of my choices, or figure out what to do with me. Their permission for me to explore the world and be whatever I wanted to be turned out to be too much freedom for all of us.

My brother was older and off to college when I was still in elementary school. My sister resented having to bring her little sister along to friends or to the playground and used every opportunity to show me how much she resented my existence and hated my guts. She lashed out at me at every opportunity with nasty words like "doodyhead" and "moron," and sometimes a hit or a push or worse. I was subjected to her reign of terror for years, and even as we grew up, she never resolved her feelings towards me. Growing up around all her anger had a long lasting effect on me. I wound up being the peacekeeper in the family, always trying to diffuse the tension whenever she was around.

I was extremely shy as a child and turned to people that accepted me unconditionally, first by befriending those not part of the "in" crowd, and later through random acts of teenage foolishness. I was tall and gangly, and my shyness made me feel different and apart, and it was difficult for me to approach others.

My friends were from the "B" crowd; they were okay, just not the choice friends. They were from the neighborhood, from school, and from other situations where we were thrown together like birthday parties and Hebrew school, even though parties were terrifying for me. I felt shy and awkward and just couldn't figure out how to act around people. I am sure that being terrified by my sister had something to do with this.

In and out of school, I immersed myself in art projects, writing stories and other creative and imaginary pursuits that were often solitary. I had notebooks filled with stories and poems and loved to act them out in front of the mirror, often with props.

When I was fifteen, my family moved from New York to Connecticut, landing me in a high school where I knew no one, a traumatic place for a shy teenager to be. It felt like I had gone back in time—the girls were wearing Peter Pan collars and knee socks, and no one had ever taken the train into New York City, which was only an hour away. Was this some sort of cruel joke?

I gravitated to the hippies, the art students, and the "outsiders". Finally, I had found a place where I fit in. I made a new best friend and we spent time cutting school to hang out in the park and drink bottles of Boone's Farm wine, and smoking pot in the darkroom of the art department. It was all part of being cool, being different, and being rebellious. For my "sweet sixteen" birthday, my parents let me use our vacation home, and I had a house party that lasted three days, filled with alcohol and drug-induced partying. I wasn't a bad kid or a troublemaker, just searching for my own identity and a sense of acceptance.

Although I loved my family, I was typical in wanting to create a life for myself that was completely different from theirs. I was a voracious reader, but leaned more towards the creative; I painted, I danced, and I couldn't envision a mainstream career. My parents encouraged me to become an architect, a lawyer, a teacher, but I wasn't ready to follow any of those paths. I was a very sensitive soul (I hated the idea of animals being killed for food, became a vegetarian at the age of 13, and have not eaten meat since) and was drawn to people, who, like myself felt like they were "outside" of society's dictates. I couldn't see where I fit in and didn't particularly want to fit in.

For a long time, my only interest was hanging out and smoking pot. For me, the euphoric high induced by drugs took away all my feelings of insecurity and not belonging. When I was high, I was calm, I was confident, and I was cool.

I started college locally and did okay academically, but still didn't have a direction. I got involved with the "wrong people," behaved badly, and was subsequently asked not to return to school. Out of desperation, my parents sent me on an extended visit to live in Israel, the cure that many Jewish parents turned to. It was a time to "re-discover" myself, and it was filled with new friendships, experiences, and adventures far from home (most of which I will never write about in fear that my mother will read this). When I returned, I headed back to college in upstate New York, and my parents were hopeful that I would "settle down" and finish school.

I became involved with a group of friends, working on artistic undertakings and projects for community and social change, including a prisoner rehabilitation agency where I developed a literary and art magazine that showcased the work of inmates from all the New York state prisons. I experienced the terrifying world of being inside a prison when I went to visit inmates. But I was beginning to feel a part of things and discovering what mattered to me.

During that time, I reconnected with a man that I had known peripherally in high school. I had never been in a serious relationship and I marveled that this person who had been so popular in high school would be interested in me, who was so quiet and shy and moved in a completely different circle. He had been the high-school football star and a gifted photographer—a beautiful specimen of muscle, strength and talent, and part of the "A" crowd.

I was a hippie, always in the art room, always a little spaced-out and dreaming. But a couple of years after high school, he lost a full college scholarship because of alcohol and drug use. Back then, there was little distinction between frequent substance use and addiction.

I was still in college in upstate New York, and he lived in Connecticut. I learned to navigate the murky waters of a long-distance relationship, and one that my parents did not approve of.

When I became involved with Jack, and they saw that this could potentially be a serious relationship, they panicked. Not only was their beloved (but troublesome) daughter losing interest in school, but she was involved with a black man who had left school and had no job and no prospects. Why couldn't I just stay in school or follow the path of both my brother and sister—graduate from college, meet someone, get married and have children? Why did I have to give them so much aggravation?

In spite of continuous arguments with my parents and their attempts to extinguish the relationship, Jack and I continued and our relationship grew. I felt abandoned by my family, and I gravitated to Jack and his family for comfort and acceptance. I never saw the difference in our skin color. I only saw a warm, loving person who cared for me and made me feel special in a way that I had never felt before. Unlike my family, his family completely accepted me.

When I announced that I was leaving school to live with him, it was my parents' worst fears realized. I left school and we wound up living in a dumpy apartment in a borderline neighborhood. I worked two jobs—at the local newspaper laying out classified ads and at a 24-hour convenience store at night. I paid the bills. He took photographs, hung out with "models" and contributed nothing.

Who was this person that I had changed my life for? Had I been so wrong about him? I hung on because I wanted desperately to be loved, hoped that things would work. But our inexperience and lack of tools to work on a real relationship took its toll, and we broke up.

We got back together several times and spent years trying to make it work. I thought that having a child seemed like the solution. (Yes, I know what you're thinking. That is not the reason to have a child. But what did I know?) When I became pregnant, I was overjoyed. Jack was not.

When I broke the news to my parents that I was pregnant at the age of 21, my mother's cries of, "How could you do this to me?" echoed the cries of many other parents. It was, after all, 1975 and middle-class, unmarried Jewish girls just didn't do things like that. And it wasn't bad enough that I was 21, or unmarried, or hadn't finished college and didn't have a job, but the father of the child was black. In their eyes, that presented a whole other set of problems that none of us were prepared for. They had a vision of what my life would be. This was not it.

Out of curiosity, I checked U.S. Census Bureau statistics and found that in 1970, white people comprised 87.5% of the population. By 2000, that number had dropped to 75.1%, and further dropped in 2010 to 63.7%.

It is projected that in 2042, whites will be fewer than 50% of the population, while people that are considered "mixed race" will more than triple from the current 5.2 million. At that time, I will be 89 years old.

But back in the 1970's, biracial children were far from the norm. And my parents feared how I would face the extreme challenges and difficulties ahead from a society that was not yet prepared to accept a single mother like me. They also feared how they would be affected and whether they would also face challenges of being accepted. What would they tell the relatives at the Passover table? What would they tell their friends at the synagogue or in the neighborhood?

Their initial reaction was not one of support and love, but recrimination and rejection. So I felt very alone. I shared my growing belly and my expectant joy hesitantly, hoping for their love and approval and accepting whatever scraps of attention I received. Like many young women, I was caught up in the fantasy of having a baby. I was completely out of touch with the reality. I left college before graduating, did not have a job, was still sharing an apartment with my college roommate, and had a boyfriend who liked to take photographs, get drunk, and was not particularly interested in earning a living. I was ill-prepared to be a parent. But I knew that no one was going to talk me out of having this child. I knew that we were meant to be together.

Against all the odds, against all conventions of society, and against the wishes of my parents, in 1976, I became a single mother. I was 22. The thinking of the time was that children born to single mothers would suffer poverty, they would be deprived of educational and job opportunities, and likely turn out to be delinquents. There was a common stereotypical image of single women having babies in order to collect welfare.

But I was not motivated by a welfare check—I came from a middle class home, I was educated, and I had middle class values at heart. I wanted my child to have the best education, and to never have to worry about having enough food to eat or clothing to wear. I wasn't sure how I was going to accomplish that, but I knew that it would involve a lot of sacrifices on my part. I was living in upstate New York, where I had returned to finish college. As much as New York City was disapproving, New York State was much worse. People stopped and stared openly. People made unkind comments. I tried to ignore them all, to not care. I tried to grow a thick skin, although it is hard not to be hurt when a stranger looks at your baby and says, "Oh my God!"

I sought out people that were accepting and brought them into our circle. My son's father continued to be a fleeting presence in our lives. I knew that I did not want to marry him (not that he was asking). What did he have to offer? He worked occasionally, still had substance abuse problems, and just couldn't seem to get his life on track.

He had grown up in a household full of women who regularly reminded him not to be a deadbeat like his father. What a perfect prescription for a self-fulfilling prophecy.

Jack's mother, a devout Christian, worked hard and raised

her children on her own. She was the church organist, the kids all sang in the choir, and she believed in hard work and discipline. Yet she couldn't help but direct her bitterness about her husband walking out on her on the one who looked most like him. They lived in the projects on Main Street because that was all she could afford. Positive role models were scarce, but angry female relatives were plenty. So I can't say that I blame the way Jack turned out. I just wish he would have wanted to change and break the cycle.

I was determined to present Jack in a positive light to our son, no matter what his shortcomings. He did not make this an easy task. I was forced to exclude him from our son's life until he got sober.

My son suffered from all the promises of visits, letters, and phone calls that never materialized. To help him deal with his anger and hurt, I provided a large cardboard box and told him that he could kick it, punch it, rip it, or throw it. I think I had a few go's at it myself. I also suggested that he write a letter to his father that we would not mail. He could say whatever he wanted, call him names, even swear at him. I promised that I would never read the letter, and I never did, but I am sure that there were far worse names in that letter than doodyhead and moron.

So I was left on my own. And I had a lot of figuring out to do. After all, being a parent does not come with instructions. Being a single parent, you don't have the support of the other parents when you're telling your child for the hundredth time that you are not buying that candy bar at the store or it's time to turn off the television; you don't have someone to take over so you can have a break after you've worked all day, cooked dinner, and read the same book six times because it's the only story your child wants to hear, and you don't have someone to tell you you're doing a good job or a lousy job or offer any words of encouragement or support.

You are on your own. I tried my best to be a consistent, loving presence in my son's life.

Ironically, I did get a lot of support from Jack's family. His sister was a single mother with three children who understood my situation and offered support and sisterhood. We spent a lot of time together and my son grew close to his cousins. Although she was a loving, caring person in my life, our choices couldn't have been more different. She had three children from three different fathers and had been on state assistance for many years. While I struggled to figure out how to create a better future, she was content with her life the way it was and wasn't particularly interested in exploring other options. I overlooked our differences, because I desperately needed her support. She accepted my son and me as family without hesitation and filled some of the void left by her brother's absence.

When my son was eight months old, I went back to finish my degree in art. I managed to find a babysitter for a few mornings a week so I could go to class, and I figured out that if I went to bed at 7:00 p.m. when he did, I could get up at midnight and paint undisturbed through the night. I balanced my studies—sometimes having to bring him to class, and sometimes being asked to leave class because of his loud babblings—with being a mother and managed to finish college.

I had been forced to go on state assistance and was subjected to some of the humiliating tactics of the welfare department. Although the "man in the house" rules had been struck down in the late 1960's, New York State continued to exercise their power to intimidate without fear of litigation. They'd show up unannounced and search through my dresser drawers to see if there was any evidence of a man living in my home (they didn't find anything). There were virtually no safeguards or protections for me or other assistance recipients. I was helpless and had to endure the humiliation so I could feed my child and pay the rent. I kept telling myself it was only temporary.

When my son was two, we moved to Chicago. I had met a man that I thought I could be in a serious relationship with and who would be a good father for my son. I landed a job running an information hotline for a women's organization, and my son and I remained in Chicago for a couple of years, even though the relationship didn't last. I think I had already become too used to being on my own and didn't see why I should have to tolerate a man who put soy sauce on everything I cooked.

I was able to get my son into a wonderful daycare where he thrived and made friends. We met other mixed-race families and felt less isolated. I joined a babysitting co-op, where the exchange of time substituted for money, so I was able to occasionally get out with friends.

As my son grew, I shared openly with him and answered all his questions. Having grown up myself in a time of free expression, I did not want to stifle my son's curiosity or his freedom to express himself in any way. Of course, this can backfire when you are standing on line in the grocery store and your three-year-old happily announces, "Mommy, I love your vagina!" Or when walking down the street, he spots an elderly woman and cries out, "Look, Mommy, a witch!" But my son was filled with exuberant happiness and brought joy to everyone he encountered. People began to overlook the fact that our skin colors were different, and they began to just see a beautiful child.

In 1979, a group formed called "Single Mothers by Choice." This was a group of mostly professional women who did not feel the urge to marry but wanted a child. I felt annoyed—who did they think they were, coming up with an idea that I had already been living? I felt that I was the original single-mother-by-choice and they were only riding on my coattails. In retrospect, I see that it was a sign that times were changing, that women were making their own choices and not feeling bound by society's dictates.

Who could have predicted that over the years, we would become more tolerant and it would be not only acceptable, but fashionable to have a baby as a single parent?

In the decades between 1970 and 1990, there was a noticeable shift in social values. Women became more independent and the stigma of being unmarried lessened. Single motherhood grew among more advantaged women, women that were educated and economically independent. The desire to be a single mother was no longer limited by a disapproving world.

As of 1970, 11% of births were to unmarried women. By 1990, that rate grew to 28%, and today it is 41%. Look around and you will see every mass-market publication and website filled with news of celebrities becoming single mothers. Now it's not only fashionable, but aspirational. You are probably thinking that I was ahead of my time, and you would be right.

Although I had made a life in Chicago, I began to feel the separation of living far from my family and wanted to reconnect with them. In 1980, my son and I took an excruciatingly long train ride from Chicago to New York, then on to Connecticut. I think it was something like 18 hours or more. He was thrilled with the ride, went off with the conductor to explore the train, happily played, ate and napped, while I endured an endless ride, not being able to sleep for fear of leaving him unattended.

When we arrived in Connecticut, there was a noticeable change in attitude. My son entered a full-day progressive nursery school where his class included children of all races and colors. No one seemed surprised or shocked that a single woman had a biracial child. On the contrary, people were accepting, warm, and friendly. It felt like a new beginning in our lives.

I can't say that over the years I did not continue to encounter stares or comments, but I learned to chalk them up to narrow-minded people. Although I had mended my relationship with my parents, (my father was an observant Jew, and family was the most important thing to him), I stood firm in my independence. I always worked, often two jobs, and struggled to pay the bills and provide for my son. I became an expert bargain shopper, always looking for deals, and learned to cook inventively with whatever I had in the cupboards.

Learning about my son, I often felt like Margaret Mead in the jungle studying the behavior of young males. What was he thinking? Why was he acting like that? I didn't have a lot of answers and dug deep into my own experience to figure things out.

I'm sure that my son turned to his friends when he didn't want to confide in me or didn't get the information he was seeking. As a single parent, my tendency was to share too much and to rely on my son too much for support, for comfort, and for companionship.

When he was young, I used to pack up the car every other weekend and head off for some destination—somewhere to take us away from our daily routine. We went to parks, museums, attractions, and any place that I could think of that would be interesting, entertaining, and wasn't too far. We went to Sturbridge Village and Catskill Game Farm, to the Children's Museum, and Kent Falls. It was a chance to spend quality time together and a chance for me to assuage my guilt from the busy week that often resulted in limited time together.

We also spent time with my parents who had grown to love my son with a special connection and cherish the wonderful child that he was. They cheered for all his accomplishments, praised every academic and athletic victory, and became his biggest champions and supporters. I think they developed a relationship with him different from their other grandchildren. And in turn, he adored them, loved spending time with them, and having them in his life. He confided in his grandfather and sought out his advice and support. As an adult, he continues to have a special bond with his 92-year old grandmother.

We settled in a Connecticut town with a good school system and lived there throughout my son's school years. He attended an open classroom elementary school which provided lots of challenging opportunities for gifted students, and he excelled. I'm not sure that I could have survived the open environment, too many opportunities to be checking on what the other classes were doing, but my son thrived. I always encouraged him to do his best because I knew what he was capable of, and that a good education was the best way to ensure a good future.

He earned a scholarship to an elite prep school, so while he was receiving an extraordinary education, he also spent every day with children from wealthy families, some of whom were not open-minded about their children befriending a child of color. But his incredible personality, warmth, and intelligence fostered many long-lasting friendships and he was able to navigate through the challenges of dealing with narrow-minded people. From there, he went on to graduate from college and law school, as far from a statistic as possible.

Looking back, I see that our society's definition of family has become more expansive and we have generally become more accepting. The opportunities for children growing up in a single parent home can be the same as for any child. However, I know that the majority of single mothers are still struggling—financially, emotionally, psychologically, and spiritually, as I did. The stresses of juggling work, paying bills, and making all life's decisions on your own can leave little time for being the kind of parent one wishes to be.

What have I learned from being a single parent? The importance of creating an extended family. Having positive people in your life that can offer support, advice, and a shoulder to lean on when you're so exhausted you just want to cry. Finding good role models for your child—teachers, coaches, friends, relatives, and others that can shift the focus from the absent parent and show your child that there are actually good people in the world. Taking time for yourself—even if it is a quiet cup of tea or glass of wine in the evening (or morning, depending on the day), it is vital to take a few moments each day to recharge so you can continue to keep moving forward. Remembering to keep things in perspective—we all make mistakes, and there is no perfect parent. But if you keep the lines of communication open with your child, you will eventually work things out.

Parenting has been an on-going journey of growth and discovery about myself as a parent and as a person. My relationship with my son still continues to evolve, and now, as a grandparent, it has come full circle. I have the joy and privilege of re-living all those precious babyhood times with my granddaughter.

I wonder why things had to be so difficult and I wonder how we can make it easier for the single mothers of the future. I know it sounds cliché, but Motherhood is truly the most important job in the world.

WHO'S TALKING ... *Suzanne Golub is a 2nd degree Reiki practitioner, an avid reader, and a serious gardener. She works at a university office, and she is a lifelong vegetarian, gourmet cook, and baker; but most of all, she loves acting like a kid with her two-year-old granddaughter.*

14: STEP-MOTHERHOOD
MARY, 60

AS AN ENGLISH TEACHER, IT IS NATURAL THAT I LOVE WORDS.
One word of special importance to me is stepmother. "The
earliest recorded use of the prefix step-, in the form steop-, is
from an 8th-century glossary of Latin-Old English words. Ste-
opsunu... steopmoder.... Similar words recorded later in Old
English include stepbairn, stepchild and stepfather. The words
are used to denote a connection resulting from the remarriage
of a widowed parent and are related to the word ástíeped,
meaning bereaved, with stepbairn and stepchild occasionally
used simply as synonyms for orphan." (http://en.wikipedia.
org/wiki/Stepmother).

"Ástíeped, meaning bereaved." I believe those words may say
it all in our world today. The etymology of the prefix *step-* recalls
the sadness of the child whose family connection has been broken
due to divorce. The word recalls the feelings of loss the biological
mother experiences due to the divorce and the feelings that the
actual stepmother encounters when she enters that role.

Being a stepmother is a difficult part to assume, one steeped
in the sadness of the actual word itself, one that comes with the
stories of cruel stepmothers from *Cinderella, Snow White*, on and
on throughout the ages. Even my own mother was raised by a
stepmother who abused her physically and emotionally as a child.

In spite of it all, in 1997, I became a stepmother to children
whose mother was engulfed in negative feelings and insecurities

about who I was and who I would become in her children's lives. Her mantra to the children was: "*She means nothing to you!*"

Here is my story, beginning all those years ago with six-year-old Amy at a neighborhood pool in Dunwoody, Georgia, and ending with how this experience led to some of my greatest joys in life as a sixty-year-old woman today.

"Mary, I am afraid to swim. I don't want to get in the water."

"Perhaps if we just sit on the stairs here together, we can play with the small children. How does that sound? I will sit right here beside you."

"Okay, but I can't get water on my face."

"Okay."

TWO WEEKS LATER

"Look, Ames, I got you a floating swimmie thing to wear that will keep you above the water. Would you like to try it? I will stay with you."

"I don't know."

"Here, let's put it on, and then we can go over to the stairs."

"I don't know. Well, okay."

We are on the third step in the water of the pool when I feel nails digging into my arm, drawing blood with their raggedy edges. I pause.

"No, No—I can't!!!" Her voice blisters the air.

We watch other swimmers, younger than her, swimming by, laughing and twirling like otters in the water. We resume our stance as we did on the stairs a few weeks before, not moving off stair three, Amy on my hip clinging as tightly as she can with athletic legs. We begin to talk with the younger children in the water, asking them about their toys. Amy leans over and retrieves a toy for a younger child and then begins to play with her from the safety of my arms.

THREE WEEKS LATER

Amy is now in the swimmie thing, perched on my hip, and we are in the pool in very shallow water. The pool is filled with young-sters splashing, screaming, laughing, throwing water on each oth-er. I think to myself that the noise alone is going to scare her out of the water on this blazing day.

She surprises me. As we walk close to the wall, she leans over and grasps the edges, with her legs still wrapped around my hips. She stays like that for a minute, and I suggest she turn and let go of me. Nope, too much, too fast, she instead turns and grasps me once more in the death grip of fingernails and toenails. I wonder at this point if she will ever let go.

As the afternoon wears on, we return to the water, play on the stairs, and swirl a little, with a little up-in-the-air motion, but not out of my arms. It is time to call it a day when she asks to play again. I say yes to the stairs and a twirl in the pool. As I head back to the landing, she turns, lets go, and grabs the side of the wall. Her face is frantic for a second. I do not move. She does not move. Then she smiles and turns to me. I say, "Super, Amy." She says back, "Super."

FOUR WEEKS LATER

She stands on the side of the pool. I am in the water. Her swim-mies drip water but snugly frame her body and arms. Looking at her standing above me, I challenge her. "Jump to me," I say.

"What?" is the only reply.

"Jump and I will catch you."

She shakes her head back and forth.

I challenge her again. "You know what I would like to see you do? You know how you can do that 'supa' thing where you touch your toes in the air? You can do that, and I will catch you before you go under the water! What do you think? You know how to do that. It is so easy for you, and you know how to land feet first, but you won't even have to land; I will catch you, and you won't even go under the water. We will yell 'supa' together when you jump. Want to try it?" I am guessing that she will run to her dad and never speak to me again, but she stands there, actually considering this crazy thing I had just proposed to her.

"How would we do it again?" she asks.

I repeat the idea again, this time with greater clarity. I break it down into three steps. "First you stand on the edge of the pool like you would to touch your toes in the air when you jump. Then you jump off the side and yell 'supa' as you touch your toes, then I catch you in the water. Number 1—stand on the side; number 2—jump and 'supa!'; number 3—I catch you. That's it. You wanna try it? We can just start with number 1."

Much to my disbelief, she assumes the number 1 position on the side of the pool for a few minutes. I just chat about inconsequential things for a few minutes like how pretty the lake looks and how we are going to eat hamburgers at the pool in a little while.

"So how about 'supa step 2?" I emphasize "supa," making it sound like the most delightful word on the planet. I say, "Let's just practice saying 'supa' together without jumping, okay? 'Supa! Supa!'" The words ring in the air a few times. She laughs, but just stands on the side of the pool.

"Well, what do you think?"

"How will you catch me?"

I show her by raising my arms and smiling. Then I think of an in-between step. "I can just have you sit on the side of the pool, and you can 'scooch' off the side into my arms," I state.

We practice a slight "scooch" off the side of the pool from a seated position once or twice, and she clamors up to the edge once more. This time she stands above me. Our eyes lock; she doesn't sit down, and I know something has clicked in her brain. Without even asking, I begin the count.

"Number 1," I say. She assumes the position standing on the edge of the pool. "Number 2," I say. I don't expect it, and am nearly late in my response, but she suddenly springs off the side of the pool with an enormous "supa" belching from her chest as she touches her toes in midair and lands feet first in the pool. I grab her before she can go under as she clings to me like a tree frog, nails digging into my arms again, but with her head thrown back in triumph. We look at each other, faces inches apart and yell "supa" together at the top of our lungs. A new game has been born; a monster has been defeated.

"She means nothing to you."

We are driving along in the car, and Amy Grant comes on the radio. "You like to dance and listen to the music. I like to sing with the band," Julie says. She begins singing the song, every word articulated like an adult from the back seat. She is five years old. Amy Grant is her favorite pop performer. Much to the chagrin of her siblings, she continues, now winding up into a full seat-belted performance, resplendent with hand gestures and a larger than life stage voice from the backseat: "I think you could be so good for, good for me baby, good for me baby!" She takes a seat bow and her siblings all laugh together, rolling their eyes and yelling over each other about how glad they are that she has concluded her performance for the day.

Days later, looking at the Sunday paper, I see the announcement—Amy Grant is coming to Chastain Park to perform. We can take Julie, no other children, just lovely Julie dressed up for a picnic dinner glittering with candles at the outdoor venue known in Atlanta for its elegant charm, a perfect Julie evening. I am on the phone to Ticket Master and with a song in my own heart, I hear the attendant say there are tickets half way up the hill, center stage. This is one time I don't mind the extra fees paid for purchasing outside of the direct venue.

I plan. First there has to be the perfect picnic basket with a tablecloth, linen napkins, plastic plates that resemble china, silverware that is neatly rolled into the napkins and tied with grosgrain ribbon, a small vase for live flowers, two wooden TV trays to create a table, and two silver candleholders with white candles to set off the table. The food needs to include Julie's favorites: shrimp cocktail, a chicken casserole, and a small salad. This is Julie's night, the child who is sensitive to aesthetics and atmosphere and who would later mature into an interior designer.

The evening dawns glorious.

She is dressed in her finest dress, a light blue cotton pinafore, below her knees in length with a slight flare at the waist. A ribbon adorns her hair, washed and gleaming in soft tendrils; small sandals peak out from under her hemline. She is the image of the small mistress out on the town in an adult world. I feel a smile on my face as her dad streaks through Atlanta traffic on a Friday evening with Amy Grant tunes scenting the air throughout the ride to Chastain.

When we arrive at the park, it is sunset. She holds my hand, and we lightly navigate the steps, uneven with quarried stone. We are two ladies dressed for an evening out on the town, and her warm brown eyes smile into mine as the elegant world of understated Chastain Park unfolds around us. Our table is carefully laid out, candles lit, and we join the audience, proudly aware that our small ensemble has added to the charm of the evening. She is proud to be part of this setting.

Tune after tune grace the night. She holds the linen napkin in her lap, carefully eats her shrimp so that the juice does not get on her dress, and sings along, this time delighting fellow audience members as she murmurs the words song after song. She is self-aware in this adult world and follows my lead as we toast the nightfall from fluted plastic goblets.

The magical evening is about to close. The audience surges

in applause, Julie is held up so she can see while she claps in appreciation. Then everyone begins to hold their candles aloft to encourage the dear Amy Grant to sing an encore. Her dad and I hold the candles high when I hear her begin to whimper and cry out, "Ohhh, you are hurting me," staring right into my eyes. I couldn't believe it. I was hurting her—how? Her dad and I place our candles on the table. He begins a frantic search of her legs. A smidgeon of wax from a candle has landed on her foreleg from his candle. There is no burn, just some wax drying on the skin. She cries in accusation that I have hurt her. I think I will cry as well at the thought. We remove the wax with some ice; fortunately, the area is not even red; then spend some time making sure she is back on an even keel before leaving. Fellow revelers stare at us and inquire if she is okay. They, too, examine the site where the wax has been and assure her as well that there is not even a mark.

A weak smile appears on her face. For a few moments, she has considered me the "evil queen" of the night, and I feel stung by the emotions I see stirred within her. Then on the walk up the cold dark stairs, she reaches for my hand. I look down at her; she smiles. I tell her once again how sorry I am that she has hurt her leg. She smiles again and in the candlelight softly says, "Thank you for bringing me here tonight," as her eyes glow with light. She trusts me again, this time stronger than before.

"She means nothing to you."

12:25 A.M. ON APRIL 8, 1998, IN ATLANTA, GA

I am asleep. A tug on my arm awakens me as I hear my voice, mine but not mine saying, "It's coming. Get the children now." It is dead quiet, so I awaken my husband in alarm. We both respond as if we had practiced this drill a million times. He heads for the boy's room and I go into the girls' room, and the dead silence ends with noises I didn't know existed. The house is being torn apart;

Julie is screaming in the top bunk; the ceiling is peeling away. I want to run away, but I cannot. I use my mother voice, the quiet commanding one. "Stop screaming." With that she listens, and I hold my arms up to her. She resides on my left hip, and I look to the bottom bunk. Amy's eyes are open and she is sitting upright. "Come here." I gesture with my right arm, and she closes the divide onto my right hip. At 5 feet 3 inches, I now have the equivalent of over 100 pounds of sprawling arms and legs to manipulate out of the room.

As I turn and take the first step, I wonder if I can physically do it. Then there is no more time for coherent thinking. The room blows apart as a 3,000 pound tree hurtles into the sidewall. Rafters tear from the roofline, and the ceiling and wooden framework pound us to the floor. The two girls lie underneath me as a second rafter hits the back of my head. I duck lower, and the three of us stare at each other face-to-face. The lightning has created a phantom-like strobe effect, illuminating the room as we try to comprehend what is happening.

Amy asks in a small voice, "What is it, Mary?" At this point, the floor is moving underneath us, vibrating as it shifts.

I respond, "I don't know," which at the time is an honest answer. All I can think at the moment, if one can even call it a thought, is of the old Atlantis movie where the island is sinking and there is strobe Hollywood lightning piercing the film set.

And then we pray aloud together. I didn't know I would do this in such a moment, but I give myself up and say, "Let's pray together." And they do; my blessed Jewish children pray with their Catholic stepmom. "Dear Lord, (Dear Lord), please don't let anything else hit us (please don't let anything else hit us), and please protect us (and please protect us)." The prayer ends as a giant waterfall of ice cold water deluges us inside our house from the now open roof. The moments seem to last forever, the unearthly feeling of being inside our home while rain pours onto us and lightning glows in the room like an unearthly chandelier.

And then it is over. We shiver in the darkness, a tree resting six inches from Julie, my old oak bureau from childhood creating a small lean-to upon which the rafters find their new home after residing above the room for nearly 30 years.

Within a few minutes the girls' dad screams our names at the door, and we climb from the carnage that a few minutes before has been a childhood bedroom, a place of safety and refuge. We scramble down what remains of the stairwell to the remains of the rooms below, where we join my stepson. The master bedroom and front porch are gone, the girls' bedroom is annihilated, and the house has been moved off its foundation.

On the weekends that follow, we go to family therapy together. We make tornado quilts; we are interviewed in articles that appear in the AJC; and we speak with teachers at the children's school, so they are aware of the trauma that has transpired in their lives. We move into temporary housing for six months with beds on floors, and the remaining furniture and belongings stored in boxes throughout the home. Eventually, we buy a new home, re-settle once again, and let the PTSD, post-traumatic stress disorder, subside from our lives.

"She means nothing to you!"

No matter the voice that is whispered, whether softly or with cruel intentions, no matter the crazy retaliations in the name of that voice, acts of love form bonds that cannot be broken, no matter where the relationship may travel. Acts of love are authentic and are embedded in our hearts whether the child is able to acknowledge them at the moment or not.

I encourage you to step up to the "step" of the word stepmother. Your acts of patience, of giving, of even heroism in the face of walls and walls of fear, may bring these children through their childhoods, to an adulthood that acknowledges that we are human, we are frail, but in spite of these flaws, we are and they are individuals who understand love, have experienced love, and who are capable of loving others. That is what happened in my case. Those little children are now treasured adults in my life.

What greater gift can a woman afford to others than to share her maternal nature with children who so desperately need to experience love in the confusing world of parents who have gone separate ways and no longer trust each other, much less a new woman who has entered their lives. *"She means nothing to you"* is only the boogey man of adults. *The truth is a stepmother can mean everything to a child.*

Be that stepmother or step-grandmother. Be everything that you can be to the children in your life, regardless of who gave them birth. They need you, no matter what anyone else says.

WHO'S TALKING … *Mary Mattson's hobby in recent years has been nesting in her cozy home on the banks of the Chattahoochee River. A former English teacher, she is now a college professor, teaching education courses to future teachers.*

15: PROVING MOTHER WRONG
INGRID, 74

MY MOTHER TOLD ME THAT I WOULD LIE IN MY BABY CARRIAGE, captivated by the sun and shade, looking into the sparkling leaves. And this is as I am today; I look at the light and shadows and wonder. I see a painting in everything beautiful.

There was very little available in art supplies when I was a little girl. It was after the big war, World War II. We had escaped Dresden on the last train out before the bombing that killed over 125,000 people. We were glad just to be alive and to have something to eat.

When I started school at age five, we didn't even have paper, but did our exercises on a small slate board with a slate pencil. My God, I sound old!

But Germany had just come out of the war and educators were trained for a short time. In the little village we lived in, teachers were emergency teachers; too many professionals were lost to the war. I don't believe they had ever heard of a lesson plan. There were no schoolbooks. Most of the hour was spent talking about the war or writing ideas in simple sentences on the blackboard.

In Sindersfeld, we had eight grades in one schoolroom. Each long bench was occupied by one grade. I still had the slate board I took with me when we escaped Dresden before the bombing, and I sat on the bench with the other children in my grade. The older students would teach the little ones, and the teacher oversaw everything.

Altogether, we learned very little about anything and nothing at all about art, except maybe Albrecht Dürer, who was one of the very best painters in Germany of the 16th century. Everyone knew his *Hare* and obviously his *Praying Hands,* although my confrontation with God came long before I learned about Durer.

I was six, and being an inquisitive little girl, I asked the priest, who came once a week to set us right, where, exactly, was God? He told me that he was all-present in the tabernacle.

This was a matter of great confusion to me, looking at the lovely sculptured tabernacle in our pretty church. How did He fit in there? Well, I could test this for sure. I figured if I would stick my tongue out at Him, He would notice. If He was truly present, He would come and punish me.

Well, he surely did exactly this. The retribution came from the whole village. How could a six-year-old stick out her tongue at the altar and at Jesus? For a whole day, I had to stand in the corner of our one-room school. Oh, the torture and the humiliation. So much for a curious mind!

By second grade I had moved to a medium-sized town and all of a sudden into a real school, still no schoolbooks but one teacher per grade. With great luck, I had a delightful and brilliant old maid schoolmarm as my third-grade teacher.

Fräulein Keller would take the class out into the fields, where she taught us botany with the plants we were surrounded by, and history by telling us stories like *The Odyssey.*

Since I received little encouragement about any kind of accidental academic accomplishment, the easiest way out was to copy from better students' efforts. This worked fine until a remark a teacher threw at me which is still very much alive in my memory. I actually had raised my hand and knew and cared to share a brilliant answer. The teacher was so impressed that he told the class: "*Ein blindes Huhn findet auch mal ein Korn.*" Meaning, "Sometimes a blind hen finds a corn, too." This remark hurt then when I was ten years old and even now.

My father rarely communicated with me about things from school, but one day he got it in his head that his oldest should know her timetables. I was eight and we actually studied them in school. Just like our history classes with its important years of wars or whatever, math had to be rote memory. I was set down at the table, and my father would ask me: "How much is 7 by 9?"

I knew some answers, but honestly, I hadn't studied, and when I got nervous, I knew even less. With every mistake—Pow! a slap in the face. Consequently, I memorized the timetables by heart—but not in my heart.

When paper, pens, pencils, and notebooks existed, I spent a good amount of time doodling. The question is was I bored in school, or was I interested in drawing? I can't say. My mother told me that I was too lazy to think. My brother was the genius, so I was free to do as little as possible in school. Which is what I did.

So I wasn't an exemplary student. But when a teacher asked me to draw the Chinese Great Wall on the board for the class to copy, I was very proud. Other kids actually complimented me.

When I was in my teens, there was a contest sponsored by the local movie theater. They were showing *Heidi* and there was a prize for designing a dress for Heidi. I won a pair of free movie tickets and my drawing was exhibited in the theater.

After this awesome success, there was nothing but a constant desire to draw women's faces—when I should have been studying.

I grew up. I learned to type and take shorthand, even while I preferred to draw or look out the window. But school was finished for me. A tumor was discovered in my left lung. They feared I had TB and sent me to a sanatorium.

For a year, I had practically no schooling at all, just an occasional hour in German, English, and mathematics. History was not a favorite subject for German teachers. After a year taking up to 50 pills a day, I survived a lung operation, which was a tough medical operation those days.

So it is easy to understand that I was not prepared to go on to any higher education, but I did end up with a fine job in the purchasing department of the world-renowned company Leitz, Inc., the makers of Leica.

At that time, Radio Luxembourg played the music of American hit parades. I listened and sang along religiously. Out of curiosity and admiration for the States, I studied and wrote pages and pages about the United States of America. I guess that proved that I wasn't all that lazy—when there was an interest that allowed me to escape.

My wish was to get far away from where I was to the country of Pat Boone and Elvis Presley. My all-time favorite song was "Young Love, First Love" by Sonny James—not corny at all, ha! These hits brought romance to conflicted teenagers like me.

At 20, I persuaded my company to transfer me to New York. Leitz sponsored me and I worked for them in New York for about a year. New York of those days was not the New York of now. I was disappointed with the dirt and confusion of the city. In fact, I was disillusioned with the USA. I was disenchanted, finding hotel rooms with gum under the desktops, and streets with garbage everywhere.

With a Swiss girlfriend of mine, I left New York and travelled to San Francisco. Of course I lost my heart there, one of the most charming and beautiful cities in the world. I had a lovely year of dating, partying, and also working. But then what to do for the rest of my life, continuing my career working in a bank? No, there had to be more of a frame to my life. What I needed was to go back to Germany and marry someone just right for the right life. That was what I intended to do. I got a job as a nanny for a family with a penthouse in Manhattan in order to pay for a permit to go back home. And guess what? On the day I got my permit, I met Wayne.

He was my dreamboat, and he proposed to me after knowing me for two weeks. He was handsome, he had a wonderful sense of humor, he was approaching his last year in law school, and he had all the right ideas for the future. Just my type. How could I say no?

I smoked a pack of cigarettes a day because of tittering nerves before I said yes. After going back to Germany to spend one last Christmas with my parents, I returned to the United States. We got engaged formally in front of his grandparents as witnesses and married soon after.

But our marriage was difficult. I felt that one of our problems was that I didn't feel comfortable about my educational background. All our friends would talk about the universities they had attended and I felt quite insecure in the simplest party situations. I remembered that my mother said I was too lazy to think; my brother was the genius. Not only that, she told me, I had married a man who clearly was too handsome for me.

I couldn't do anything about the "too handsome" part, but I most certainly could prove to my mother that I was not a lazy thinker. I could earn a college degree.

My husband insisted that I didn't need to work, and so I had time to start painting again. My first real attempt was a picture I saw in the *New York Times* for the "neediest". It was a mother with child, and I was pregnant at the time, so I felt a connection.

I think I did a fairly decent job in the execution on my first "real" painting, but it turned out to be too depressing—after all, that mother was one the *Times* called "neediest."

From then on I only concentrated on subjects that made me happy: flowers or happy people and landscapes. Most of all, I loved to use color.

I was enamored of a German painter named Franz Marc. I love his use of color and his wonderful rounded shapes which he used in his animal paintings. He was one of the key figures of the

German Expressionist movement and one of the founders of the well-known "Blaue Reiter", a group of great painters.

Over the years I had the good fortune to be close to the Metropolitan, visited the Prado, the Munich Pinothek, the London Tate, the Parisian museums, and lots more. I loved impressionism best. When I stood in front of a Monet or Renoir, I felt like I was eating ice cream, just such pleasure! To look at the painting close and just seeing dots and stripes, and then standing back and having the paintings come together and alive filled me with joy.

When we moved to a new house and I found the dining room dull, I decided to make it more stimulating by creating an 8' x 12' mural imitating Monet's garden. I left the house out, since I didn't want more neighbors and had wonderful flowers, trees, and rose trees on my wall. I copied it from a Monet art book and was proud of my work. We could eat our dinner in Monet's garden!

But when I saw the original work in Paris, I was shocked how different the colors were. The print in the book had not done it justice at all. That is why I need to see the originals.

But having a baby—and then two—killed my not-so-promising art career. How could I protect my precious toddlers from oil paints and turpentine? How could I protect the house from their curious fingers and oil paints? Overshadowed by a practically all-consuming love for my children, my need to paint took a backseat.

However, I was free to concentrate on getting an education. I enrolled in night school to get a high-school diploma, and after I received my GED, I was accepted at Western Connecticut State College. I decided I wanted to become a teacher. I would have the same vacations as Kirsten and Kenneth, then three and five years old. I could spend more time with them, which I longed for, and I wouldn't have to worry about babysitters.

I was excited because I was able to handle college courses in a foreign language. It wasn't easy. I broke down in tears. How could I continue to handle five courses, insurmountable amounts of homework, children at home, cooking, and housework? Furthermore, Wayne had gone into politics, which presented us with a busy social life. We designed and built a new house. And when I told my mother my plans to get a college degree, she told me that it was a great idea, but I would never make it.

I thought I had figured out what professors wanted. But "works cited" and "foot notes" were foreign territory for me on top of a foreign language. When I got my first A on a paper about Ophelia in *Hamlet*, I couldn't sleep for two nights. I could do it, and I could do it well. Hallelujah! With a college education, I could still have the social joys of talking about the weather in New England, but now I knew other things to talk about. I was going to college.

Painting, raising children, going to college, and accompanying my husband—who was then a senator—to social functions kept me wildly busy, but I earned the degree I needed to become a schoolteacher.

I was the proudest graduate. Wayne, the children, and my in-laws came to applaud. I went on to earn my master's, but that meant very little to me compared to the first American college degree.

I was hired as a high-school German language teacher. This was amazing, since very few jobs in foreign languages were available around the state. I even taught Spanish for two years.

I bloomed as a German teacher. What wonder and excitement to teach students my own language and culture. Even though we had textbooks, I preferred to design my own classes: travel in German-speaking countries, literature, art and architecture, music, and history (my least favorite, for obvious reasons).

I got the students to sing and dance with me, write poetry, and hike. We spent three weeks in Germany as exchange students— and I was presented with the honor of best German teacher in Connecticut.

After earning a BS degree, two masters' and one sixth-year, which provided me with the certification to be a school administrator, and working as a dean of students in my high school for 10 years, I had proved to my mother—and to myself—that I was somebody.

And so I taught school for 31 years, during which time, for many reasons, the man who was too handsome for me and I divorced.

My second husband, Jack, is a rabbi and a clinical psychologist. He's not only brilliant, but he's also a great support for me. For the last 31 years, he still thinks I am the smartest, most charming, and beautiful woman he has ever known; and he's a man with whom I can discuss any topic—theatre, literature, history, philosophy, everything cultural. I learn from him, and he is my number one fan when it comes to my painting. He had a small book published which combined his love poems to me and paintings I did that he loved. It's our book of blessings.

So, married to Jack, I felt more interested in broadening my art. The paintings I used to like best were Georgia O'Keefe's sexy flowers, and ironically, now my last name is Bloom and I can sign my paintings, "I Bloom".

Painting murals has become a hobby for me. Give me a wall and I am happy! When my son moved into a small condo, his kitchen was separated from his dining area by a beam in the ceiling and then again the same way from the living room area.

I painted a harbor scene with a boardwalk, some boats, and a lighthouse in the distance, clouds and birds. I was surprised when his dining room area looked about three times as big and pleasant. My upstairs TV room became a studio overlooking Manhattan. Doors became bookshelves. Our king-size bed was converted into a four-pillar bed surrounded by meadows and grapes.

Then I helped some friends change their views. I painted a balcony overlooking the Long Island Sound onto two large closet doors. Oh, what fun! My "customers" loved sitting in a new and cheerful environment.

Almost every room in my house has something I've painted. The master bathroom is marbleized and my front door has mosaic panels. My entrance floor looks like inlaid wood. My daughter told my son not to let me into the house with paints. Too late, I already had converted his bedroom into a room looking out onto the Mediterranean.

I was wife, mother, *housefrau*, artist, and schoolteacher; and by 65 I was exhausted, but was I really looking forward to retirement? I was becoming increasingly worried about my future without a formal job. I saw myself sitting around the house in a robe, getting up from an endless breakfast to go to Turner Classics once again and spending my day between the chair, the couch and the bed.

But retire I did, and I did not spend my day eating breakfasts and watching the BBC.

Always interested in painting, I signed up for every available art course for seniors at a local college. Not only that, I signed up for theater classes and was astonished by the quality of the teachers. What fun I had, taking classes with very little financial burden, not worrying about grades, but just for the joy of learning.

But wait a minute. This was too easy. Why not tax my brain a little?

I signed up for courses just like all other students, responsible for the homework, papers, tests, and quizzes. I signed up for Spanish, English literature, poetry; you name it, anything I found interesting. In art class, I made sculptures out of clay, transparent tape, and Styrofoam. I made a wonderful fool of myself in my improvisation class where the other students were four or five decades younger than I was! Instead of taking the elevator, I bounded up the stairs two at a time to prove to myself that I was still young enough to do that!

What surprised me was the ease of writing papers on the computer. You have spell check and grammar check. I cannot tell you how long it used to take me to come up with one paper so many years ago. Of course, my knowledge of English had improved in 50 years!

Some courses have been a challenge. Memorizing lines in theatre class was difficult. It took me ten hours to memorize twenty lines out of Moliere's *Tartuffe*. I would practice my lines while I walked around the block. Exercise for head and foot! Then when the final performance came, much to my horror, I kept stuttering and forgetting my lines. My poor fellow actors!

The accomplishment I am most proud of is my resilience. I stuck with it.

The professors told me that with my enthusiasm I was a teacher's dream. I got all A's. I earned my associate's degree at 73.

I have reason to keep my brain going. My mother died of Alzheimer's, which showed up just about at the age I am now.

My mother was still fine when she gave herself a wonderful 70th birthday party. My daughter and I made the trip to Germany for the big event. At the party, in front of all of her important friends, my mother announced that she was proud of me and my brother and our accomplishments. She said it, but it was too late. It didn't mean much to me at that point. I already had proved to myself that I could do it. I always used to feel judged by my mother, but as Albert Einstein said, "Everybody is a genius. But if you judge a fish by its ability to climb a tree, it will live its whole life believing that it is stupid."

I keep going. I stretch every morning, walk with my friends for an hour, twice a week jazzercise, painting, and college classes.

My challenge now is, and I know it is considered a platitude, to enjoy life and live in every moment. It is not easy, but it could be a learned behavior. How many wonderful days do we have? When I lift weights, I try to think of the feeling in the muscles. When I brush my teeth, I think of the movement and pressure. When I see the beauty of nature, walking in the woods, at the beach, or anywhere, I ponder the magnificent loveliness of it all, instead of mostly wondering how long I should be walking to get enough exercise and what I need to plan for supper. When my grandchild smiles at me, I consciously think about it and thank my fate to have some of these wonderful creatures like grandchildren to smile back to.

I don't think I keep going to school just to stave off dementia. I still love painting—portraits, especially, even though they are by far the most difficult. It is so trying to find the soul in a person.

And I still love flowers. Yet I have to watch out for subjects, like the needy mother and child, that can spoil the joy. When I had breast cancer, I was sent the most lovely flower centerpiece I ever saw. I painted it, and that should have been good for my terrified mind. But I never, never, liked the painting, even when I tried to improve on it, adding more and more color. It still oozes discomfort and I still don't feel good about it. It is hidden in my basement.

I have started to concentrate more on painting, taking courses, and having shows or participating in fairs. I don't like being judged, though. I feel criticized when I don't sell right away.

I did get a few lonely awards and my painting of the American Eagle hangs in the town hall of Fairfield, Connecticut, but I don't like the work of preparing, framing, and setting up. I just want to paint beautiful flowers and children, the shadows in trees and rivers.

I try, but I never understood abstract painting. Looking at a totally black canvas made me feel that the audience was ridiculed. But last winter, I read an article about Ed Reinhardt's black canvases in the *New York Times'* art section. One should contemplate them, the article said, and in time you can see colors and shapes. Perhaps I wasn't looking hard enough.

One of the most emotional impacts I ever had was in 2006 at the Massachusetts Modern Museum of Art, where we saw an installation by Carsten Höller.

It was called *The Amusement Park*, installed in a 300' long room, which was kept in the dark. In the room were several items which are familiar to us from amusement parks: bumper cars, a carousel. They were lit up and active, just as they would be in real life. However, there was no noise.

Jack and I were alone, walking towards a long mirrored wall at the end. We saw the whole amusement park in duplication, but there was no sound. I felt like we were the last people on earth. The feeling followed me all day and it upset me no end with a feeling of alienation. I guess that this is what art is meant to do, capture your imagination and make you feel.

I am grateful for my interest in art. It fills my life with imagination and beauty. When I paint, it is meditation and relaxation.

But above all, my greatest satisfaction involves my first grandson. When his kindergarten teacher asked him what his colorful scribbles represented, he answered her, "This is Monet's Garden". You know who taught him.

WHO'S TALKING ... *Ingrid Bloom is a retired schoolteacher whose exercise regimen includes yoga, walking, swimming, and jazzercise. Staying fit is not limited to physical fitness; Ingrid continues to go to college and the opera. She can still fit into her wedding dress.*

16: THE MAN IN THE FAMILY
JILL, 66

I'M THE MAN IN THE FAMILY. I WASN'T BORN THAT WAY. IT JUST happened. My father wanted a house full of children—boys and girls. Instead he and my mother raised three daughters. Although we were a great joy to my father, we were an incomplete family without sons. At least that was what my mother said. Even the dogs were female.

I must have felt the lack very early in life because I remember clinging to my father's knee (at 6'3", he was a giant to me) and begging to go everywhere with him: hunting, fishing, and—he was a builder—his construction sites. I imagined that every time my father left the house, he went on a great adventure.

I was so excited when my father took my sister and me on his Saturday trips to the lumberyard to choose the building materials for his next project. My fondest memories are the earthy aromas of freshly cut maple and oak, concrete mix, and paint. Carefully chosen paintbrushes, saws, planes, and drafting supplies were my greatest source of entertainment. I kept treasure boxes of #2H pencils, slide rules, and compasses to assist my father in perfecting the angles and straight lines of his craft.

Being girls did not deter my father from encouraging intelligence, athletics, and self-confidence in his family. Dinner table conversation centered on history, politics, and social justice. Leisure time focused on the batting averages of the Boston Red Sox and practicing our pitches across home plate, hitting home runs, and catching pop flies. We grew healthy and strong to please him. He taught us to be proud of our accomplishments, especially our schoolwork. So my sisters and I returned his confidence in us with straight A's, awards, and leadership roles. He was quietly known for his leftist thinking, but expected us to examine all points of view.

But one of us had to step up and be the boy.

Cultural pressures of the 50's deterred my older sister from making the break from traditional female roles, and after much protest on her part to buck the mainstream of marriage and family, she relented and got married. My younger sister was the tomboy, but this didn't stop her from realizing her dreams of being a mother, and she cooperated by producing a granddaughter and grandson for my doting father.

So there I was, a child of the 60's, radicalized by The Movement, Martin Luther King, John F Kennedy, and my father. And thank the Goddess for that. These influences provided the impetus for what was to come.

In spite of the mixed messages that all women were getting in those days—join the revolution, but march behind the men—I used my youth and optimism to struggle through the challenges of social change. I remember being 14 years old and visiting my father's philosopher friend, John Gregory, owner of the local saw mill. They were discussing the future generation and what could be expected from them. On the way home, my father told me that I could do whatever I wanted with my life, even if it did not include marriage or a family. I was so relieved! I was free! I now had a chance at a real career, but what was it?

I aspired to be my father's only son. I was not to be outdone by any x chromosomes. I ate like my father—heaping plates of meat and potatoes, I fished like my father—casting perfect handmade lures off the Sasco Beach jetty, and I thought like him—a leftist through and through. The natural progression of my life led to the study of architecture, because my Dad was a builder and engineer.

Of course, he discouraged me because such professions led to a life of hardship and isolation. Besides I would be the only girl in the class, and I was! Even my guidance counselor in high school wouldn't let me enroll in a drafting class because the class was for boys! It was one of the first battles I didn't win, but I kept trying.

The close-minded conservative society of Connecticut in the 60's was the last to change during the cultural revolution, so straight out of undergraduate school, I made tracks for the west coast. It was time for my first real adventure and I was determined to prove to my father that I could survive on my own. I was both afraid and excited to step into the breach.

At first the breach wasn't exactly as big as I thought. I followed my east coast boyfriend to Los Angeles because he wanted to explore the alternative lifestyles so appealing to the hippie generation. I pushed my Waspy school girl conventions aside and chose any adventure that came my way. I applied to graduate school at The California Institute of the Arts—the new Ivy League College for the arts, and I majored in architecture, finally achieving my childhood dream.

It was a marvelous new world, full of free-thinking professors, unfettered by east coast conventions. I was in heaven and I thrived and, supported by my mentors, I had new hopes and dreams that promised a future of professional accomplishments equal to any man's. I was armed with a master's degree and financial independence from men—my father and boyfriend. I was ready to make my own decisions.

The Women's Movement was also in full force and I became an integral part of The Feminist Art Project in Los Angeles, raising funds for the founding of an independent Woman's Art College in downtown Los Angeles—The Woman's Building. It was a hotbed of radical change for women and I was proud to be a part of it. Once again, I stepped into the breach of change and found a new source of strength in the solidarity of women. It was a slippery slope trying to navigate my new direction, integrating my architectural aspirations with radical feminism, but I charted a course and set sail.

Men were a part of my life, but permanent relationships seemed to fall by the wayside. I had live-in boyfriends and they were fulfilling the need for social and intimate liaisons, but I could not succumb to marriage just yet. I knew that I was on my way to bigger and better things. I viewed marriage as an impediment to my career and I was afraid that motherhood would hinder my chances of success in a man's world. I was soon to find out that these weren't the only potential hurdles.

I entered a competitive high-powered work force in New York City during the 70s and 80s where I was the only woman in the room. Men humored me and thought I was attractive, but they were also impressed by my intelligence and strong work ethic, so they let me stay. I rose to a level in a corporate world where only men were in the boardroom and I struggled to advance and achieve the financial rewards that I deserved.

Part of what seemed so daunting during this period was the constant battle for recognition. When a man completed a project and did a good job, he expected a promotion and got it, including more income. If I did the same project, I was a good team player. If I asked for a promotion, a bonus, or a company car, I was either expected to sleep with the boss or step aside for a family man who had children to support. My hopes and dreams were beginning to dim.

I bought a boat. This seemed like an appropriate reward for myself. I could navigate my personal life for a change, fish with my father, and entertain my friends. Of course, I was the only female boat owner in the marina, and it was one of the crowning achievements of my life.

I had to make some more adjustments. I had to get tougher. Men alienated each other, so I figured why not me, too? I was so male-identified, I didn't see the difference between them and me, so I proceeded to act like them. My strategy got more complicated and I left some wounded in my wake, but I thought the sacrifice was worth it. I was determined to be successful and I pushed even harder.

I lost track of time and the years slipped by. I became an executive in an entrepreneurial world, and although I was proud of my progress, I was struggling to survive. Mergers and acquisitions were profitable, but outsourcing became a way of life. Women executives were the first casualties of the corporate world during lay-offs, and it became increasingly difficult to replace my high-paying jobs.

Because I was pioneer in my field, I was one of the senior women at my level and I needed a woman mentor. They were hard to find. So instead of connecting with one mentor, I found other women and we supported one another.

The struggle that women had then, and still have now, however, is how to balance their roles as mothers and wives with their professional lives. I was never able to take that plunge because I never found a man I could trust to share half the domestic burden. I looked around and saw all those women who thought they could do both, and they either lost their careers or lost their husbands. I was not about to lose my career for a man. I was already the man in my life.

And I became the man in my family's life.

My younger sister was very accommodating to my strange and irregular career plans. She married and had two children. I was so relieved that one of my immediate family members was willing to fulfill another one of my father's dreams. Now I didn't have to do this, either. Being the man was challenging enough.

I wanted to be an example to my niece and nephew, and I suppose I was, but I have learned some very valuable lessons from them. Once when my niece was ten years old and we were taking a bicycle ride one Sunday afternoon, she told me that it would have been nice if I had children for her to play with, but then she and I wouldn't be able to spend so much time together. I have never forgotten those words. The women from my generations were torn.

My niece is from a new generation. She is confident that she will be able to have her medical career as a doctor, her marriage to an engineer, and raise children, without sacrificing her aspirations to be director of The Center for Disease Control.

Her whole generation is focused and comfortable with their expectations. I fought the war of the sexes, but I am hopeful that my niece will not have to. She will have professional battles to fight and she should be free to do so without social battles, too.

My niece doesn't have to be the man! She can be a woman, a career woman, a wife, and a mother without compromising her gender roles. She will realize her dreams and achieve them all in the context of her marriage and family. I am pleased to be a part of her life and to have played a part in her accomplishments. I know that she benefitted from seeing me go to an office every day, pay the bills, and reach my career goals. I often check in with her on these matters, just to be sure that I did the right thing.

I know my mother had career goals, too. She wanted to be a nurse, but her father did not think that it was an appropriate profession for a "nice" young woman. My mother became a reluctant wife and mother because she fell in love with my father. It would have been much more fulfilling for her entire family if she could have done it all, been a nurse, wife, and mother.

So I became the man in the family. I gave up a dual role of wife and mother to achieve career goals. I paired my mother's disappointment with my father's encouragement to be independent and came up with my own plan.

To be the man.

WHO'S TALKING ... *Jill Soderholm started collecting worms and stuffing them in her pockets at age two. She was preparing for the day when she could go fishing every day and be captain of her own destiny. She's definitely captain of her own destiny, but fishes only on the weekends.*

17: GETTING TO KNOW MY FATHER
JENNIFER, 63

MY MOTHER ALWAYS REFERRED TO HIM AS *your father*. SOMETIMES happily, sometimes quietly, and other times with a stiffness in her throat that I later came to realize was sadness.

Your father—what a mix of emotions those words held. Beautiful. Dreamy. I worshipped him. I wanted to claim him as *my father*. But it was impossible, especially when I heard discomfort in my mother's voice. My tongue would seize in hesitation; still determined to say it, I would stumble over the words. *My father* seemed both too formal a title, and yet too intimate a name for a stranger I would never meet. I just wanted to be a regular human being, able to say those words without having to sweat or gulp.

Dad? I thought about calling him that, but that was what I called my stepfather. Even had he been kind, I would never have wanted to confuse him with my father.

There had to be something I could call my father. My mother and I were in the kitchen when I tried it out. I was about eight. She opened a small bottle of maraschino cherries; I could smell them across the room and watched her halve the brilliant red balls then stir them into the batter. It always amazed me, no matter how well mixed, they always sank to the bottom of the cake. She poured juice from the jar into the batter for color.

"Did Daddy cook at the snack bar?" I said it as fast as I could and still remember the rush of heat to my face.

"Sometimes he'd help with breakfast; sometimes he'd pump the gas." Her tone sounded odd. Was it disapproval? I already felt my own. I did not like to think of my father as having any similarity to my stepfather, a mechanic who ran a White Rose station downtown and sometimes pumped gas. After all, my father could read Greek and Latin. He spoke French so well the Parisians took him for one of their own—and he wore flannel pants to mow the lawn.

My mother opened the oven door. I ran to the window and drew a picture on the condensation, sucking on the tip of my braid to distract myself from how embarrassingly cute "Daddy" had sounded as it had come out of my mouth.

In college I tried a new tack. On a visit to my mother one weekend, I tested out my fledgling bohemian cool. She was in a different house with a different husband, but we were still in the kitchen when my father came up.

"So I want to ask you some questions about Stephen," I began.

My mother's rounded shoulders stiffened.

"Since when do you refer to your father by his Christian name?"

I shrugged. He'd been dead for so long, how could it possibly matter? The truth was I still longed to find some comfortable place where the two of us could share him. The next time we spoke about him I went back to saying "my father".

There is a photo in which my father is dressed in a suit and tie. He's in his late teens, his hair slicked down and higher on the left side of his part. He stands between two mounted equestrians. His feet are in first position, suggesting not a dance posture but a sense of awkwardness. The photo has been taken at a distance; he measures about an inch and a quarter high. With a magnifying glass, I study his face and for the first time noticed that his ears stick out like my brother's.

Beside him, mounted on a black horse with a small white obelisk shape on his forelock, a rider sits straight-backed holding the reins with soft hands. The top of her head is missing. I presume by the posture and slim body that it is my Aunt Josephine.

My father holds the rein of a white pony. The rider of this horse is in pigtails. She is smiling and dimpled—my mother. I see how my looks had mirrored hers at eleven or so. My father would have been in the Upper Sixth form, as it was known in the English school system, and ready to graduate from high school. I knew there was an age difference but seeing it shocks me.

The Worthams, the father's family, and the Robins, my mother's family, met socially. My father's family had a "cottage" nearby where they summered, which was how they came to attend my grandparent's lawn tennis parties and summer soirees. My Aunt Josephine and my father were the same age and spent time together, but they could never have fallen in love and married. She was rough-and-tumble. Once she discovered a rat in the stable and dropped a brick on it. Skinned on one side of its body, the rat leapt straight up, snapping its teeth into her hand. It hung on. Aunt Josephine did not utter a sound, but went to work banging and smacking the rat against the stable door until it was dead.

WWII began and Aunt Josephine fell in love with a mechanic who had joined the Air Force and was soon shipped to Europe.

My father, twenty-two-year-old Second Lieutenant Wortham, was sent with his regiment, the Royal Sussex, to France. Aunt Jose, as she was called, no matter how close they had been, refused to write to my father, so my mother, who'd just turned fifteen, wrote instead.

When he reemerged she was 21. He was still in uniform when they married. It's a good thing for me that Aunt Jose dumped my father for the man who later became Uncle Jimmy; otherwise I wouldn't be here.

Licensed London Taxi Drivers are required to know every road and place of interest in the main London area; that is

anywhere within a six mile radius of Charing Cross- a major
railway station which is moments away from 'King Charles
Island'; the official centre of the capital. Although Taxis in
London were first licensed during the time of Oliver Crom-
well, [17th Century] the requirement of studying this vast
area is a relatively recent one- it was only introduced during
the Victorian Era; in the 1850s!

View from the Mirror: A Taxi Driver's London

"Your father did it on foot." My mother always chopped the
walnuts first, then the dates because they stuck to the knife; she
was stirring them into the batter that would become my favorite
loaf. My mouth watered at the thought as I knelt on a kitchen
chair watching her and waiting for the moment when I would get
to scrape the bowl.

"He learned London by walking it. When you took the test,
you were not allowed a map."

On hearing this, my stomach was a tumult of excitement,
awe, and incredulity. I tried to imagine walking those streets day
after day, the strength of will involved to keep learning, memorizing landmarks, reading all the signs and noting the direction of
one-way streets. Did I even know the names of all the streets in
our neighborhood? I could barely study for a spelling test without
fidgeting and playing with the cat.

Passing The Knowledge [the shortened form of The Knowl-
edge of London Taxi Examination] involves detailed recall
of 25,000 streets . . . The locations of clubs, hospitals, ho-
tels, railway stations, parks, theatres, courts, restaurants, col-
leges, government buildings, and places of worship are also
required. It can take three years to pass the test, including the
six months it takes to be tested.

The History of the London Black Taxi Trade

As my mother swung open the door of the oven, a soft wave of warmth reached me. The loaf pan made a muted clang as she placed it on the rack and slid it in. She handed me the bowl and the scraper.

"The examiner said, 'Take me to 3 Cherry Lane.' It was some tiny buried dead-end street." My mother's tone grew more animated, her admiration palpable, something I am now realizing encouraged mine.

I scooped up the one bite of date my mother had missed, or purposely left, and put it in my mouth. "He did it just to test himself, to see if he could. He never drove a cab after he passed."

The sweet smooth batter, combined with the richness of the date and the slightly bitter fizz of the baking soda, slid down my throat as I absorbed her words. This made it official. My father, always a wonder to me, was truly crackerjack smart and had something I recognized, though I didn't know the word then, as grit, and I had some of him in me. Maybe that meant something.

Dunkirk, 1940 . . . Approximately 400,000 British troops as well as significant numbers of French, Belgian, Polish, and Dutch were trapped near the harbor by the German Army and Luftwaffe. At least 39 British destroyers and eight hundred "small ships," the very smallest believed to have been an 18-foot open-topped fishing boat, came to rescue and transport over 330,000 soldiers to safety in Dover. Winston Churchill called the success of the evacuation a miracle.

When I was six I knew nothing about Dunkirk. One Sunday, too cold and wet to play outside, our mother sat my brother and me around the coffee table and placed our record player on it so we could hear a special story. I was very excited as she lifted the needle, blew it clean of dust and placed it on a slowly turning black vinyl record. It bounced, there was a scratching noise, and then came a deep English voice announcing a story called *The Snow Goose*.

The story begins in the marshlands of England where an artist is living alone in a deserted lighthouse. A young neighbor girl finds a snow goose with a gunshot wound and brings it to him; they nurse it until it can fly once again. Every year during its migration, the snow goose returns to the lighthouse.

Then WWII is declared. In the late spring, the artist tells about the thousands of soldiers in Dunkirk Harbor trapped by the Germans.

Enthralled, I listened, leaning towards the man's voice as he tells us the "men are huddled on the beaches like hunted birds."

The artist maneuvers his small sailboat back and forth through gunfire to big ships waiting to carry the men to Dover, the goose faithfully guiding him. After saving and ferrying several hundred men, the artist is downed by machine guns. By the time the snow goose leaves, having circled the body of the artist three times, I am sobbing.

"That's where Dad was, wasn't it?" Tim asked.

My mother nodded, motioning me to her lap. She stroked my hair.

"It's all right, Poppet. It's okay," she soothed.

"Was he in the artist's sailboat?" I spluttered.

"No, he wasn't," she answered quietly.

My father spent his 24th birthday waiting for a ride that never came. Instead the day came and went, as he, along with 62,000 other soldiers, was never rescued from Dunkirk Harbor in France. My father literally missed the boat.

Germany's windfall of POW's left them incredulous at their luck but completely unprepared. Their first priority was to feed their two and a half million German soldiers. Rations were not to be squandered on thousands of enemy captives who had to be forcibly marched across France, along with the other thousands of prisoners of war, half starved, 20 miles a day. Instead, the Germans relied on meager Red Cross supplies available in towns en route, but the scarcity of food, exhaustion, and painfully blistered feet made the captives less likely to attempt escape.

Germany treated its British, French, and American prisoners comparatively well, but treated Soviet, Polish, and other Slavic POWs with genocidal severity. Over two million of the over five million captured starved to death. The German treatment of the Dunkirk POW's included kicking, beating, and sometimes murder. They knocked over buckets of drinking water left for the POW's at the roadside by French citizens.

After reaching Germany, my father spent the rest of his twenties in Stalag 383, a little-known prisoner-of-war camp, and when he returned home, his stomach had shrunk to the point that he was only able to eat very small meals a few times a day. My father joked that it was due to the camp cooks' attempts to make cabbage soup, to which they always forgot to add the cabbage.

In one of his plain brown Sandhurst Training notebooks, my father, an officer, had written: *An officer's responsibility is keeping up morale as well as maintaining technical equipment.* He knew that boosting the spirits of those around him was a terrible and formidable job, but maintenance of technical equipment was not an issue. On the shores of Dunkirk, the British had to abandon enough armored tanks, vehicles, motorcycles, supplies and ammunition to serve eight army divisions.

I hated getting my hair washed. The ritual involved having to stick my head under the bathtub faucet, which invariably sent clumps of shampoo suds straight into my eyes. My mother must have had a long day as she had scolded me, threatening to push my head under the tap when I hesitated. Afterwards she sat on the edge of the tub, planted me, still crying a little, between her legs, dried me off and then started toweling down my hair that reached the middle of my back.

"You're lucky, you know. Hard as I would try, I could never grow my hair past my shoulders. It just stopped, too thin. And your father…" On hearing this might be about him, my crying ebbed completely. "I told him he mustn't try and grease down his curls for our wedding. He was always trying to tame his hair, but it was so thick and strong, he never could."

I turned and looked at her, knowing I was being treated to a story to make up for what had happened between us earlier. On catching my eager eyes, Mum continued. "He lived in London and I lived with my parents in Kent. There was a law everyone had to have lived in the same county for a month before publishing wedding banns in the paper." She responded to my puzzled look, "That was what we called marriage announcements in those days. So your father rented a room, placed his shoes under the bed, had his mail directed there, but never stayed. That did the trick, but his hair was still unruly that day."

It did the trick for me as well.

"The men are out," my mother said, in a pleasant confiding way.

Her smile was conspiratorial. I deduced from that, and her lumping my older brothers, not quite teenagers, into the manly bracket of my stepfather's realm, that this would be a special afternoon—just us women.

We sorted through a box of old photographs. From a large yellowed envelope, she pulled an 8 x10 photo, with a slight curl at the bottom.

"Careful, Pet! Hold the white part."

It was a full-length black-and-white shot of my father and mother, striding down a street. Mum had what I later came to recognize as a fresh English girl complexion. She was wearing a smart-looking three-quarter length coat over a patterned dress belted at the waist. My father wore a suit with his tie in a Windsor knot, and an overcoat.

"A London photographer snapped us unawares and put our picture in *The Daily Telegraph* with a caption about our being newlyweds after the war."

"In the paper?" I was astonished and wondered why they weren't famous.

"We were looking a little grim. We'd just had a row," my mother said benignly.

It was true; neither was smiling. I noticed my mother would have been a tad taller than my father, who was saved by a wave of hair cresting three inches at its highest peak. Even though they were at odds, he was lightly clasping the strap of my mother's purse so their hands were almost touching.

Whenever I run across a 1930's Charlie Chan movie, I want to be like Keye Luke, who played Charlie's Number One Son and called the venerable and old-fashioned man "Pop". The heck with the word "father". Why hadn't I experimented with that insouciant title when my mother and I talked about him? Maybe the fun of it would have appealed to her.

It pleases me to imagine my tempering his upper-crust British manners and accent by calling him Pop, especially during a political conversation when our views diverged or when asking to borrow the car. The best part always being the sensation of heedless nonchalance in taking the safety of our family for granted.

My mother and father married immediately after the war. My father, not yet discharged from the Royal Sussex Regiment, wore his officer's dress uniform, complete with sword and scabbard. Nine months later, in 1946, fair-haired Robin, their first-born, arrived. He had long fingers and kept himself amused in his crib. My mother thought he might be a musician.

The rest of his story I was told only once. My mother had her back turned to me.

"It was the middle of the night. Your father and I were sound asleep. We were exhausted. Your brother let out a terrible scream. I started to get up to go to him and your father caught my arm and said, 'Don't go. He has to learn. So I got back into our warm bed." Her voice trembled a little. "Early the next morning I went to him. He was stone cold. . . he'd died in the night."

The post-mortem reported the cause of death—cerebral meningitis. Robin had lived ten months. My mother said that my paternal grandmother blamed her. Was that real or imagined? Even had she gone up, she wouldn't have been able to save him, but she would have been with him.

Some women would never have forgiven the husband, who had uttered those words, nor herself for listening. But my parents survived their grief and fifteen months later, my mother gave birth to a second boy, a healthy eleven-pounder. They named him Timothy John Simon Michael Wortham. Perhaps they gave him such a long name in the hope that it would hold him to earth and they would not lose him as they had their first. My father even talked about when he would be able to sign Timothy up for membership at Lord's Cricket Club. But then he changed his mind.

Here the tenor of the story shifted.

"Your father visited me in the hospital and announced we were moving to Canada." She was at the sink peeling potatoes she would later slide in beside the roast beef sizzling with its drippings. I was coloring a picture, trying to stay inside the lines.

"I certainly didn't appreciate that he didn't ask me." Her brow furrowed, her tone still annoyed as though it was happening in that minute.

I was just relieved they managed it all.

There's another photograph of a store and two gas pumps. There is a sign printed in quiet squared letters:

GROCETERIA. SNACKS. CABINS.

MR. AND MRS. S.B. WORTHAM PROPRIETORS.

PEACE VALLEY

I peer at the small black-and-white print, remembering my mother's words.

The London we left behind had been devastated during the blitz. After the war, food shortages made rationing worse. We had taken responsibility for so many other countries where people needed food because their land had been destroyed. I think your father wanted to start fresh, away from reminders of the war, of losing Robin, and to put some distance from your overbearing grandfather. He went ahead of your brother and me and found a piece of land in Southern Ontario. We started a small business and we named a tiny corner of Canada—Peace Valley.

Mother could still get worked up about their 1950 trip to New York City when my father declared the $800 fur coat he'd bought for her. "Your father was far too honest. Customs confiscated my coat!" Less sympathetic to my mother's plight than to my father's, I admired that his character contained such a broad streak of honesty even when caught off guard.

When I was still just a kid, I found my brother, Tim, working busily with something in the dim dead-end hallway by the bathroom. He was hanging a funny-looking wooden shield he'd just made.

"What's that?"

"Our family crest, our coat of arms."

I gawked in awe even though I didn't like it with its single paw and bared claws atop what looked like a twisted piece of rope on a dull grey background. I was silently critical of the ragged edges and nicks of his labors from cutting a piece of scrap plywood with his fretsaw. Still I felt a swell of pride that we had a family coat of arms. His audacity in making it and then hanging it without permission, despite his placing it in a dark useless bit of space, made me brave enough ask.

"Do you miss him, too?"

His face clouded and I was a coward again.

The rest came out in a strangled voice. "I mean . . . our father."

He answered with a stiff shrug and something gruff I can't remember. It was obvious; I had trespassed.

I was too young to understand what Tim's curtness was hiding and that the answer to my question lay in his actions. He wore our father's army jackets before they became the style; he built a replica of our family crest and collected as many English town badges as he could when my mother took us on a trip to meet our cousins.

Here's a dream I had.

My father and I are in a hut, cataloguing ancient artifacts. We line up dozens of small stone figures on a wooden work bench, examine them, note date, location, and write a short description. A few of the figures are whole. The rest are worn smooth where their heads or legs have broken off. Occupied, we don't speak. I just finish tagging one when my father swings around and strides out the door. Our hut is perched on a rickety slat bridge slung with ropes across a huge gorge. I follow in time to see him dive into the violent rapids far below us. Without a thought, I follow right behind.

I woke with a start in my college dorm, full of pride, feeling the dream was evocative of our connection. None of it seemed related to any story I had been told about him, which made it all mine and as close to meeting him as I would ever get.

Years later, I told a friend about the dream. She was quiet for some moments then said, "I think it meant when your father died he took an irretrievable piece of you with him."

I never did tell my mother, although in hindsight, I see now how my mother's way of telling stories brought me into my father's world, in a way I could never have otherwise experienced.

This man, whose hand I never held crossing a street, whose knee I never sat on, who never scolded me for misbehaving, this man came alive in the moments she talked about him. I have been most fortunate because my mother was not one of those who refused to speak of an absent father. Instead, her stories helped plant the seeds of my feelings for him.

There were men who came after. They came to mind when I saw Ingmar Bergman's movie, *Fanny and Alexander*. I identified with the brother and sister, who were deprived of their exuberant, well-to-do family when their father suddenly dies and is replaced by a severe and sadistic bishop. The story was all too familiar—though I lived the glorious part only in my imagination. Like Alexander, I often fantasized about getting rid of my stepfather and having our happiness restored. Although Alexander's stepfather died and mine finally left us, neither of us was set free. At the end of the movie, Alexander is knocked to the ground by the ghost of his stepfather. And I have never been able to entirely shake the effects of being raised by a rigid authoritarian stepfather, who made me yearn for a home where I wouldn't be afraid.

After I left home, my mother married her third husband. Don was loud and swaggering. He never finished high school but was exceedingly smart. We couldn't stand each other. Once after I'd been away for a summer, Don and my mother picked me up from the train. Mother and I wrapped our arms around each another in a long hug. He stood observing. After a minute of watching and listening to us, he barked, "Okay that's enough."

My mother pulled away immediately. I felt forsaken.

It came to a head a couple of months later. I was in the midst of divorcing my first husband. When my mother came to help pack my books, she arrived at the door with Don. I bit down my outrage. Why did she bring him? Didn't she know I was vulnerable and didn't feel like being exposed? Within less than an hour, he made some remark I took amiss.

I stood up, grabbed my half-full coffee mug and smashed it against the kitchen wall screaming, "How dare you tell my mother and me how long we can hug!" It was a short visit.

About a year later, he said, "We might not ever like each other, but maybe we can tolerate each other for your mother's sake." He was right, and we did.

I thought that settled the issue of me and Don, but my mother proved me wrong.

Spring was beautifying the world on a Saturday at my mother's farm, prompting us to saddle the horses for a ride. After cantering along a field of fresh green spring wheat, we slowed the horses to a walk and mounted a hill. Lake Ontario lay in the distance, the waves little bits of glitter. In front of us was a gate. When I dismounted to open the latch, my mother sat up straighter in the saddle. What burst out of her caught me completely by surprise.

"And what do you have against Don, besides the fact you don't think he's fit to lick your father's boots."

I stuttered, making those helpless involuntary gestures people do when caught in a futile attempt to find an answer that is not an obvious lie. If only I had been able to pull some words of kindness from a secret cache kept for just such contingencies and say, "What matters is that he makes you happy."

I think my father would have wanted that.

Years later, I went into a used and rare books store on a whim. "Do you have any of H. E. Wortham's books?" Perhaps on this particular day in New York City where I've spent most of my adult life,

I wanted to feel some connection to family. Otherwise, why was I in this musty place filled with ancient atlases on glass counters and hundreds of books with yellowing pages? The clerk's intelligent eyes peered at me from under a Buster Brown haircut and then turned to the computer.

"He's my grandfather," I blurted.

Her curt nod of acknowledgement dampened any further urges to tell her that he'd been a British journalist and biographer. She read off his available books in a disinterested manner. I already had *Edward VII* and *Gordon: An Intimate Portrait* that earned a book review in *The New York Times* in 1931 and *Three Women: St. Teresa, Madame De Choiseul and Mrs. Eddy* and *The Mustapha of Kamal*. I chose one that was not sitting on my shelves at home.

Two weeks later, I went back and zipped out of the store with a copy of *A Musical Odyssey*, a collection of his essays written when he was the music critic for London's *Daily Telegraph*. Cradling the book tight to my chest, I hurried to the subway in time to catch the No. 1 train squealing to a stop.

I grabbed a seat and studied the book's table of contents. A chapter titled *The Youngest Opera-Goer* stopped me. A pulse in my stomach banged against my innards. I hoped, while trying not to hope, that the youngster might have been my father. With clumsy fingers I fought through the thick sturdy paper to page 23 and scanned the piece. No name. Then on page 24, line three, I saw it, Stephen. Still incredulous, I paused to do the math, grateful to H.E. that he had named dates allowing me to calculate that it would have matched my father's age. Although my grandfather, an Edwardian gentleman, referred to his son as "my young friend, Stephen", most likely to guard their privacy, it was about my dad! Oblivious to the crammed bodies around me, the conductor's announcements and the screech of steel wheels against steel tracks, I read on.

Transported, I was in London, 1923, where my grandfather had just taken my father, a six-year-old, to see the opera *Hansel and Gretel.* H.E. described his young friend as being "tough-mind-ed and philosophically sensationalistic." I tried to imagine what it would be like to have a father, who would use such huge words to describe his son.

My mother had once told me she was afraid of my paternal grandfather.

"But you wouldn't have been," she said. "He would have liked you." Words I had preened at, though I was relieved that I didn't have to prove the truth of her words.

Further on, my grandfather's tone changed. H.E. writes, "The moment that Hansel put his fingers into the milk-jug and then licked the cream off them, our empiricist gave him his whole heart. . . . anybody who could do such a glorious thing was amongst the noblest of his kind." Was my grandfather touched by the expression on my father's face? Or was he reminded of himself as a boy and in that glimmering understood my father down to his bones?

The only childhood picture I have seen of my father is a miniature portrait painted when he was two, held in a locket surrounded by seed pearls, several of which are missing. Still, when I closed my eyes in the subway car I had no trouble conjuring the look of ecstasy that must have lightened my father's young face when Hansel becomes his hero.

While my father asked many questions about the opera, never once did he refer to the depraved and evil witch. H.E. envisioned my father having reached the age of 73 years in 1990. Teasingly, he wrote that only then would *his young friend* trust himself to describe the witch to his grandchildren. I could hardly breathe. 1990 was only a couple of decades back. By then, I was a grown adult with a husband who would be dead in three years, and Stephen Bache Wortham would have had no grandchildren to tell the story of the witch.

Or am I wrong? Perhaps he might have had grandchildren. Might my brother still be alive had we not had the "evil stepfather" who so angered Tim that he walked off his rage in the unmarked gravel pit dumps of the local uranium plant and die of cancer before his seventeenth birthday? How different might our lives have been had our father lived to raise us.

But I did not want to deal with that mystery now, for my grandfather had reached out from the pages of his book and offered me an invaluable gift. He talked about my father and the year 1990, making me consider him as an aging adult. I tried to picture his hands. Would they be wrinkled or shiny, freckled with liver spots? I imagined his slightly formal yet jovial British accent that would no longer have the power of a young man's voice. I thought of how might have been the stereotypical male Brit, so good at avoiding their feelings, and how I would have made it my business to sometimes let him know I saw through his humorous asides and other times just glory in our volley of witty comebacks, trying to outdo each other's straight face.

All the while there was a riot in my gut. Grateful I was in the subway surrounded by human energy and so jubilant I wished only for a drum to bang. Had I been alone I didn't know if I could have endured all the turmoil and gratitude I felt, as I, an adult, met my father as a young child, yet who in reality I have never met at all.

My desire for my father to grow even more alive, I ran my finger under the questions he asked his father, mouthing his words to edge just a little closer. When I read, "Why did the conductor wave his stick?" a bark of laughter escaped me. Unnoticed by the teenager on one side and the man on my other, both plugged into their ear-buds; hip-hop music spilling out caused me to smile at the difference in our worlds as I read my father's query: "Why did the orchestra play so loud?" His curiosity did not abate. "Were the angels' wings made of feathers?" And perhaps my grandfather was right that the young Stephen was an empiricist, "a lover of facts in all their crude variety" as his final inquiry asked, "How had all the children learnt to sing?"

Here is what I learned. On a Sunday afternoon in May 1951, my father, my mother, who is pregnant, and their son, Timmy, pile into their Chevy for a drive with a special destination. Three-and-a-half-year-old Timmy is bouncing up and down in the back seat. He has been promised the choice of his very own pup from a new litter at a neighbor's farm. The bright afternoon sun warms my parents in the front seat. Perhaps my mother thinks about putting my father's hand on her belly to feel the baby but resists as the seat is wide. My father is going a comfortable 50 miles an hour.

Something makes him squint. A fraction of a second passes. And he knows. A single-axle three-ton truck, hauling a load of lumber, is careening around the curve towards them.

Then it is over. The car is no longer recognizable. My mother's head has smashed into the windshield, missing her left temple by an inch. Both of Timmy's legs are broken. Ambulances arrive. At the hospital, staff focuses on my mother, five months pregnant with me—my father's condition beyond hope.

Six decades later I visit a close friend in Canada, who grew up near Peace Valley. She gives me a short newspaper article stating the cause of the crash was a construction sign that had blown over. It read *Caution: Single Lane Traffic Only.*

A few days later we visit a 95-year old woman, a close friend of my mother's, and who had outlived her by almost two decades.

I ask her what she remembers of my father.

"Well, this once, it was my birthday. Your mother and I are outside gabbing, he marches out of their snack bar with a triple scoop ice cream cone and hands it to me."

I am grinning.

"He liked to make people laugh." Nodding to herself. "A friendly man."

Flushed with an unearned sense of pride verging on a rare feeling of bliss, I wait to see if there is more.

"But sometimes he would go very quiet, the war you know, his nerves."

Sadness fills me.

"Your mother and I talked a lot. After the accident she told me..." the old woman pauses, her voice a little hushed.

I strain towards her.

"There was the truck all of a sudden and nowhere to go. Your mother told me the instant your father saw it, he threw himself across her lap to protect her." She is quiet, then adds, "And you."

I am able only to both shake and nod my head. Nothing can direct this information which I am hearing for the first time. The crash was always too painful for my mother to talk about. No breath, let alone words, escape me. I am enveloped with a bittersweet acceptance: My father was a complex man. I keep him close to me.

WHO'S TALKING ... *Jennifer Wortham is a social worker in a psychiatric ER. For relaxation she maintains a psychotherapy practice. When visiting home in Canada, she peppers her conversations with "eh" so Canucks won't disown her for being an uppity New Yorker.*

18: FAMOUS COUSINS
BRENDA, 63

IT WAS THE SUMMER OF 1954 IN GEORGIA. AS WE RODE DOWN THE country dirt road, fighting the dust and smelling the fresh-cut grass through the open windows, I listened to my favorite person in the world.

My grandpa, Joe Daniel, was the most wonderful person I've ever known.

As I sat on the passenger seat of his green 1953 Chevy pickup, it was just him and me out to explore the world. Only four years old and not knowing any better yet, I happened to touch the buttons on the radio. Grandpa exclaimed, "Look, if you don't behave, I'm gonna take you over to Mayhayley!"

I looked out the window as we passed what was left of cousin Mayhayley's old burned-down log home. There were other buildings around, old sharecroppers' cabins, in just as bad shape. Scared to death, I thought, "She must really be bad."

Little did I know how many times Amanda Mayhayley Lancaster would come to touch my life. In fact, I had no idea how much "cousins" in general would touch my life.

For a little bio about Mayhayley, she was my mom's cousin, so my cousin, too. She was a teacher, lecturer, lawyer, and landowner, but most of all a fortune teller. Some called her a fortune teller and some called her a witch!

As I grew up I learned a lot more about my famous relative. Born in 1875, she died a year after my grandpa threatened me with a visit to her house. She was 79 years old when she passed, after living a very colorful life. For one thing, she was one of the richest women in Georgia.

At age 39, in 1915, she was involved in the high-profile case of Leo Frank in Marietta, Georgia. She was one of the few people to publicly defend Frank, who was Jewish. He had been accused of raping a girl who worked in the pencil factory where he was a manager. Anti-Semitism ran wild in the South at that time and Frank was eventually dragged from his jail cell and hung in Marietta's square by a group of vigilantes. In 1986, the Georgia State Board of Pardons and Paroles pardoned Frank. I'm sure Mayhayley was up in Heaven saying, "I told you so!"

Mayhayley was the first woman to run for the Georgia Legislature. In 1926, when she was about 51 years old, she ran on a platform asking for better roads and schools in rural areas and supporting a law forcing doctors to deliver babies to women who couldn't pay. She lost the election; however, many of her ideas were later adopted.

But she seems to have spent a lot of her time being what she called the "Oracle of the Ages." I've heard countless stories about how a hundred people would be lined up at a time to meet with her. She charged a dollar and a dime. The dollar was for her and the dime was for her beloved dogs.

Mayhayley's most famous attribute came from her part in a murder case that took place in 1947 in Coweta County, Georgia, a case that involved her fortune-telling skills. To make a long story short, a landowner, John Wallace, was found guilty of murdering his hired hand.

Mayhayley told the court where to find the ashes of the body. Yes, the hired hand had been burned! The sheriff went right to the place she said to go to, stuck his pocket knife into the dirt, and came up with ashes.

The landowner was later electrocuted. This story was made

into a book and movie, *Murder in Coweta County*, which starred Johnny Cash and his wife, June Carter Cash. Johnny Cash bought the rights to the movie; he played the sheriff and June played Mayhayley.

So many things have come to my mind about her during my life. I have researched her, visited her grave, and studied her, but she was just too complex to figure out.

I will close her story with one final episode that I think is fascinating: She told a movie star of the day, Tallulah Bankhead, where to find a ring she had lost. And as always, Mayhayley was right.

I don't know how many times, too many to count, this odd cousin has passed through my thoughts and I've wondered about this "Oracle of the Ages." As I stare at a photograph of her with my Uncle Tommy playing at her feet when he was three years old, I just wish I could have known her.

Many times through my life the "cousin factor" has been there. Listen as my other stories unfold.

I have wondered why these events have occurred in my life. Well, I did have a strong-willed drama queen for a mother. Her family ties seem to have started a lot of the excitement.

The next cousin I want to tell you about is Evelyn Keyes, Sue Ellen in the movie *Gone with the Wind*. Yes, Scarlet O'Hara's younger sister in the movie was my cousin in real life. She was my mom's first cousin and therefore my second cousin.

Just like Mayhayley, I had heard about Evelyn all of my life. In my mom's final days, she insisted that I find Evelyn. I did find her; she was in a nursing home in Santa Barbara, California. I had a chance to speak to her on the phone but dementia had already taken its toll.

But there were many in our family who claimed that Evelyn was always a strange person.

When she left Georgia for Hollywood, she also left all her family behind. She considered them to be "Bigots of the Old

South." Once when I was little, I was so excited to watch her on *The Johnny Carson Show* on television. Joan Rivers was guest host. When they finished talking about Evelyn's movies and Hollywood life, Joan asked her, "What about your family in Georgia?"

In typical theatrical *Gone with the Wind* fashion she turned up her nose, lifted one shoulder, and said, "Po' white trash." It hit me that she was talking about me!

Evelyn was seventeen years old when she went to Hollywood. She eventually married many men, including "Big Band Leader" Artie Shaw and movie mogul John Huston. Oh! Let's not forget her eight-year relationship with Mike Todd, who later married Elizabeth Taylor. Evelyn said she knew when Mike Todd brought Elizabeth Taylor on the set, it was over for her. Years later, in her autobiography, she wrote that she had many love affairs, saying, "I always took up with the man of the moment and there were many such moments." Men of the moment included Glenn Ford, Dick Powell, Anthony Quinn, David Niven, and Kirk Douglas. She was a busy girl.

As years went by, Evelyn had fifty-eight movies under her belt. *Here Comes Mr. Jordan*, 1941; *The Jolson Story*, 1946; *Mrs. Mike*, 1949; and *The Seven Year Itch*, with Marilyn Monroe in 1955, were some of her more famous films. Although she is most re-membered for *Gone with the Wind,* in her book she said that she believed that *Mrs. Mike* was her best film.

It's interesting that after all of those marriages, relationships, and movies, by the time I contacted her later in her life, she only had two real friends: movie star Tab Hunter and his domestic partner, Alan Glasser. They took care of Evelyn until the end and we became very close friends. However, when she died they dis-appeared.

When Evelyn passed, I received two boxes. One had family photos, mementos, and an 18-carat gold broach that John Huston had given her. I have her movie stills from *Gone with the Wind* and also in that box of photos were pictures of my grandfather, aunts, and uncles. So maybe she hadn't completely forgotten her Georgia roots after all.

The other box contained her ashes.

My mom was a brunette with olive skin, yet from old photos I could see that they looked alike. It's a shame my "drama queen" mom never made it to the silver screen.

I treasure the photos and mementos I have, but most of all, my heritage.

I guess the one thing that bothers me, though, is that Evelyn was an atheist. I believe in God. Strange again, because her grand-father was a minister.

The final cousin I want to tell about is not my blood cousin, but still a famous cousin who has had a tremendous impact on my life. I was twenty-four years old when I had a date with a man who worked for rock 'n roll star Jerry Lee Lewis. Little did I know that I was about to meet the most famous cousin of all. My date said, "You wanna meet Jerry Lee?" as we were entering the club in Atlanta where he was playing.

I thought to myself, "Yeah, right," as we waited in a hallway talking to a friendly guy who wore dark glasses. I had no idea who the rather short man was, but he was real nice and we chatted for a while. Later I learned that he was the wildly popular singer, Tom Jones.

My life of meeting famous entertainers had just begun.

Finally, my date and I were welcomed into Jerry Lee Lewis' dressing room. As the guy introduced me he said, "Brenda is a hairdresser here."

In a moment I will never forget, Jerry said, "Oh, really? Hon-ey, would you mind cutting my hair? I've been on the road and no time to do it. I'll pay you anything you want."

Would I mind? Would I mind?!

That haircut started a friendship that has lasted some forty years! Included in this friendship are also Myra, Jerry's ex-wife; Phoebe, their daughter; Lois and Jay Brown, Myra's parents; and Rusty Brown, Myra's brother. These people have hearts of gold. I will always treasure the friendship and time I've had with my "other family."

I was Jerry Lee Lewis's hairdresser…wow! Just to think… at eight years old I remember watching this rock 'n roll idol on *American Bandstand*! Who would have thought I would grow up and have this friendship with him? I travelled in the music business for many years, doing hair for many other artists along the way.

The thing I take with me is that I got to witness the talent of this wonderful entertainer and to know him and call him friend. I can't tell you how many times I sat on the floor of a hotel suite and hung on every note he played on the piano. The show was the best after the show was over.

As I reminisce about my life in the music business, I think the best part is the friendship I have with Myra Lewis Williams. She is my friend, one of my inspirations in life; I love her and will always treasure our friendship. She is one of the strongest, most successful women I know today.

At age sixty-three, as I look back on all of my relationships with "cousins," I can see that each of them impacted my life in ways I didn't always realize when I was younger. I've learned something from each of them.

Amanda Mayhayley Lancaster was a strong woman, especially in a time when independence was not encouraged in women. I like to think that knowing about her since the time I was a child has fostered in me strength as well. My life has not been free of tragedy, like the suicide of my first husband, the drowning of my little two-year-old grandson, or the accident that has left me crippled for the rest of my life. Like Mayhayley, I know that life goes on. We as women go on. If I woke up one morning and there was no challenge to living, I couldn't go on. Survival has been my bread in life. Like so many women before me and since, I get up, brush off, and go on.

Even cousin Evelyn Keyes, the actress who disowned us as her family, may have influenced my love of being a bit dramatic and looking good. As a hairdresser, I've always believed in dressing up, doing my hair, and putting on some makeup. As the old saying goes, "Everything looks better with a new coat of paint."

And my adopted cousins, the Brown and Lewis clans, have taught me that loyal friends are family, too. They are the family that we get to choose.

Each experience I have had has taught me something about each person I've encountered. My loves at home... my husband, Michael; my children, David and Brooke; my precious grandchildren... all of them make my life worth living. To them I am just "Mimi."

Thank you my friend, Linda, for the chance of a lifetime. I will never forget you for letting me write this.

I've been a lucky person to experience all of this. And thank you, my friends, for reading my story. I hope it touched you in some way.

WHO'S TALKING ... *Brenda Cox was a hairdresser all of her adult life, until an accident a few years ago left her unable to work. Cane in hand, she hasn't let that keep her down. She still manages to do some of the things that she wants to do, her indomitable spirit keeping her going.*

19: BUYING THE FARM
CHERYL, 65

OCCASIONALLY I CATCH MYSELF CONDUCTING IMPROMPTU QUALI-ty-of-life assessments, usually during the prolonged black hole of depression northern Michigan residents with better mental health than mine simply call "winter." Realtors advertising upscale area properties write, "Winter in northern Michigan is a time of breath-taking beauty when snow-fairy forests are cloaked in sparkling diamonds" or, "In winter, Michigan's panoramic blue waters rest beneath a glittering cover of ice, interrupted only by the Beaver Island Archipelago visible from your cottage windows." *I'm not kidding.*

The people targeted by these ads will not live here year around. They say things like "the devil is in the details" and "what is my exposure?" Their "cottages" start at around 7,000 square feet and might typically feature a $30,000.00 AGA range, in-floor heating, and a spa-room sporting his-and-her massage tables upholstered in white leather. Most of these seasonal residents will only be here between the second week of June and the first week of September.

A summer highlight is the annual "Race to Mac," a 333-mile mid-July race to Mackinac Island sponsored by the Chicago Yacht Club. Over a two-day period, 300 sleek racing yachts sail north past the cottage windows of seasonal Lakeside and Lake Bluff dwellers, providing plenty of thrills and another reason to host a cocktail party with full-service staff and a harpist. Occasionally some of these seasonal residents jet in to briefly celebrate the

Christmas Holiday when they again will host and attend many catered parties and down copious amounts of well-aged Glenfiddich while working custom wooden jigsaw puzzles that feature one puzzle piece special to them, such as a cutout of their 1958 mahogany Cris-Craft Classic.

LIVIN' THE DREAM

Winter on our small farm, tucked away in extreme northwestern Michigan's Lower Peninsula, is defined by less impressive events. During a thirty-year career as a city police officer, my husband (known to many of our friends and family as 'poor Pete'), nurtured a dream. In this dream, he was retired and reborn as a farmer, standing waist-deep in leafy vegetables eating a perfect, juicy, just-picked, sun-warmed red tomato. Nearby, contented white-faced Hereford cattle grazed knee deep in fields of clover while their beautiful red calves played together and steadily gained weight on their way to the market.

As retirement neared, weekends and vacations found us increasingly making the three-hour drive north to the Lake Michigan area where Pete had spent his childhood summers. Unlike the area's wealthier seasonal residents, Pete's family had purchased an unremarkable old farmhouse that came with a long neglected barn, out-buildings, and acreage. But the property sported a swell view of the big blue lake and provided refuge from the city's summer heat for his mother and Pete and his siblings. Pete's father, a hunter and fisherman, remained at home downstate working in their mid-Michigan city during the warm months, enjoying the farm during the cooler days of autumn when his painting business slowed down.

For Pete, summers spent at "Island View Farm" had been heaven. The youngest of ten children, most mornings he stuffed his pockets with apples and headed out alone to roam free and look for adventure in the steeply rugged hardwood forest surrounding the old farm. He swears his tired mother usually didn't even realize he was missing. Pete's happy memories of northern Michigan summers include mornings walking barefoot down a leafy two-track to Lake Michigan, picking juicy wild strawberries in the afternoon, and lying on a grassy hill watching shooting stars in a diamond-studded night sky. Fueled by his stories, we soon began looking for a similar property in earnest.

Weekends and vacations we headed north to spend countless hours scouring the area. Eventually we responded to a hand-painted "land for sale" arrow that had, as it turned out, been blown and buffeted by the late winter winds so that it now pointed to the property across the road. As we tramped around the snow-covered fields the arrow was pointing to, the property's surprised owner informed us his land was most definitely not for sale. Eventually we tracked down the elderly seller of the property the sign was *supposed* to be pointing at, and learned he also owned unadvertised property a bit further up the road. It seemed he and his wife had originally planned to build their own retirement home there, but had ultimately built at the lakeshore. After some discussion about the parcel's price and number of acres (we thought 40 sounded appropriately "farmy" and his unadvertised property, he told us, was nearly 35), we agreed to take a look at it with him.

"Taking a look at it" began with a wild ride in the backseat of the seller's bucking Jeep, straight up a small mountain while our heads bashed into the ceiling and our spines compressed as we were slammed back down into the seat. We finally crested the peak. There before us stretched a nearly 180-degree panoramic view of Lake Michigan and all the islands of the Beaver Island Archipelago we'd read about in the advertisements. Beneath a bright sun, the sky and the big lake were impossibly blue. Tiny sail boats passed by under billowing cumulus clouds while just beyond Skillagalee Island Lighthouse a thousand foot Great

Lakes freighter moved steadily north with a load of coal headed to Minnesota. Our driver explained that "Skillagalle" was the local pronunciation of the "Isle aux Galets," or "Isle of Pebbles," a gravely outcrop named by the French explorers, traders, and Jesuit missionaries who originally settled the area in the 1600s. Goggle-eyed and slack-jawed in the backseat, we clutched each other's hands, nearly drawing blood. *Unreal! Unbelievable! Things like this don't happen to people like us!* Without even getting out of the Jeep, we bought the 35 acres of hardwoods and fallow, rolling fields that would eventually become "Beckon Hill Farm," and our year-round home.

Soon after, we began to claim the property as our own. After the first of many nights spent tenting, we realized we needed a good mattress and a fire pit. As it turned out, the mattress would be a long time coming, but the fire pit, needed partly for cooking and partly for comfort, was doable. I say "partly" because during that first night we were awakened by a series of other-worldly screams, accompanied by a muffled, steady drum beat.

The next morning we found the open fields were teeming with rocks of all shapes and sizes. Using a homemade lever and fulcrum, we learned how to pop them out of the rich black soil, dragging them to the site of our proposed fire pit with our truck and a heavy logging chain. We kept replacing the smaller stones we'd first used with increasingly larger ones until before long we had pretty much built a boulder fortress with a fire in the center. Sometimes I actually *sat inside the fire pit.* Nearly every night and occasionally even during the day, we continued to hear the horrible eerie screams.

We discovered our steeply ridged and gullied highland property had originally been part of the picturesque old farm next door. It sported a creaking, vine-covered windmill, a multi-storied chicken coop, and a huge, ancient barn. A few weekend trips later, we decided to introduce ourselves to these neighbors. Their farm house was badly in need of repairs and paint and the stone fences were neglected, but the place had loads of charm. We had seen children, dogs, hanging laundry, and a pony that, we later learned, had pointedly been named "Sober." It seemed clear these folks were bona-fide year-'rounders.

After hiking down from our hill to the road below, Pete and I headed toward their place. Just as we started up the walk toward the sagging front porch, the door flew open and a large, dark object slowly began to emerge. It completely filled the doorway. Finally, what turned out to be a well-used upright piano cleared the sill. Next, several small children and large dogs emerged, followed by two men pushing the piano, two women, numerous cats, and at last, a huge male peacock dragging his impressive tail behind him. It was an honest-to-God classic Clown Car.

Eager to demonstrate what good neighbors we intended to be, Pete volunteered to lend a hand, but the group seemed to have a plan; we watched as they wrestled the piano across the porch, down the cement steps, along the walk and across the road. Then it slowly moved along a second walk, up more cement steps, across another porch and at last, to the front door of another neighboring farm, through which the entire entourage promptly disappeared.

Eventually the piano's original owners, their children, dogs, cats, and peacock reemerged and made their way back across the road toward us. After introductions, we stood on the walkway making small talk. Suddenly a horrible and eerily familiar scream interrupted our conversation as the peacock, his magnificent tail now upright and fanned fully open, snapped his beak at us. We've always considered that to have been our official welcome to the neighborhood. Although we never did identify the source of the distant drum beat which we still hear occasionally, I stopped sitting inside the fire pit.

MYSTERY RIDGE

Admittedly, we live in a very extraordinary place. During its 1600s settlement, the French Jesuits built a series of missions along the shores of the Great Lakes to bring Christianity to the indigenous people who had already been seasonal residents here for thousands of years. Unlike Pete and me and Father Marquette, who froze or starved to death one winter along the shores of Lake Michigan, the savvy native people knew to head south each year well before the arrival of the "the breath-taking beauty when snow-fairy forests are cloaked in sparkling diamonds" and the "panoramic blue waters rest beneath a glittering cover of ice, interrupted only by the Beaver Island Archipelago."

Besides its historic and obvious visual charms, it is pretty well acknowledged that for reasons unknown, really strange places exist here in which really strange things occur with such regularity they have come to be considered normal. One of these local anomalies provides marginal entertainment for those of us who are unable or unwilling to enjoy more sophisticated adventures. Pete's family learned about Mystery Ridge when his mother inherited a 1940 Chrysler coupe from a cousin. In those first heady weeks when she was celebrating the freedom of having her own "wheels," she often gathered whichever of her children were available, stuffing two or three of them into the open trunk if necessary, and headed for the beach or an unexplored two-track in search of wild huckleberries.

Downstate, Pete's family had lived for generations in the totally flat farm country of eastern mid-Michigan. The only hills in their home-turf were and are the temporary mounds of sugar beets waiting to be processed at the local sugar plant every fall. And so, irresistibly lured by the many stomach-dropping hilly roads surrounding their summer neighborhood farmstead, Pete's mother soon developed the habit of speeding up, then suddenly throwing the little coupe into neutral and coasting down whatever hill she came to. Eventually this type of thing was developed by Walt Disney into a big business in California and Florida.

The kids could always be relied on to scream and beg for more; even the ones choking on clouds of road dust in the trunk. But one day, something amazing, something astounding, incredible, and downright astonishing happened the first time Pete's mother coasted her little car down a long, steep hill near their farm. As always, when it at last reached the bottom of a hill, the coupe slowly came to a stop. However on this particular hill, after coasting to a complete halt, the car suddenly lurched backward and slowly began to move back *up* the hill it had just coasted *down*. The car was still in neutral, yet it was unmistakably gaining speed as it coasted backward uphill until it almost reached the crest it had just been launched from, before once again slowing to a stop.

Over the years, numerous friends and relatives have tried to demystify this "illusion" for us with determined skepticism and a variety of methods and tools. Whether relentlessly staring at the feet of the driver to be sure there's no "hanky-panky" going on with the gas pedal, or walking slowly up and down the hill while wielding levels, plum bobs, powerful magnets, and portable balance beams, each summer friends and members of our family arrive with a new theory to test, and leave still scratching their heads.

We've learned that it makes no difference whether the humidity is high or low; the gravel road is wet or dry, freshly graded or rutted. No matter if the vehicle involved is a fully-loaded eight-passenger cargo van or a lightweight two-seater; after coming to a complete stop in neutral gear and pausing for a second or two, it will slowly begin backing inexorably up the hill it has just coasted down. The driver's feet remain firmly planted on the floor, well away from the gas pedal; his or her only involvement is occasionally nudging the steering wheel if necessary to keep the vehicle from drifting off the road.

For years Pete's family believed this phenomenon had truly been discovered by his mother. This gave her a certain mystique, and increased her already formidable power within the family. Eventually, though, they learned that local residents had long been aware of the strange properties of the hill that Pete's family by now called 'Mystery Ridge'. As with many other curious places and events here, 'the Ridge' is rarely acknowledged. If pressed, often a resident may uncomfortably admit that the hill 'has a very powerful spirit.' They might even add a warning reminder that it really isn't a good idea to speak about such phenomena. For this and other reasons, I have always discouraged Pete from acting on his impulse to somehow, someday, parlay it into a money-making venture.

HE WHO SHALL REMAIN NAMELESS

Around here, not speaking about strange goings-on seems to be about the only accepted way to gain any control over them. A local legend features "He that shall remain nameless," a spirit creature who lives in the deep of Lake Michigan and is believed by many to be responsible for taking the lives of those unlucky fishermen and sailors who venture across the big lake and never return. I should tell you "He" not only shall remain nameless, "He" shall not be referred to *at all*. However, if you feel you really must, it is only permissible to talk about this creature in the winter when ice covers the lake, and you are still basically stupid if you do. In fact, the only reason I'm sharing this now is that as I write, Lake Michigan is completely frozen over, so if anything happens, don't blame me.

THE BIG MOVE

After counting down each day to retirement for eight years, we packed our furniture and belongings into two big moving vans, turned the keys over to the buyers of our house, and one early June morning, with a caravan of helpful friends and family, finally headed north. The previous summer we'd hired a crew to build a large garage with semi-finished quarters above.

During the six or seven months it would take to build our house next door, we planned to live there with our teenaged daughter, our cat, our nearly blind 15-year-old sheep dog, and the new puppy that our oldest daughter had insisted we take with us at the last minute. Afterward, the little garage apartment would accommodate the overflow from vacationing summer visitors. If the first part of this plan sounds like the worst idea you ever heard, you probably just passed some kind of mental health test, but at the time, it seemed perfectly reasonable to Pete and me.

With plenty of help from our family and friends, by the end of the day the garage was filled to the ceiling upstairs and down with furniture and boxes. Exhausted, we sprawled at the fire pit.

Our crabby-pants, never-been-outside, city housecat, Felix, had disappeared as soon as someone opened the cat carrier door upon arrival earlier that day. By now, he'd been gone for hours, and we figured we would never see him again. Suddenly here he was, with his back to us, sitting ramrod straight like an Egyptian tomb cat on the low stone wall we'd built just beyond the fire pit. And just like us, he was staring intently at the spectacular, panoramic sunset. We realized that having lived his entire life in a house in the city, he had never seen a sunset of any kind, let alone a spectacular one like this. He sat there motionless, watching the lake and blazing orange sky until the fire died down and we finally began to gather ourselves to head in for the night. Then he stood, stretched, jumped daintily off the wall and with his tail straight in the air, followed us across the yard to the garage and upstairs to bed.

FELIX SHARPENS HIS HEAD TO A POINT

From that first day onward, we couldn't keep Felix inside unless it was pouring rain. He proved to be a talented hunter and kept us constantly supplied with dead mice, voles, and shrews. One minute he was napping in a grassy nest in the sun, the next he was stalking grasshoppers or climbing through the gnarled branches of the big old maple tree next to the fire pit.

But a few days later, I realized that something was very wrong with Felix. We'd been so preoccupied with the start of the building project that somehow no one had noticed that he had developed ugly, bleeding wounds on each side of his head, just in front of his ears. I learned there was a veterinary clinic about twenty-five miles away and we took Felix there the same day. The veterinarian examined him thoughtfully, and then asked us if we had recently moved into a new home. *Why yes, yes we had, only about a week ago!*

"Well," the Vet said, "he must really like it." He went on to explain that cats have powerful musk glands at the base of their ears which they use to mark their territory. It seemed that Felix had been grinding his head against every rock and tree in an all-out effort to claim the place as his own. As the summer wore on, Felix's head finally healed up and we realized the ill-tempered, pouty cat we'd hauled north with us was gone forever. We would eventually come to understand that, like some of our new neighbors, Felix had apparently been replaced by a stoner look-alike, happily adrift on his own perpetual high.

PETE STEERS ME INTO A HOLE AND BREAKS MY BACK

Summer passed in a blur of building and suddenly it was September. Our teenaged daughter hated her new school, hated the bus she had to ride to get there, and most of all she hated us. I still can't understand how we could have been so selfish as to completely uproot her just at the beginning of her high school years. After all, this was our dream, not hers.

Her temporary "bedroom" in the garage apartment was a just a tiny dormer, and with only a curtain hanging against the footboard of her bed for privacy she didn't even have a door to slam. How could we have torn her away from her friends, cheerleading, and years of ballet lessons for life where, as one of her older sisters still describes it, "the ozone layer ends and space begins?" Our three grown children had remained downstate, but they too were unhappy about our move. The oldest was married and a young mother and the other two were in college, but they all felt we had abandoned them. Ah, guilt; the gift that keeps on giving.

Mostly as a result of our unfortunate decision to serve as general contractor, by the end of October the project was hopelessly behind schedule and over-budget. We were working with the builders every day, doing whatever we could to help us get into the house before real winter arrived. The tiny apartment had been designed for fair-weather use and would be impossible to heat once the temperatures plunged. Despite everything, we were taking things one day at a time and trying to enjoy the journey.

I'm totally lying. By then we were way beyond all that crap and fighting a growing sense of dread as the days grew shorter and the grey skies filled with thousands of Canada geese headed south.

Then one day in early November, Pete and I were walking arm in arm through the frozen and rutted minefield of clay clumps that still remained around the building site, when Pete steered me into a hole and I broke my back.

This is probably an exaggeration. Mostly I believe him when he says he didn't steer me into the hole and break my back on purpose, plus I only ruptured a disc, which hardly paralyzed me at all. Although the pain was unbearable and I couldn't walk, I refused to go to the hospital because when you are paralyzed and in unbearable pain, a day or two of bed rest will usually take care of it.

Somehow Pete managed to carry me up the steep, narrow stairs to our bed in the garage apartment. Suddenly, besides Poppy, our faithful old English sheepdog, who was having age-related incontinence problems, and the young pup, Dahlia, who was terrified of stairs, Pete was carrying three creatures to potty several times a day. It may have been during this period that people began calling him "poor Pete."

About three o'clock one morning, when the gales of November were howling outside the garage, I decided that I had to go to the hospital, and I had to go *right then.*

Within minutes, sirens could be heard and suddenly half a dozen first responders in full fire gear stormed up the stairway and tumbled through the door, filling the apartment. (God bless our volunteer fire department. They've saved our bacon several times during the past twenty years.)

The nearest hospital is thirty long and difficult miles away, so it took a while for the ambulance to arrive. By then, time had lost all meaning for me anyway, so I wasn't even annoyed.

That is a total lie. It turned out the narrow stairway and its clever pie-wedge landing couldn't accommodate their gurney. Eventually the firemen and EMTs managed to strap me, in a sitting position, to an L-shaped backboard. With my flannel pajamas flapping in the wind, I rode down the steps and to the ambulance on their shoulders like Cleopatra on her barge. The next day a kindly neurosurgeon completely fixed the exploded disc with tiny tools and a little fat from my butt and I've been in agony every minute of every day since then.

I'm kidding again. I only say this when I want Pete to feel guilty about steering me into that hole and breaking my back. The truth is I'm hardly ever in agony.

WARK AND THE COWARDLY BULL

For years we kept a high-quality, registered, Bluefaced Leicester breeding ram. Wark was a powerful animal, and he could be a real handful when his interests didn't mesh with ours. He sired many beautiful lambs over the years and contributed a lot to the success of our farm, but we learned to never turn our backs on him. Once, as breeding season approached, we stupidly put Wark and a younger ram in the same pen; then watched in horror as they nearly killed each other. Again and again they ran full speed at one another, crashing head-on until finally the younger ram fell, unconscious, cerebral spinal fluid leaking into his grotesquely swollen head and neck. One of our neighbors, a strong, good woman who survived a miserable battle for her life against breast cancer during which her weasel husband left her for a much younger woman, calls such events "tales from the dark side of the barn." Somehow the young ram lived, but he never played the piano again.

We felt terrible about what had happened, and from then on we respected the male animals on our farm as the dangerous creatures they can be. With the grandkids here so often, I didn't want Pete to keep a bull here, so each spring we leased a Hereford bull just long enough to breed our cows, then quickly sent him packing. Our ewes were usually bred between mid-September and late November. By this time, the leased bull was long gone, so when Wark completed his duties, we always turned him in with the Hereford cows for company.

Wark loved the ladies; any ladies, all ladies. When he wasn't eating, he could usually be found dozing in the pasture in that peculiar way of Bluefaced Leicesters, legs tucked neatly beneath him, eyes closed and nose straight up in the air. The Hereford cows never left him untended in this state. Instead, these nearly one-ton beauties positioned themselves closely around the two-hundred-pound Wark, either quietly grazing or napping like him. But the strangest habit the big red girls had was their licking of Wark's face and ears until his head was soaked. Sometimes two of them went at it together, and there he would lay, head in the air, eyes closed, lost in bliss.

Although in the past we had always managed to get Wark moved out of the cow pasture a few days before the leased bull was delivered, one year Pete didn't get this task taken care of in time. Before we knew it the stockman had arrived and unloaded a huge red bull the size of a locomotive straight into the pasture with Wark and the suddenly timid cows that stood cowering behind him. With head up and blood in his eye, the giant beast charged into the pasture and headed straight toward Wark and the cows.

I was horror-struck, positive that my prized Bluefaced Leicester ram was about to be run down by the enormous bull and stomped into mutton puree. Instead, Wark put his head down and charged the bull, who turned and fled at full speed down the hill toward the road and disappeared into the dense pines at the bottom of the pasture, where he remained in hiding for several days until, presumably, Wark gave him permission to come out. We didn't expect the cowardly bull to have much luck with the cows after that miserable show, but whether out of pity or desperation they must have forgiven him; every cow gave birth to a red calf the next year.

DIVING FROM PONIES

When our grandchildren were younger, on summer vacations a sunny day sometimes found us all on a picnic at Spirit Lake. Wearing bathing suits and beach shoes, the kids rode their ponies overland through the woods to the little inland lake. Pete and I would load the SUV with a bale of hay for the ponies and sandwiches, chips, and drinks for the rest of us, often sinking a big watermelon in the lake to cool while we waited for the swimmers to arrive. After paddling out far enough to reach deep water, the ponies swam in big, looping circles and served as diving boards for the kids while Pete and I watched safely from shore; it turns out both of us are terrified of Lima beans and water.

4TH OF JULY

The 4th of July is a really big deal here, possibly because by then the snow is usually gone. Out in the Bay, armadas of wealthy summer people host all-day soirees on their sleek boats, boarding one another's vessels to visit with friends and sample the sushi. Later, after a spectacular sunset, darkness falls and the evening is capped off with extravagant fireworks displays over the big Lake.

Our small village celebrates almost exactly the same way, with a parade of kids riding decorated ponies or stuffed into little flag-draped garden wagons pulled by grandparents on riding lawnmowers. The whole thing is led by the volunteer firemen who blast the pumper truck's siren, wave tirelessly, and throw candy to everyone. Some years kids walk their spiffy 4-H animals on leashes behind the ponies. The village is very small so the parade goes around the single block several times but everyone watching pretends not to notice.

KIDS IN THE OVEN

Besides horses, ponies, and cows, we bred and raised a variety of purebred fiber animals including several breeds of wool sheep and registered Angora goats. Every year the farm's greening pastures filled with twin and sometimes triplet spring lambs and their patient mothers. Sheep are the oldest domesticated food animal. For over 10,000 years sheep genetics have been controlled by man rather than nature. Without the benefit of natural selection, a modern sheep can't survive on its own; it can no longer defend itself, find food or water, and often can't even give birth without serious assistance from a shepherd.

Unlike rams, which have been selectively bred for other qualities, ewes are generally affable and meek, with no real defense mechanisms other than practicing safety in numbers. Any physical or behavioral deficiency a sheep exhibits invites derision from those who don't appreciate the many fine qualities sheep *do* possess. If we had a dollar for every time we've heard, "stupid as a sheep" or "a sheep is an animal looking for a reason to die," we could get out of here in the winter.

On the other hand, the smart little Angora goat is a natural clown and ours were hands- down favorites with almost everyone. Goats love to perform for any audience; they routinely play leapfrog with each other, give delicate kisses, and boldly search visitor's pockets for treats.

Angora goats also produce mountains of curly white, silky mohair, and just about the cutest babies, called "kids," in the world. Generally, sheep and goats are wonderful mothers. But occasionally circumstances are such that a mother rejects or can't care for her offspring, and that's where "bottle babies" come from. Most flock owners consider them to be a flat-out nuisance, but we raised more than a few "bottle babies" through the years, and I had fun with them. I always made it a last resort, because a bottle baby loses out on a lot; powdered milk replacement is a poor substitute for mother's milk, and a lamb or kid raised by humans misses valuable info that only their real mother can teach them.

Some years a diapered bottle baby following me around the house while I dusted or folded laundry was a common sight. As sometimes happened, when a doe or a ewe rejected her newborn baby, if the weather was bitterly cold, or the lamb or kid was smaller or weaker than normal, the little one's chances of survival in the barn were greatly reduced, even with me traipsing out to give it a bottle several times a day. For this reason, I brought them into the house, gave them a warm bath, and broke out a jumbo pack of disposable diapers. They bonded to me because I had the food, which meant they wouldn't voluntarily leave my side; whenever they were hungry they cried and I fed them and sometimes when all of this made me miss mothering my own babies too much, I wrapped them in an old baby blanket and rocked them to sleep.

I'm not kidding. In my own defense, I was usually still in the throes of end-stage winter poisoning at this point. Usually after a week or two the baby could be successfully grafted into the barn flock again, and I always missed them.

The puppy we'd brought with us when we moved north had grown up to become our much-loved friend and official stock dog. Dahlia was smart, kind, faithful, and a great surrogate mother to the bottle-fed lambs and kids. She rounded them up when they cried if they couldn't find me or became lost behind furniture. Gently holding them down with her paw while administering an all-over grooming, Dahlia could quickly calm down even the unhappiest baby.

Although I usually tried to time our sheep- and goat-breeding seasons so that their babies would be born after the worst part of winter had passed, sometimes I purchased a new animal that turned out to be pregnant. One such year, I was surprised to discover a young Angora doe I'd recently purchased was unmistakably pregnant, and it looked like she was carrying twins. She would be a first-time mother; without a clue as to what was happening to her, she would be terrified, and her lack of experience meant I had to be extra vigilant and ready for anything. I made sure my "go-bag" was packed with everything I could possibly need to help her deliver live kids.

Like most flock owners, I made increasingly frequent barn checks around the clock as the little doe developed the tell-tale signs that delivery was ready for launch. The late February temperature had taken a dive to the low teens one night, and when I checked her just before I planned to go to bed at 11:00 p.m., I realized her labor was well underway.

Everything went better than I expected; before long twin kids, a doeling and a buckling, were struggling to get to their feet under the heat lamp. The new mother, pressed into a corner of the pen in an effort to get as far away as possible from her shivering children, clearly had no intention of mothering them. After several attempts to turn things around and despite the warmth of a blow-dryer and the heat lamp, vigorous towel rubbing, tube feedings of warm colostrums and time spent with me inside my barn jacket, the kids were limp; a finger thrust into their tiny cold mouths told me they were dying.

It was definitely time for plan B. By now the doe had passed her placenta so I quickly re-bedded her. Dahlia and Pete met me in the kitchen and Dahlia immediately began licking the babies' cold heads as Pete and I began filling the big sink, planning to submerge their bodies in warm water to raise their body temperature. Then we realized one of the kitchen's gleaming stainless steel double ovens would be so much more efficient! Pete kept a hair dryer blowing on the kids while I quickly lined the lower oven rack and sides with several thick clean terry barn towels, turned the oven on low just long enough to get it toasty and then turned the heat off. We laid both kids together on the padded single oven rack and tucked more of the warmed towels close around and over them, left the oven door ajar with the light bulb to maintain heat, and pulled our chairs up to watch and wait.

I kept feeling inside their little mouths and soon the kids both had their heads up and were coming to life again. When they began to try to stand up, we took them out of the oven and turned them over to Dahlia. As soon as we spread an old comforter next to the oven for Dahlia and the kids, she lay down, pulled them to her chest and busied herself becoming their nanny. After a vigorous licking, she kept nudging them until she managed to get them both on their feet and soon they were tottering around the kitchen behind her. I gave them each another tube feeding of warm colostrum and before long they were practically tap-dancing.

Before calling it a night I went to the barn once more to make a final check on their mother. Despite her ordeal, she was blissfully munching hay under the heat lamp without a care in the world. That kind of mental muscle could get a person through a northern Michigan winter. A few minutes later, the snow squeaked and crunched as I walked alone back from the barn that frozen, starry, February night and it struck me that the unusual life we had chosen was, well… unusual, but it was really *life*.

LAZARUS RISES

Once another of our neighbors, a veterinarian, who raised Black Angus cattle, came home from work late one winter afternoon, and found a nearly dead calf that had been born hours earlier and gone unattended all day by its first-time mother. Our neighbor and his wife carried the cold, limp calf up the steep hill to their house.

Once inside, a warm bath was drawn and the calf was placed in the tub. Our neighbor started an IV in the little animal and took turns with his wife keeping its head above the water. They continued this therapy for three days as best they could, but it seemed hopeless.

On the fourth day, they left for work, expecting the calf, still in the now waterless bathtub, to be dead when they returned later that afternoon.

In the spirit of all things weird that residents have come to accept here, when they came home, the calf was on his feet walking around the living room. They named him Lazarus, successfully raised him with the herd as a bottle baby, and as far as I know he's still alive.

This last part about him still being alive is probably not true because we are a nation of meat-eaters. Which makes me realize that although for some people, the take-away here would be "never give up" or "miracles do happen" or some such crap, now that I think about it the efforts of our neighbor and his wife were probably a waste of time because in the end, everything dies anyway.

I'm only kidding; it's mid-February and I have end-stage winter poisoning.

ALL GOOD THINGS MUST COME TO AN END

The heady days of raising cattle, sheep, and horses have been over for several years now. We only winter a few chickens for their brown eggs and three geriatric Bluefaced Leicester pet ewes. Each spring, Pete buys two or three red-and-white Hereford calves to fatten on pasture grass but sends them off to market at the end of fall grazing to avoid the difficulty and expense of cold-weather cattle feeding. The long grey winter eventually disappears each year with the intake of a single breath. Suddenly, the breeze is filled with soft, warm promise and sometimes, just for a minute, I see our grandchildren when they were small; and the ghosts of lambs, calves, and ponies; and kids in the oven.

WHO'S TALKING ... *Cheryl Reed is an artist, farmer, mother, grandmother, and former 911 operator. She has awards for saving lives. Her beautifully realistic paintings of children and the out-of-doors are snatched up by Michigan's seasonal residents and visitors.*

20: DOG LESSONS
KARENE, 61

I'VE NEVER THOUGHT OF MYSELF AS A PATIENT PERSON. I DID, AF-ter all, inherit that embarrassing family temper. Remember the dad in the movie *Christmas Story*, down in the basement having the "conversation" with the furnace? Yup, that was my dad.

My mom used to have her own conversations with the sewing machine and I was well into adulthood before I knew sewing didn't involve #$%X@# words. My sister once told me of the time she was putting up curtains in her bedroom, conversing with them as well, when her husband came into the room, calmly looked at her and asked, "Do you need a pill or something?"

And me? Well, I'm the one who has a little conversation of my own with the Microsoft gods who have pre-determined that I can't possibly know what I really want so they auto-correct for me. Don't even get me started on cable and all those remotes.

So imagine my amazement in learning that I do indeed have a very patient side. All it took to discover it was fourteen pounds of spunk and tenacity named Chelsea, followed by a goofball named Barnaby.

Although I grew up with a variety of dogs in our family, I had never adopted one as an adult. Living alone, it's quite a commitment, always having to adjust your schedule around them. So when my sister-in-law, Val, suggested I adopt her sister's eleven-year-old Westie, Chelsie, I hemmed and hawed. Val and my brother, Tom, had two dogs of their own, which I often dog-sat, and they knew I loved dogs. Val's sister had remarried, had several children, and had started a day care in her home, so Chelsie, being an older dog, was having trouble adjusting to all those children and their commotion.

I knew Chelsie from our family get-togethers and yes, I finally adopted her, but only on a trial basis. I wasn't at all sure how this would go. Well, of course, I absolutely fell in love with her in no time at all. Loving and loyal, she was such a curious and happy dog that she was a delight. I went from worrying about adopting her to worrying about the family wanting her back or her wanting to be with them and not me. As it turned out, she was always very happy to visit them, but right by my side when I headed to my car to go home. It was a perfect match for all of us.

If you know anything about terriers, you know they come with a surplus of personality. While they may be stubborn, that stubbornness can also represent a tenacity that I came to deeply respect and admire. Little dogs don't see themselves as little. They're ready to take on the world. Chelsie was such a character, she always made me laugh, and I never grew tired of watching her watch the world. She was very territorial. In fact, she would leap off the couch and bark at any animal that appeared on TV. I was amazed she could even recognize them, but she could. Even a horse in the background would warrant a bark. It was actually quite fascinating.

One day, though, I was sure she had it wrong. A commercial came on with a man fishing from a boat. Chelsie planted herself in front of the screen, stomping her feet, and barking ferociously. I laughed and told her, "Sorry, Chelsie. There are no animals in this one." Just then, the fisherman's cell phone rang. He answered it and heard, "Meow, meow, meow" and the screen changed to a cat on a cell phone calling him. Okay, either Chelsie was way too smart or had been watching way too much TV!

If you Google Westie (aka West Highland White Terrier), you find such definitions as independent, alert, curious, courageous, hardy, active, affectionate, happy, and always in the thick of things. Their original function was vermin hunting, so they developed a fearlessness in the face of foxes and badgers, among other critters. Like vicious mice.

I always keep a trap set under my kitchen sink—just in case. One morning, I heard a commotion in the kitchen. I went in and found that Chelsie had opened the cupboard door, something I didn't even know she could do, and had discovered a mouse with my little trap hanging off the end of his nose. She was in full hunter mode. She herded him out to the center of the kitchen, then circled and circled him, keeping him in place, looking continually at me with an "OK, it's your turn" expression.

Me? I shrieked and started hopping around. Chelsie looked at me with utter disbelief. Here she was doing her job and the master hunter was falling apart. I finally got it together, put my work gloves on, picked the trap up by its corner with the mouse kicking and squirming and took it outside, opening the trap and letting the mouse go. I swear Chelsie's jaw dropped in disbelief. She stomped her feet, snorted as loud as a bull, and took off after him.

No, she didn't catch him, but she sure came close. I think she was planning on mice meat pie for dinner but didn't get it, certainly not for a lack of effort on her part.

Chelsie and I spent almost two years together and she became an important part of my life. I never tired of her adventures and grew to love simply watching her confident, adventuresome self while in the yard or on our walks. Often I watched her in awe. How on earth could so much attitude, affection, and just pure *life* be encompassed in that little fourteen-pound body?

When Chelsie neared thirteen, she developed kidney disease. Hospitalized for several days, I was so in fear of her dying. Once home, on meds and a new diet, she required subcutaneous saline injections several times a week to keep her hydrated, a necessity due to her disease.

I've always been afraid of needles. In fact, as a child, I'd literally faint dead away whenever I had to get a shot. If you had told me I'd ever be hooking up an IV bag with saline, gently inserting a needle just under the skin on a dog's neck, then comforting her for the time it took for the saline to drip in, I would never have believed you. Yet three times a week, Tom or Val would come by to hold her while I set things up. Chelsie took it with an amazing tolerance and her characteristic toughness. How could I not honor that with my own patience and tolerance? A whole new side of me emerged.

During this time, as I knew her health was declining, she became slower and slower on our walks and in our activities. While I always appreciated a good steady walk, I now slowed down, letting her set the pace. The truth was I grew to admire and respect her tenacity and attitude. Here she was, having come so close to death and now in declining health, and yet she was still curious about the world around her and anxious to get out there and be a part of things.

As she became slower, stopping more often to sniff (her way of resting), I came to appreciate this slower pace myself. I noticed this interesting tree with wildly twisting branches that I'd never really noticed before. I'd stand and watch birds building a nest or see the first little crocuses making their way up through the snow. All things we'd simply marched by before. I came to appreciate this gift Chelsie was giving me.

Chelsie started to lose her interest in eating. Each meal, I sat on the floor next to her, putting morsels of food in my palm, offering them to her and encouraging her to eat. Mealtime now had to be planned for and could span a half hour. Instead of just letting her run about the yard on her own, I'd stay close, keeping an eye on her in case she needed me. My whole world slowed down along with hers and, more and more, I found this to be a blessing of its own. I enjoyed simple moments in a way I hadn't in quite some time. I quit rushing so and became more patient with life itself.

When I realized Chelsea was failing and there was no more the vet or I could do, I took the day off work and spent it with her. It was a beautiful, sunny day in June. I got a blanket and we lay in the sun. I just stroked her, sang to her, napped with her, and even sketched a picture of her. When Tom and Val got home from work, we all went together to the vet's. It's hard to explain, but I know that Chelsea knew, and that she really was ready. The vet put her to sleep with us all stroking and talking to her. She went very, very peacefully.

I learned a lot from Chelsie. I had worried so about it being too much of a commitment (okay, a bother) to have a dog on my own, yet quickly found that the companionship, joy, and unconditional love she offered were so much more fulfilling than I ever imagined. It truly amazed me to discover that patient side of me as well. I've thought about that a lot since. Part of it is that our dogs are truly so vulnerable and dependent on us. How could I be impatient with that? They have no hidden agendas, no ulterior motives. That's the great things about dogs. They live in the moment with absolute honesty. Somehow, that makes whatever they require from you so much easier to give. I learned a lot from Chelsie. I had no idea how much more I was about to learn from Barnaby.

I found Barnaby in our local animal shelter. He was such a happy fellow, I actually wondered if something was wrong with him. Didn't he know how awful a place he was in? Yet he'd been found as a stray, so regular meals and a warm dry place to sleep must have seemed pretty good to him. And I have a sense the people there really liked him. How could they not? He was such a joyful little guy.

He looked like he might have some Westie in him, with huge pointy ears, big black eyes and nose, and white scruffy hair. (Actually, a DNA test would later show poodle, keeshond, and schnauzer.) He was the last dog I looked at that day and he made me laugh when I saw him. Those rabbit ears! And that tail wagging so hard it thumped. He seemed so genuinely happy that I thought, maybe I don't need to rescue the most needy dog. Maybe it's okay to rescue a happy, healthy dog! So I did, and eventually learned I was going to laugh at this initial assessment.

I adopted Barnaby, a young, healthy, happy dog. Young? Yes, in fact a bit younger than the year old they said he was. Happy? Yes, perpetually. Healthy? Well, as it turned out, Barnaby was born with cataracts, an extremely rare condition, so he saw movement and shapes, but nothing very distinct (more on this later).

To add to his uniqueness, his head bobbled, and if you looked closely, you could see his eyes bounce a little bit as well. Our vet referred to this as an ocular bob and said that it and the head bobbing were most likely caused by maybe just a little brain damage, but nothing really to worry about.

Oh, and he was also lacking a stomach enzyme, so for every meal for the eleven years I was his chef, I mixed an enzyme with water into his food, letting it incubate for 15-20 minutes before I gave it to him. It appears I had more to learn about patience and commitment and caring.

Yes, Barnaby was genetically challenged, but as our vet said, "Oh, but he's got all the cute genes!"

And the happy ones, as well, for throughout his life, with all his health issues, he never lost that goofy, happy guy attitude that was pure Barnaby. How could I not admire, respect, and even be a little envious of such a joyful take on the world?

Just as Chelsie didn't see herself as small, Barnaby didn't see himself as lacking in any way. In fact, he always acted like he'd just won the jackpot. Watching Barnaby proved every bit as enlightening as watching Chelsea.

Soon after bringing Barnaby home, I noticed he was afraid of even the two steps into my house. If he jumped up on the couch, he wouldn't jump off. He'd reach down with his paw, feeling for the floor, but since he couldn't feel it, he wouldn't jump off. This actually came in handy at times. Instead of having to crate him when we visited overnight with family, I could just put him on the couch and he'd stay there.

But at home I accommodated him with stools next to the furniture he was allowed on. My challenge was to take the time to see the world from his point of view so I could protect him from anything that he couldn't distinguish (a street grate with openings his paws could fall into, a thin pole he could run into). Here was another new perspective for me, to truly slow down and see the world through Barnaby's eyes.

Barnaby continued to be the happiest, most joyful of dogs. He slept at the foot of my bed, but in the morning, he'd come up and put his head on the pillow next to me, lying on his back, legs spread wide, his tail whomping. I'd try not to laugh. If I succeeded and didn't respond, he'd reach over and lick my ear, definitely making me laugh. This led to a full-body massage and belly rub for him, a great way to start his day and really, what better way for me to start my own day than with laughter?

Barnaby made others laugh as well, often with those ears of his. Walking him one dark night before Christmas, all bundled up, we passed a woman with a Brittany spaniel, saying hello as we passed.

The next night we passed her again, this time under a street light. She stopped and stared at Barnaby, then burst out laughing. "Those are his ears!" she exclaimed, still laughing. "I went home last night and told my husband I'd seen a lady walking her dog and he had white fluffy antlers on his head and how impressed I was that she'd gotten him to wear them!"

On another day in early summer, stuck in a traffic jam with my car window rolled down, I heard a male voice in the car next to us say, "It's a rabbit." I looked over and saw he was looking at Barnaby.

I laughed and said, "Hey, you're not talking about my dog, are you?"

The guy laughed back, saying, "My buddy asked if that was a dog or a rabbit in that car. I said it was a rabbit!"

Barnaby barked at him, wagging his tail all the while. Another thing I learned about life with Barnaby was that I often found myself in conversations with people I otherwise would have just passed by.

Some of what I learned from Barnaby was the simple things most dog owners learn in one variation or another. Like the time I visited with friends one evening, later finding out Barnaby had discovered their laundry basket of dirty clothes and very quietly and methodically eaten the crotches out of their underpants. Yes, all of them. Fortunately, they found this quite hysterical. I covered the cost of new ones and spent the next couple of days inspecting Barnaby's poop to be sure everything "came out" okay.

When Barnaby played with my neighbor's golden retriever, tugging on her long hair, I'd awake at 5 a.m. the next morning to find him hawking up a nice big hairball.

Even though I learned to keep paper plates in my bedside stand, I never once got him to actually hit one when hawking up.

When we visited Tom and Val and the cover was on their pool, Barnaby thought he could walk across it, only to discover he slowly sank and had to be rescued.

On our nightly walks in the winter, little snow balls would form between the pads on his paws and he'd stop, hold his paw in the air, and refuse to take another step until I removed my mittens and worked the balls out with my own freezing fingers.

With Barnaby in my life, it wasn't only patience and tolerance I learned more about, and it wasn't just coming to accept that these little adventures would occur on a regular basis. It's that I actually appreciated and in some weird way came to enjoy these little mishaps. Sure, they could be ill-timed, frustrating, and even expensive. Yes, there were times I got angry. But overall, they gave a texture and variety to daily life that still makes me smile. These were the experiences, after all, that made our bond grow stronger as the years went by.

One of the most amazing things I learned from Barnaby was unexpected to me. As I mentioned, Barnaby had congenital cataracts, which is extremely rare. In fact, the animal ophthalmologist we met with (yes, there really is such a thing) was totally geeked about meeting Barnaby. Even though he had been a professor at Michigan State University's vet school, he hadn't seen a case in eight years. "And that was a cat," he said. So for only the cost of an arm and a leg (i.e. a home equity loan), when Barnaby was three years old and his cataracts had matured enough for surgery, I had them removed. Life was soon to become very different for him and for me.

Even as a puppy, Barnaby never had clear vision. It was like looking through a milky glass that became more blurred as time went by. He could distinguish shapes and movement, but nothing in much detail. He couldn't even chase a ball and was very hesitant in unfamiliar places.

The surgery was outpatient and the staff did the most incredible thing. They brought him out to me in the waiting room to hold until time for his surgery. I propped my feet up on a chair and made a place for him on my lap. He was sprawled across me with his head full against my chest. The meds they'd given him made him sleepy and he just relaxed into me and let me hold him close as he fell asleep.

I had never held him like this. Barnaby was an independent little fellow whose idea of cuddling was to lie across my lap on the couch and have me hold his chew bone so he could wrap his paws around my hand while he chewed. Eventually he'd stop and just lay there, letting me pet him, but then he'd be done and off he'd go. So this was an unexpected gift. How wonderful for him as well, to be with me rather than in a kennel while he waited.

After the surgery, for the first time in his life, he could truly see the world around him. So what does he do on the ride home? He sat straight up, faced the back of the car seat and stared at it the whole way. He may have still been a little spacey from the anesthesia, but I actually think he may have been trying to limit stimuli.

Barnaby was very subdued, staying close to me and sleeping most of the evening. The next day, he was frustrated with the cone he had to wear, trying to figure out how to eat and drink with it on and discovering he couldn't get through his pet door. I had to laugh, though, when he also couldn't figure out how to pee. He usually peed along the fence or a tree, but when he'd get near, his cone would bang against them and startle him, so he'd walk around and around. He finally figured out how to be near the fence but turn his head so the cone wouldn't bang it and he could pee. Whew!

The next two days, Barnaby remained subdued and slept a lot. He greeted people when they visited, but then went back to his bed. I wondered how much of that was the aftereffects of the medications and how much was his instinctive way of reducing stimuli.

On the third day, I put his harness on to see if he wanted to go for a walk and he refused to take even one step out of the yard. What he did begin to do, however, was sit in the yard in his favorite spot and just look. He'd look in one direction for a long time, barely turning his head; then he'd re-position himself and look in another direction for a long time. He'd do this for hours at a time.

I began to realize the most amazing thing. Barnaby's whole world now looked different to him. His brain had to take each image, translate it to how he used to know that image, and create an entirely new frame of reference for that image. He had to take all the smells and sounds of his world and form associations to images he'd never seen in this way before. I found myself pulling up a lawn chair and just watching him watch his new world. I was fascinated with the miracle that was taking place.

On the fourth day, Barnaby was back! Those crazy, exuberant circles he'd turn. That happy dog, non-stop tail wagging. My goofy guy was back. He would still sit and look intently about him for long periods, but when my neighbor came out with his golden retriever, I opened the gate and Barnaby ran straight over to them. Heading back home, Barnaby ran full-tilt towards our house, dodging a small thin tree at the last minute, barely slowing down. He'd have hit that tree before his surgery.

Barnaby tired easily, but each day brought renewed energy. He still sat outside for long periods, just looking and looking, even after dark. I couldn't imagine what it would be like to have this gift of renewed sight, but I never grew tired of just watching him.

Once his cone was removed, the ophthalmologist said he was looking great. Since he was clearly feeling better, we started our daily walks again. He walked with a confidence I'd never seen before. Crazy, I know, but he looked physically different to me. He looked erect and more handsome (in a dog sort of way). His eyes were more open and focused, giving him a more alert look, a more assured look.

My amazing little Barnaby. He taught me to see the world differently in so many ways. It's hard for me to put into words those hours of watching him relearn his world, but they were a gift to me as well. I'm aware even now what a privilege it was to witness that.

I never anticipated that and certainly wouldn't have expected it to come from adopting a scruffy little shelter dog. But maybe, after all, that's the most important thing I learned from Barnaby.

Just when you think you're the one who is giving to someone else, it turns out you're really the one who is doing the receiving.

Barnaby and I shared eleven joyful, loving, goofy years together. He was around twelve when I lost him last summer, his age and medical issues catching up with him. I still miss him dearly. We were so very well-suited for each other in so many ways. Truly, a day never went by when he didn't make me laugh right out loud. We were both very lucky to have found each other.

So yes, I'm "between dogs" right now, but I dog-sit often and know that when the time is right there will be another little four-legged friend to come along and teach me what I don't even know I have yet to learn.

WHO'S TALKING ... *Following her MoMo's recipe, Karene Hughes makes the best wild blackberry cake, with thick caramel frosting, on the face of the earth. She enjoys camping on the lakeshore in Northern Michigan and volunteering at the world's largest radically-open ArtPrize competition in Grand Rapids. She invites everyone to join in this amazing annual event.*

21: BEING BIPOLAR
JAN, 63

I FIND MYSELF IN STRANGE COMPANY.

Edward Elgar, Marilyn Monroe, Kurt Cobain, Carrie Fisher, Patrick J. Kennedy, Elvis Presley, Jean-Claude Van Damme, Lord Byron, Ben Stiller, Jackson Pollack, Catherine Zeta-Jones, Ted Turner, Richard Dreyfuss, Abbie Hoffman, and probably Beethoven, Van Gogh, Moses, Nietzsche, and Napoleon Bonaparte.

We're usually either promiscuous, drug users, financially irresponsible, or some combination of all three, and given to cycling through wild mood swings. We're all mentally ill, we're all bipolar, and we all have faced potentially life-threatening consequences without diagnosis and chemical help.

Some, like Cobain, never make it because of non-compliance with treatment. And some, like Van Gogh, never get diagnosed and ultimately find life too painful to cope with. And we all experience mood swings between manic highs and depressive lows.

According to the National Institute of Mental Health and the Mayo Clinic, the manic highs include overestimating our abilities, talking rapidly, thinking we're the most charming people in the room, euphoria at the same time that we're also extremely irritable, taking on lots of projects and even producing a great deal, racing from one idea to the next, having sleep disorders, and engaging in impulsive, often risky behaviors that feel good, such as spending sprees, casual sexual encounters, and alcohol abuse. (I am told by friends that the "high" sounds very similar to that of cocaine, which I have never tried because I was absolutely certain I would not be able to stop).

The depressive lows are marked by deep sadness, hopelessness, and loss of pleasure in things that once moved us (including sex), being tired, unable to pay attention (we get distracted very easily), anxiety and guilt and, as with the high, irritability and sleep disorders, not being able to concentrate, poor performance at work or school, and most catastrophic, thinking about death and even attempting suicide.

It's a hell of a way to live. Literally. And I have lived that way almost from the beginning.

My family was fully dysfunctional. My father ruled with an authoritarian iron hand when he bothered to pay attention, and my mother was given to angry outbursts of verbal abuse.

When I was five, I was sexually abused by the teenaged boy next door, twice. My parents discovered it the second time, and I was so terrified of my father's reaction and my mother's anger by this time, that I lied about the actual details, not knowing what would happen if I told the truth.

When my mother demanded to know what *I* "had done," I simply answered that I had taken my panties down. That was the end of the interrogation. There were never any questions about what *he* had done. I remember my parents arguing about what was to be done about the episode. My mother wanted to tell the mother of the boy, but my father said no, so in 1950s fashion, my mother conceded.

My father's ultimate solution was to whip me with the flat side of a wooden clothes brush. I never forgave him or my mother for not protecting me, for even at five, I knew something had gone really wrong there, so I bitterly resented it.

From then on my existence was a study in avoiding drawing my father's attention, and in the years I lived with him, I remember him hugging me only once. When my parents divorced the year I turned sixteen, I cried with joy that I was out from under his thumb.

I don't know what the onset of my bipolar disorder was, or whether the sexual abuse was a precipitating factor, but I can remember being depressed as early as age eight.

I couldn't sleep at night, and even as a pre-teen, I was already cycling, labeled by my family as "Pepper-Pot" for my irritability and hot temper, and when I entered adolescence, I was a nightmare, not merely difficult. My explosive disposition was honed to a fine edge, and then my depression would cause me to withdraw, being even more remote than most teens.

To my parents and siblings, it was always just drama on my part, but my intermittent rages complicated a family life that for me was already in ruins. I was so alienated by my father's distance and iron rule and my mother's anger that I retreated from any sign of affection that might have given me any relief. I hated my parents, and so I couldn't stand to be touched by them. Moreover, because my father punished me severely if my fury was directed at him, I pushed most of it in the direction of my mother and my brothers.

I wasn't to know for decades what fueled my mother's own anger. She did love her children, but she could barely cope with them most of the time. When my father made her miserable, she passed her misery on, unbeknownst to herself, I am convinced, as later in life she had little memory of events that remained vivid to me long after I was into my forties. So I grew up believing, as I was told, that I was extraordinarily difficult, a problem child. Profoundly guilty and angry, just like my mother.

I married, but it only lasted seven years, a miracle in itself given that I married a man like my father, moody and emotionally distant.

My illness progressed rapidly during that time. I had more highs than lows, but I never had more than a very close coterie of only a very few friends because I went through people like a hurricane. I was arrogant and impulsive in my treatment of others, self-centered, and blind to others' needs and wishes, imposing my will with a Napoleonic ferocity. I was very smart, so I developed a strong set of coping skills that included managing everything in my space that I could, including people, just to keep the storm within at bay, and I justified it by thinking that I was brighter than everybody else around me. Yet, always, at some level, I was guilty, for I knew that I was an abuser.

And no matter what I did, I could not hold back the swings. I cycled between believing that I was unstoppable, a force of nature, and thinking that I wanted to die. When I was up, I felt that I could do anything, and when I was down, I felt worthless and unsuccessful. Everyone around me thought I was confidence squared, but I knew that I was the most insecure person on the planet. I was lucky that during the early part of my career I was cycling up for longer periods than down, so my down episodes didn't impact my work significantly, ultimately enabling me to have a very successful career.

But my impulse control problems plagued me at every turn. I had one-night stands from time to time. I had affairs. I drove drunk because once I started drinking, I couldn't have just one. Somebody would say, "Have one more," and, impulsively, I would do so, even when I knew that would put me over the limit. I would smoke, quit, and then take it up again. At one point I was chain-smoking four packs a day. (That was in the days when it was possible to do so in public without censure.) In my early 30s, I got so deep in debt, without having the faintest idea *how*, that I ended up in bankruptcy.

It wasn't that I didn't try to do something about my "problem." I was in and out of therapy for years. Most often I was diagnosed as depressed and given something like the talking cure. I would "work through" whatever "crisis" supposedly had precipitated my most recent round of depression, and that would go on for as long as my low lasted, and then I would stop therapy, thinking it was the therapy that had done the trick. I had no idea that bipolars are most likely to seek treatment when they are depressed, thus causing therapists to miss the manic symptoms. And I don't think I ever actually saw a psychiatrist, but instead saw a string of MSW's, counselors, and psychologists.

Then came the event that changed everything. When I was 38, I made the decision in the span of a few days, impulsively again, to return to graduate school. It seemed reasonable at the time, and I cannot say now that I made a mistake, but had I known what was coming, I am not sure that I would do it all over again. Graduate school was the most brutal experience I have ever been through, although I think I experienced it that way because my illness took such a prolonged downward turn. For a number of years I had been cycling regularly, but almost as soon as I entered my PhD program, I began falling into a depression that lasted during all the years I was there.

I went to the Midwest to get my PhD, and that was the first time I had lived outside the South for any length of time. I was away from what few friends I had and an extended family that I relied on, completely on my own with no support network, a bipolar's worst-case scenario when she is falling into depression.

It was complicated by the fact that during the second year I found my teacher, a young woman whom I adored but with whom I had a very thorny relationship. I was initially terrified of her: she was authoritative, demanding, and brilliant. She made me want to be the best I could be, but secretly insecure as I was, I *knew* I could never live up to her expectations, despite the fact that I was making all A's in her classes. We became friends and colleagues, but we fought and made up and fought and made up. Nevertheless, she gave me extraordinary attention and training for which I was profoundly grateful.

It helped that I had become friends with another student, a young man who was just as unstable as I, but someone who in retrospect I think recognized me as I did him. We hung out, talked about our work, listened to music, drank too much, sometimes studied together. We developed a very small coterie of friends, but like me, he went through people like a hot knife through butter so that in the end, he had only one or two very close friends there.

In the meantime, as I devolved further and further into depression, my teacher's own life unraveled. She went through a messy divorce, and at the same time, her beloved mother quite unexpectedly developed breast cancer and died at an early age. She herself fell into a depression, and the combination of the two sets of struggles began to make our lives diverge. Compounding my growing sense that I was alone, my friendship with the young man became antagonistic, and he and I, too, eventually parted ways. I learned later that he also was bipolar, and much to the sadness of many of us, he was unable to stay compliant with his treatment and eventually committed suicide.

Despite the forces pulling in opposite directions, as the only woman on a faculty of men who were for the most part patriarchal, and who fundamentally made my life miserable, my teacher had become my lifeline in graduate school, and I had become unhealthily dependent upon her. That she was willing to let me hold on to the degree she did, for as long as she did, is a testament to her concern for her women students. And an indicator of her regard for me.

However, as I finished my coursework, our relationship had become so volatile that our working together had become exceedingly difficult. When she told me that she thought it was in my best interests that another professor direct my dissertation, dependent as I was, I felt betrayed. But I agreed, nevertheless, and in the long run, I came to the conclusion that she had made the right call. (The irony of all this is that she is now my dearest friend.)

At that point, all I wanted to do was escape from the university. As in the past, I was trying to outrun my illness. My mom and I still had a conflicted relationship, but we were making uneasy progress. Thus, when she offered me the apartment in her house, where she had always welcomed her children when they needed a place to retreat to, I took it. So I returned home to Tennessee to write my dissertation.

I had been thinking a lot about dying in those last months that I was at school, but I had done that almost all my life. What had always saved me from attempting suicide was pure intellect: I knew from experience that the cycling would eventually turn upwards. In other words, there would come a moment when it would not hurt quite so badly. However, in all honesty, I thought that once I left the university that I would never complete my degree, that in some way my life was over because I don't think I had ever been lower. Yet it was the decision to go home that in the end made all the difference.

I was out of the environment of graduate school, utterly depressed. Nevertheless, I began to write a dissertation on the exceedingly difficult work of the French feminist philosopher, Luce Irigaray. (The irony was that Irigaray herself had been in and out of psychiatric treatment for years, which I did not know at the time.) I finally began to cycle again, and during the next four years, I did successfully write a dissertation.

My director, an extraordinarily kind woman, managed me with a deft hand: understanding that something was very wrong with me, she skillfully guided me without demanding more than my limits permitted. During my highs, I would write like a maniac, sometimes for 20 hours on end. Then I would crash and not be able to write for weeks, even months. But eventually I would have another high, and the process would begin all over again. Irigaray's anger at the Western tradition of philosophy fueled my own anger about the masculinism of my own field and the kind of education I had received from the greybeards at my school, and it all came pouring out onto the pages. (The first question my first reader asked at my defense was, "Now that you've had your rant, what do you think?")

As I wrote my dissertation, other life-changing events were occurring. While I had been a feminist for decades, it wasn't until I went to graduate school that I fully realized the limits of my understanding of what that commitment entailed.

I had begun trying to come to terms with why my mom had been so angry when I was growing up. Once I moved back home, we began to talk, very tentatively at first, about what her own past had been like. For the first time, I learned that part of her anger derived from infidelity on my father's part, including an early affair with her best friend.

But the deepest reserve of her rage came from having been denied the opportunity in the 1940s to accept a scholarship at an art school because her father decided it was "too far from home," leaving her with no other option but to get married and have children (she had four living, two who died), when she really did not want to do either. When all she wanted to do was become an artist. To paint and to study art. She painted all her life (she was a watercolorist), never giving up on her desire to become an artist but burdened with the corresponding guilt of her wish not to have children. For the first time, her behavior made sense to me, and over time I slowly, painfully, began to uncouple from my own anger at her.

In the midst of that development, despite the fact that I was grinding out a dissertation document, I was getting increasingly desperate. I had always known something was wrong, but it was getting much worse. By this time, I was nearing my fiftieth birthday. In and out of therapy for years to no satisfactory outcome, never diagnosed beyond depression, and never medicated, I was by then in so much pain that I was willing to try anything. Because I had no health insurance, through just dumb luck, I found my way to the Helen Ross McNabb Mental Health Center in Knoxville, a community mental health facility.

By the time I got through intake to the psychiatrist, he already had a diagnosis: I was bipolar. The first question he asked me was if I had ever been institutionalized or in jail. Already blind-sided by the diagnosis, I was completely taken aback by his question. Here I was, a middle-class, college-educated, middle-aged woman, and he wanted to know if I'd ever been in a mental health hospital or incarcerated?

When I responded vigorously with a negative, he just shook his head, and said, "Remarkable." The only thing I could think to say was that I had a really good skill set for coping (and in my mind, a terrific fear of authority, a legacy of my father, so I had been careful to avoid behaviors that would bring me under too close scrutiny of the authorities), but I did have the presence of mind to ask him why it was so remarkable. Apparently, very few bipolars whose conditions were as serious as mine could get to that age without institutionalization or incarceration if they were untreated.

But I was terribly disturbed by the diagnosis. Bipolar disorder sounded so final: I had a mental illness, and there was no going back from it if he was right. Yet, as he described the symptoms, there was no discounting the reality that he was describing *me*. In that session, however, I discovered that bipolars can tell within a fraction once they are medicated whether they have the right dosage or not, and that *with* the right drugs and dosage, bipolar disorder can be controlled. He promised me that I would feel better soon. I cried.

And cried. For the first time in my life I felt genuine hope, not the giddy euphoria promising something that experience had taught me was a fantasy full of sound and fury.

I don't remember the combination of drugs he put me on that first time, with the exception of Prozac and Depakote. But I did learn that it sometimes takes time to get the cocktail right, as it's different for every bipolar because the same drugs don't work the same for everyone, and there are a number of combinations that can be tried. The cocktail *wasn't* exactly right for me; however, he was correct: I did get better soon.

In the meantime, my mom and I had reached détente, and after I moved to Arizona to teach in 1998, she soon joined me. Over the next years, she continued to paint on a daily basis, to study art, and I taught. I tried different drug combinations with different doctors, trying to get it just right. At one time or another I've been on some combination of Prozac, Paxil, Seroquel, Buspar, Wellbutrin, Depakote, Lamictal, Zyprexa, Abilify, Effexor, Xanax, and others I can't even remember.

Over the years, my mom had already come to terms with her demons, and with medication, *my* entire personality had changed, so for the eight years we were in Arizona, we learned to genuinely enjoy each other's company. By the time we moved to South Georgia in 2004, we had, as she put it, learned to "rub along well" together. I had come to love her and appreciate her in a way that I simply could not in my early years and was able to forgive her for not being able to mother her children or to protect them from the authoritarianism of our father.

Moreover, she had stopped being afraid that my own anger would suddenly erupt and take over our lives again.

By 2008 I had come very close to reaching that perfect drug and dosage combination. And then my world crashed. In February, my mom fell and broke her hip and wrist. Because the wrist break was so bad, she had to be anesthetized, which turned out to be a death sentence.

Her lungs filled with fluid, and she eventually succumbed to its effects in March. My response to her death was eerie. Over the years, I had learned to deal with loss by simply swallowing it, and when she died, I was totally calm, completely unable to grieve.

Those around me thought it "just hadn't hit me." They were, of course, right.

For reasons I still don't fully understand, she had left me her small estate. She had told me some months before her death that that was her plan because I had taken care of her for those ten years. I had challenged her about that decision, but she was adamant. However, she knew better than anyone that I was financially irresponsible, and she had always been so careful with her money that I could not figure out why she would entrust me with what she had managed to put together over the years. It wasn't a great deal of money, but it was enough that it could have made a difference to my retirement if I had managed it well.

Instead, I began to spend. I had tried for years to get my mom to go to Europe to see the great art that she had studied all her life. Her excuse had been that she didn't have the money, although I knew she did, and then later, when she admitted she could afford it, she realized she was too old to handle it. I was registered as an art student, and when a slot became available in a study abroad program in May, I decided to make the trip that my mom never did, to do it in remembrance of her.

So I went to Italy. We were based in Florence, and for four weeks I drank in the beauties of the Italian Renaissance. I lived in a 16th century palace (not as glorious as you might imagine), walked where Michelangelo had tread, lit candles for my mom in the most gorgeous Catholic churches I had ever seen (even though she was a Southern Baptist and was probably twitching in heaven), stood in awe of the *David* in the Academia, spent breath-taking hours in the Uffizi, dined under the stars in Sorrento, marveled at the Amalfi coast, trudged up the narrow streets of the ancient town of Montepulciano, passed through the corridors of the Coliseum, stood in the Roman Forum, imagining the great speakers who had orated there (I teach rhetoric), wandered through the charms of Siena, blinked back tears at the Pietà, and missed my train in Venice where I had to stay overnight and so took a photograph of the canals at dark that won a prize in an art show.

And I spent. Whatever I wanted, I bought. Expensive gifts for family members. Jewelry. Clothes. Expensive meals rather than cooking in. Cooking lessons. Crates of red wine to send home. The rate of exchange was high: for every euro, I was spending $1.60 American. But I told myself that I would worry about that later. I wrote postcards home to my mom. I told her all about the art, the museums, the architecture, the experiences, the food, and the wine. The red wine, which I couldn't drink at home because it gave me migraines. (I drank Nobili Montepulciano at every meal, no matter what I ordered because it was red, and it was Italy.) One night I sat out on the balcony of the palace with a bottle of wine and a pack of cigarettes, drinking, smoking, and crying for her. The only time I grieved for her. Ever.

And when I came home I went to see my psychiatrist, telling him that I thought I was having a manic episode because I had spent so much money in Italy. But he thought not because I had no other symptoms. None of the euphoria, no rapid speech, no sense that I could do everything. I know now that I was having a mixed episode, that I was depressed over my mother's death, but was also having total impulse breakdown.

And I was right. In little more than four months I had taken all my mom's artwork that had never been framed to my master framer and had him complete it with archival materials. I had taken all her framed work that wasn't archival and had it redone. I had bought more clothes, I had had my bathrooms remodeled, I had bought a new computer and expensive peripherals, I had loaned my niece $10K that I knew I was never going to get back, I had bought a second home in the Smokies (another mortgage, but who was counting?).

And then I had spent some more. I had a terrific screaming fight with one of my brothers on the phone that came out of nowhere, a breach that five years later has not been fully healed. In the midst of all this, I had legally changed my last name to my mom's maiden name, in honor of my mother, severing all ties to my former husband and my former father.

By the time I was through, I was in bankruptcy court for the second time in my life. My lawyer included in his brief that I was bipolar, that my mother had recently died and that her passing had triggered a manic episode. The court saw those cases often enough that the judge took it in stride in granting my petition.

Soon thereafter I moved north to the Atlanta area, and seventeen years after my diagnosis, I now live as "normal." I say that knowing that I have no idea what normal really is, for I have never *been* normal, and I cannot pretend to know what kind of lives people experience who are not bipolar.

All I can really say is that I now live a life that is bearable. I can stand to be in the world without considering dying on a routine basis, without always feeling sandpapered by the daily grind of living, without continually feeling the impulse to exhaust my resources, whether emotional, mental, or financial. This is to admit something that I have avoided for years: my illness defines me. It shapes the kind of relationships I can have, the kind of work that I am best doing, the judgments I make. Perhaps the most important dimension of my illness is that it has given me a kind of empathy that I doubt I would have developed without it.

I am most fortunate now when it comes to friendships. I have *good* friends here. Plural. Kay, Barb, Tonya, Rebecca, Bill, Susan. They know my limits and love me anyway. I am able to love as well as I can in return and not feel the compulsion to manage.

My illness has made me careful in relationships with others because I know how easy it is to cross a line from asking for help to demanding attention. It has also made me reticent to ask for help sometimes when I should because it has made me overly cautious, but that's something I just have to live with.

At least two of them are always sensitive to my moods and ask about where I am, am I beginning to swing, do I need to think about adjusting my meds, do I need to slow down, am I being suddenly impulsive. It's good to know that others are looking out for me, and since this is the first time in my life that I have had that, it is precious to me. I appreciate it all the more for knowing that friendships are fragile and have to be nurtured, that too much pressure can break them, that the will of one imposed on the two can be ruinous for the relationship.

This may be something that non-bipolars simply already *know*, but I came to this knowledge very late in life, and because for so long I moved through people as if they were paper dolls, my relationship to friendship is particularly fraught with significance. My friends are crucial to making life bearable for me, and I am sensitive to the nuances of friendship now in a way that I think I might not have been able to be if I were not bipolar, given the kind of family I grew up in.

Perhaps nowhere does my illness shape my responses to the world than it does in my work. I am a professor at a local college that is open access. We take the students who often cannot get into another institution and who come with varying degrees of preparation for college, oftentimes not quite college-ready. Generally, these are not privileged students. They often don't come from the best high schools or out of college prep programs. Many of them are first-generation college students, and many of them do not speak English as their first language.

Almost all of them work, many of them full-time. A large number of them have children at home, and some of them have the responsibility for caring for other family members. If they are women, married, and have children, they frequently have the responsibility for running the household as well as going to school, sometimes full-time. Yet they aspire. They want better lives than their circumstances often would otherwise permit.

Because they come with such complicated lives, these students bring their struggles with them to the college doorstep, not always having their best game on, and it sometimes can be frustrating working with them. But it's not usually because they aren't *trying.* That's what I attempt to keep at the fore when I am teaching them. So I go the extra mile with them: I find myself explaining things repeatedly, even when I think they should have "gotten it," meeting individually with the same students to provide additional support, cutting students slack on late papers, and checking up on students who seem to be having special problems.

I doubt that I'm doing much more than many of my non-bipolar colleagues, but I *am* sure that before I began to accept my relationship to my illness that I could not have done this kind of work. I had always worked at institutions where students were largely privileged, were ready for the college experience, by no means having the disadvantages that my students now struggle with every day, and *then* I didn't have the patience with my students that I do now.

To be sure, my judgments about others are tempered by the realization that there are people in the world who suffer and struggle on a daily basis with their own demons and conditions, often without the kind of support that I am now lucky enough to have. I look around me, and I see 46 million living in poverty, one of the key stressors for producing mental illness, two million incarcerated (and am outraged that the jails in some of our biggest cities have become repositories for the mentally ill), and 26% of the general population in any given year living with a mental illness.

That's 81 million this year, and these are *not* just the celebrities that I named at the beginning of this piece, but our mothers, our fathers, our brothers, our sisters, our *families.* I no longer have patience with a society that regards the poor, the lost, the mentally ill without profound concern, unwilling to devote the required resources to solving the problems. Indeed, I have come to the conclusion that a society can be measured by how it treats its weakest members and that ours fails miserably.

What I have finally realized about myself is that I am undeniably impatient with a self-centered world where people are more concerned about their own well-being than that of their fellow human beings. I am *not* suggesting that being bipolar has somehow given me the mantle of righteousness. God forbid. It's just that my relationship to my illness has made me conscious that behavior is a thoroughly complicated affair. I am less inclined to blame the "bad behavior" of others before I know their specific circumstances (sometimes people *are* just bad actors) and more willing to accept the possibility that forces move within people's lives that shape their actions and words in ways that they don't always have full control of.

This is not to say that we shouldn't be held responsible for what we do and say; only that perhaps it's time to get over the notion that we don't have any collective responsibility for each other. As the remarkable Helen Keller put it, "Until the great mass of the people shall be filled with the sense of responsibility for each other's welfare, social justice can never be attained."

WHO'S TALKING ... *Jan Odom is a survivor of the culture wars and currently teaches at a liberal arts college. She pursues hobbies as an amateur photographer and sewist and reads as if her very life depends upon it. One of her joys is Phoebe, a Chihuahua who thinks she's queen.*

22: A SPIRITUAL JOURNEY
KATHRYN, 63

I AM A GEORGIA-BORN GIRL OF THE FIRST ORDER. I AM THE DAUGH-
ter of a seventh daughter. In other words, I entered this world
with the *cellular* reconstruction of my ancient ancestors intact. I
know this for many reasons. First, there have been throughout my
life the graphic moments when mental imprints unfold. These are
seconds in time in which I stand so close to the cosmos that I feel
the slight jolt of a door opening to my future. This happened the
first time I saw the man I would marry. I saw him in the distance
as he walked through a parking lot at a school. I did not know his
name. I had never met him or his two female friends. Yet I knew
I was looking at my future.

How do you explain such abilities? I could not. But I knew
that I was delving into a controversial terrain, given my Baptist
upbringings. So in the end, I chose as a profession (the only con-
formist career) in which such foreshadowing might be broached
without any meddling or prying when it came to my unconven-
tional research methods or abilities: I became a historian.

Even as a child I sought out adult conversation by asking my
parents the angst-ridden question, "Why?" Over time, the "why"
of youth turned to the "why" of life itself. Of course, by the time I
turned six I had received from the Christian community the "one
acceptable answer" to the question of life. I, like most Southern
children, found myself deluged with the precepts of organized religion. Immersed in religion at an early age, the Revelation of how

God worked to develop man (and woman) was interrupted by the byproducts of rejecting this philosophy: all the "hell, fire, and brimstone sermons" delivered inside the walls of a small Baptist Church. The message for me was simple. If you obey God, you live long enough to find your way to heaven and the good life. If you disobey God, you go to hell on the fast train!

The sermons were never ending and began and ended every week of my childhood. And during the summers, they were festooned via these intense week-long church revivals. This was where new speakers arrived to offer their rendition of "hell on wheels." And then there were the Vacation Bible School days. Intense week-long experiences designed to draw the little children to God, ending in a stage production.

The Vacation Bible School trend was a rather peculiar core of the twentieth century Baptist Church religious institution. Set up as a special time when children were subjected to what was seen as an organized play time with the church leadership, in actuality it was all a disguise! In this one week indoctrination sprint, cookies and Kool-Aid, Bible lessons, scripture memorization, and calls to the mission field were all interlaced. And the real give-away for me was the frightful "sing-song blasts."

Every Sunday, the regular church hymns contained graphic and unexplained words for the children to interpret, words like "I am washed ... I am washed in the blood of the lamb." After the blood-washing, there were the summer school sessions when we were drilled as if we had signed up for the newest leg of the Nazi Youth movement. Days when the "blood-splattered" lines were replaced with action-packed howls of aggression which would have pleased my Confederate ancestors. In one song, we all were taught to stomp our feet and lift our arms and pretend to fashion make-believe weapons. So while we turned in circles shouting "I may never walk in the infantry, fight in the cavalry, or shoot the artillery, but I'm still in the Lord's army!" the piano player would suddenly speed up the rhythm and we would get louder and turn frantically, almost to the point of collapse.

For me, these training camps for a war against the Devil and his invisible army proved to be just a little too real. Throughout my childhood, my sleep was disrupted with recurring images: one vision of me trying to make a faltering slapdash attempt to escape the fires of hell by running around the grave stones in the church cemetery toward home. And then there was the one where I slid down embankments with a rifle in hand, moving beneath barbed wire fences, to find safety in a deep gulley.

The sad part of this story, at this point in my life, was that I was left to trust the accumulated knowledge dispersed by the experts: the pastor and the deacons. And when I questioned God about these tactics, I received absolutely no feedback. Thus I had to figure out God's role in my life.

For years I merely resorted to asking "my God" for help when I got in trouble (bad report cards) or for ways to cover up my daily transgressions (calling my brother names). Later, I would learn to quietly subjugate myself to the extremes of religiosity while secretly seeking out truthful answers to why we live at all. Organized religion fell to the background during my childhood and I moved forward to take control of my own destiny by looking inward.

As a spiritualist, nature became and today is still my natural palate. It was my earliest experiences with nature which steadied me on my journey toward finding the "inner self."

I first began to rely on my inherent abilities while roaming the fields, the creeks, the forests, the cemeteries, and the mountains of Georgia. Thus it was the natural environment which strummed the strings of my heart long before all the social institutions twisted or confused or distorted the direction of my life.

By age six, I spent more time outside the house than within the four walls of my room. I examined every inch of the world that was readily available to me. Marching through the briars and brambles, I scrutinized the smallest creatures and the plants. I caught grasshoppers just to see if they really spit up brown tobacco juice as my brother had said. I waited intently on the wild strawberries to sprout under the huge fig bush while at the same time considering my brother's warning "don't eat those wild strawberries." I noted the depth of my exploits by counting the scars mounting up quickly on my sturdy legs.

In the spring of each year, I ran to town with my brother to buy ten-cent kites to send upward on the March air currents. When the kite string came to an end, I would watch it shift, dip, and finally tumble from the sky. All the while, I watched faces form in the moving clouds. I especially liked signs of the many creatures I had read about in books. In the early summers, I awaited the glow of the first lightning bugs. In late summer, I gathered "goat grass" and chewed the sour mesh, just because I could. During the early fall, I along with my brother and Carolina cousins, collected rabbit tobacco, stole matches, and smoked the furry green leaves in a broken pipe.

Summer evenings were the most special of times for every family on Vickery Street. By the late 1950s, black-and-white television screens flickered from inside a few of the homes; nevertheless, all summer long, screen doors would slam as the neighbors entered their porticos for face-to-face conversations with family and visiting friends. The summers were the most exciting because that was when the kids from far-away places like Sparta, Georgia, and New York visited their grandparents. Most of the Vickery Street homes, except ours and one or two others, housed retired school teachers from the town school, so during the warmest days of summer, the backyards were filled with the laughter of children on what seemed to be for many of those grandparents a "rather too long school recess."

Of course the New Yorkers were the odd lot. Raised on cement, these kids were the most curious of our visitors for they knew nothing of nature, animals, or outside games other than the one they called hopscotch. Obviously a game best played on the cemented worlds of places like Queens. These were the grandchildren of marriages between World War II servicemen who took home to New York their Georgia brides. Some of these childhood friendships lasted for years, while others were caught only by black-and-white flashes, those Polaroid camera portraits where the faces would eventually fade and, worse, names lost.

In the late afternoons, it was the games we played at dusk that were the best: nerf-baseball, 1-2-3 red light, and my favorite "fox and hound." And all the while we played, the rockers and porch swings squeaked up and down Vickery Street as the adults roamed from porch to porch to share news (gossip, mostly) or debate political issues like the legitimacy of a Catholic president. At a young age, even in the darkness, none of us had any fear, because in the background of our shrieks and yelps, the porch chatter along our avenue mingled and created a low soothing hum—a hum only occasionally shattered by my dad's boisterous Carolina laugh.

I remember there was this one evening that Daddy allowed us all (the New Yorkers and the kids from Sparta) to stay out later than usual (past the nine o'clock bath time). That particular evening we ran around shoeless on the cool green grass playing 1-2-3 red light near the front porch while Daddy watched over us on the front porch swing. Mom was by his side.

He stopped the game to give us a mission. He sent us searching through the damp grass and shrubs which surrounded the long columned porch for the largest "toad frog" we could find. From the hazy light of the street lamp, we beat the bushes at every imagined gruff or croak. From the darkness at the end of the porch, I could only hear the creak of the swing and see the red embers of Daddy's cigarette, but every once in a while we could hear him chuckle.

As he laughed at our failed exploits, we would work even harder to find that toad. After more misses than successes, we finally caught the largest and ugliest toad in Georgia. We took our catch to the edge of the porch. That's when red glow moved upward. The swing stopped creaking. And we watched curiously as that red glow headed our way.

We watched curiously as Daddy walked to the end of the porch where we had gathered to show him our prisoner. He looked down at the toad which we now surrounded in a circle with our bare feet. He reached down to pick up the frog as we looked on curiously. He then took from his mouth his half-smoked cigarette and gently placed the cigarette in the mouth of the toad. He placed the toad back on the damp grass. Nothing happened. "Patience," daddy said. Then after several minutes that dumb-founded toad sucked in the tobacco and spouted forth a huge puff of smoke. We jumped back in utter amazement! We watched as that toad sat there and smoked that "joint" right down to the nub! Then "Mr. Toad" hopped off to his well-hidden shelter near the porch.

One late fall afternoon, after paying Mr. Simpson for bush-hogging the pasture, Daddy gathered us all together once again. He walked us down to the creek bed at the end of the field.

A huge briar patch growing along the bed had now been slashed to pieces, leaving only unbendable stubs poking from the earth. Daddy stopped to stand near the edge of the embankment where a small stream ambled by during most of the year. He told us to look down at a particular spot on the ground where the sawed-off blackberry branches poked up so sharply.

At this place a few soft white pieces of white fur was visible. While Dad stood aside, we stared anxiously at the soft white patch. And that's when we all jumped backward—for we had seen the earth move!

This nest on the earth was breathing. It moved up and down with the rhythm of our own heart-beat. At first, our limited knowledge of this phenomena made us suspect. "It's a snake hole," yelled Billy Sewell."

"It's a big snake," my brother added knowingly, "probably an African python!"

That's when I screamed because my brother knew just about everything. When he had a question, he went to a book. He had even learned to play tennis by reading a book.

All the others took off running. But Daddy, he stepped forward and bent down to touch the soft white patch while we edged back to the patch. As the earth moved up and down, he began to softly brush away the furry covering and just beneath a few pieces of this white fluff, huddled almost on the top of the soil lay five baby rabbits.

The bush hog had removed their "fire wall" or their briar patch of protection against their world of intruders. It was a magical day, a real life adventure when for a few minutes the books of my earlier years like Beatrice Potter's "The Tale of Peter Rabbit" and "Br'er Rabbit and the Briar Patch" tale of the safety of the briar patch took on a new and profound meaning.

On another very special summer day, Daddy gathered us all in the back seat of the "woody" and whisked us off to a local store where it seemed that we bought everything in sight. He even allowed us to purchase something which had caught my eye—an Indian head dress with one tall black feather attached to the back of the band. That summer, at night, my brother with flashlight in hand read to me under the covers *The Last of the Mohicans*.

Later that day, Jimmy and I watched in amazement as Dad positioned a tin tub filled with ice in the back of our station wagon. He filled it with bottles of Pepsi Colas (He was a Carolina boy, so he did not drink Coca Cola) and in minutes we all (even Mom) were headed down the road at full speed ahead toward Currahee Mountain, the mountain which from town we could always see from a distance.

In town, Daddy slung the car toward Highway 17 north. Soon we could almost touch Currahee Mountain. As it grew larger, Dad said it was the mountain the Cherokees had mined silver from.

Years later, as a freelance writer, I would remember that special day as I stood beneath the shadow of Currahee Mountain. I was working as a writer for a Georgia magazine and I had made the trip to interview a man who bragged to me that the Cherokee blood line remained strong in Georgia still.

"I am 1/8 Cherokee," he said. In the late afternoon as we walked his land, he told tales about his Cherokee heritage, including how he had re-created a Cherokee "blow gun." He illustrated its force by sending a feathered point into the trunk of a nearby pine tree.

It was indeed a superb weapon. That sharpened arrow made a deep two-inch wound in the tree trunk. It could have easily killed a small animal.

It was late afternoon and as he talked, every so often, he would bend to pick from the ground a broken pottery shard or an arrowhead. He placed them in my hand.

Daddy loved to push the limits. And we learned that he liked to watch us push the restrictions of our world as well. So as I now look backward, I think Dad liked to modify the constraints of life just so he could laugh! Daddy was a man who, beneath his wavy grey mane and thick dark eyebrows, held not only a beautiful broad smile but a boisterous laugh which still echoes through my every memory of him.

Of course, as most dads from his generation, he worked all the time in order for our family to survive. And true to that generation, I thought his favorite word was "overtime."

Still, when my Daddy had those few rare days off, we all knew that we might have some fun. So by the age of ten, I had learned not to beg. Just stand by. Wait—wait for the right opportunity. I had to carefully wager on the exact moment to strike with, "Daddy, let's go to the sliding rock on the Tugaloo River."

As I look back, this was a trip far more dangerous than any faced by the characters on the television, even the ones who were said to "soar tall buildings in a single bound."

The ultimate challenge of my childhood had nothing to do with tall buildings. My challenge was having the nerve to climb and then slither down the river Tugaloo's ancient "sliding rock" formation. You see, before the advent of dam building up and down the Savannah River, from Augusta to where the Tugaloo and Seneca Rivers met, the hot Georgia summers pushed everyone on both sides of the Savannah to fill up the car with kids, towels, inner tube floats, and even the dogs, and head for a river.

There are still Carolina parks that boast of "a sliding rock" but my sliding rock was born of the ancients, the ancestors of those who lived on Currahee Mountain. Those who had obviously founded that first Tugaloo River crossing site eons earlier before the first bridge spanned the site. The Tugaloo River was one of the places where the ancient ancestors of the Cherokee had roamed and built mounds. Most of these huge hills now rest beneath the waters of the once great "Savano" river near places like Tugaloo and the ghost town sites like Petersburg, Georgia.

Describing our sliding rock is difficult, but the Tugaloo sliding rock formation looked like a wide spout created by the forming of the Georgia fall line. Over time this spout had been carved out by the waters. Then it was further fashioned by the ancients sitting at the top and hoping for a safe arrival on their bottom at the bottom. Thus at the top of this falls, in between several major boulders, for ages, human bodies had sculpted a slick but still quite jagged incline which at the end dumped every challenger into a pool of cold water coming down from the upper reaches of the Tugaloo and Seneca rivers.

The excitement generated by watching a friend (or the hated enemy of the day) climb to the top and then slide downward to the pool was awe-inspiring! Yes, the scrapes were many. And the rips to already worn bathing suits proved embarrassing at times. That's why by the early 1960s, a more substantial bottom or cut-off blue jeans were the preferred swim wear for the Tugaloo rock slide.

Our dog made the trip with us. Our three-year-old calico dog named "Butch" (named in honor of one of the meanest of the characters from "Our Gang" reruns) loved to swim in that pool as well. She loved even more to paw her way onto our one inner tube float for a trip down the river with us all. As we all clung by one arm to the tube, the current moved us downward toward huge oak leaning ever so slightly over the river. A swing was tied to a tree branch overhanging the somewhat muddy water at this spot. We turned the float completely over to Butch while each of us climbed the bank, swung out over the river and bombed Butch where she awaited our return.

Even as a child, I knew this alcove was a special place. A life-time later, while searching for primary documents on early Augusta, I found the needed evidence to back up my childhood intuition in the *Journal* of William Bartram. His journal was written long after the ancients or ancestors of the Cherokee had disappeared from this place along the river.

In the 1760s, beginning at Savannah Towne, young Bartram had headed toward the Cherokee Hills. William Bartram, like all early naturalists, made his hike alongside the Savannah by following the Indian paths. In fact, it was near the Cherokee Hills, and I like to think near my sliding rock, that Bartram recorded coming across two Cherokee boys fishing near a falls. Taking a break from sketching exotic plants and animals, Bartram attempted to make a trade with the boys for a fish. They were not interested. They moved away. Bartram recorded watching them as they turned slowly and disappeared into the bushes and trees.

For these two Cherokee lads who fished on the Tugaloo that morning, Bartram's appearance must have been a graphic moment. His appearance signaled for the Cherokee yet another European intrusion.

In summary, just like "Scout" in *To Kill a Mockingbird*, for several summers I had been a southern tom girl. As a child of the outdoors I learned that I possessed unlimited inner capabilities. But like those two Cherokee boys who disappeared into the woods near the waters of the Tugaloo, I knew that my sunny childhood days were limited. There was no going back.

I found consolation in reading *To Kill a Mockingbird*. For just like Harper Lee and her young partner, Truman Copote, I had hit that pending demarcation, that thin line which separated the innocence of childhood from the ordeals of the adult life.

Years later, well into my marriage and the raising of my two sons, like sleeping beauty, I awoke from the social paralysis of the cult of domesticity that I and so many women around me had fallen into. Right in the middle of my established life, I realized that I wasn't where I wanted to be. I felt as if I had wandered onto what was said to be the right path for all young women, but instead I had landed in a very, very bad neighborhood.

That was the point wherein I stopped to review my early years. For obviously, like so many women of my generation, I had adopted the social context and had left my own path to take the road most traveled. It was at that point in time when the idealized version of domesticity fell from my shoulders and melted on my kitchen floor.

When I awoke from my epiphany that day, I remembered that I was a Georgian-born girl of the first order. I am the daughter of a seventh daughter. I have the strength of those who came before me to build my own life. I harbor the wisdom of the Cherokee culture that has always fascinated me. I hold near and dear my childhood days spent barefoot in the grass and swimming in the river. I respect and feel connected to nature. This is still the life that appeals to me today.

I finally looked past the institutions and social movements and looked inside my heart for direction. I reviewed my every endeavor. I asked myself which of these endeavors had given me peace.

I decided that the second time around I would strive to understand life from as many vantage points as possible. So in 1981, I returned to college and eventually earned advanced degrees in history and education. I became a college professor which gave me the opportunity to roam around archaeological digs, explore historical sites, and, my favorite, peruse old cemeteries. I have an excuse to bury myself in my favorite books.

Most importantly, today I worship in my own way and according to my own study of the history of religion and science. I honor nature. I am truly amazed at the spirit of the universe that vibrates around and within me. So rather than acquiescing to "one acceptable answer" to the question of life, I believe life is a marvelous mystery to be cherished, day-by-day, every day of our lives. And I will plan to repeat and even leave this very message for others, those who dare seek out the rational answers to human existence. The tombstone in my hometown cemetery shall read: *C'est la vie, and what a great adventure!*

WHO'S TALKING ... *With degrees in journalism, history, and education, Kathryn Gray-White has served as contributing editor and writer for several magazines. She is a college professor, her specialty being local history. Direct her to an old cemetery and she is one happy girl.*

23: A DAY IN THE LIFE
OF A PSYCHIC
DEBORAH, 62

A QUAKER PREACHER GRANDFATHER ON ONE SIDE OF MY FAMILY and a Wiccan Baptist grandmother—yes, you read that right—on the other side. No wonder my life has been different.

My name is Deborah. Being a rather ordinary-looking woman in this mortal body, you might find it hard to believe the type of work I do and the life I now lead. I also find it hard to believe. I am an eclectic Druid elder, a professional psychic, and a hypnotherapist.

Today my day began as I stumble to the bathroom with my first cup of black coffee that I desperately need, more so than usual. Looking into the bathroom mirror, I feel my age of sixty-two today. My eyes appear puffy and red; yes, that's what I get for zooming through the universe at night, out of body. Some would call it dreaming; I call it reality.

As I stand there whining about how bad I look, I hear my guides telling me to can it. I'm experiencing exactly what I asked for. Looking at my reflection, I shock myself at times with the square jaw and pale skin with a hint of rose in the cheeks which yells of my Scots/Irish descent. Since the first time I can remember, looking at my reflection, I've felt uncomfortable with this face and body. My generally hazel eyes look almost entirely blue today. But, of course, they do tend to change very easily and quickly according to my mood. I have been told they can turn brown at times, but I've never seen it.

Thinking back on my crazy life, I never forget I was born in a small town in North Carolina in May of 1950. Thank the powers that be, our very dysfunctional family was positioned out in the country on a farm away from the population, so they couldn't hurt anyone but each other. I found myself the oldest of five children, none of whom was ever planned for or wanted. My mother was the daughter of a Quaker preacher and my dad was a possessed child from redneck hell! Bet my mom was shocked when she married into this family.

As I grew older, I realized I wasn't like any of my immediate family. The only soul I connected with was my paternal grandmother who helped raise me. Leona was my grandma's name and it suited her very well. Much later in life I was to realize I had many of her psychic gifts. My grandma was the hands-on healer and herb woman of the neighborhood. She was also very Baptist. What a combination! I think the minute I was conceived she must have known I'd be hers to train in the old ways. Even before I could talk, she spoke to me of the secrets of life, animals, and of humans. I was taught never to harm any living thing.

My grandmother revered the energies that ran the universe and connected all people, plants, and animals together, all the same but different, each deserving of respect and love. She told me that the gift we had was a special gift from God and should always be protected to keep us safe.

She taught me to be free with my mind and to allow my mind to soar in the heavens, even if my child's body was connected to the earth. She kept secret the joy I found in communicating with plants, animals, and birds. She never called me crazy or insane; she loved me unconditionally, even when I was a brat. She taught me the meaning of immediate karma. What you sow you will reap.

My childhood flew by quickly with as much of my time as possible spent outside in the pasture and the woods or at the barn on the family farm. I always sought the company of animals over humans, where I had incredible days on end.

Of course I was considered as odd as my grandma by the neighborhood. I took this as a great compliment. We used to laugh good-naturedly at people who feared us, and looked with sorrow on those who had no idea what life held ready for them to find. My mother was very stand-offish when it came to me. With her Quaker upbringing, my connection to my redneck dad's Wiccan Baptist mother was totally confounding to her.

I learned to tell when adults lied to me and even to themselves. It wasn't mindreading exactly, but really close. I was but a child, what did I know? My education continued with my grandma. I couldn't wait to get bigger so I would be taken seriously. Little did I know that no matter how big you get, it's hard to be taken seriously when what you are is very different.

I loved talking with chickens, cows, and horses; they look at life from an entirely different viewpoint. Their viewpoint was very simple and straight forward: You love me and I will love you back. This was my escape from a very unhappy mother and a father who had been brought up to hit and think later. To me they were hell on earth. I now realize they were trapped. After five children, there was no escape for either of them.

Time and space has eased my pain of mental and physical abuse at their hands. I actually feel sorry for them now and wonder just how they made it. A good part of my childhood was spent being afraid. At sixteen, to escape, I married the first boy that asked me. This turned out to be a case of jumping out of the frying pan into the fire.

This was just the first of my many bad moves. This proves to me that spiritual people still have to evolve and learn the hard way at times. I was determined to escape the poverty and feeling of hopelessness that surrounded everyone I knew. I did whatever I felt I had to do to survive. This amounted to marrying two more times to totally unspiritual, mean, redneck drunks. I must have had a sign hanging in the astral level over my head that read, "If you beat women and cheat like hell, pick me. I'm your girl." Some of them were entertaining, but generally they showed me I didn't need them to survive.

My grandma left this dimension in her eighty-seventh year. At that time, I knew I was now truly alone with my gift. Or was it a curse?

During the years that followed, I did go back to school, got my GED, and took some college courses. I tried to polish off some of my own North Carolina redneck ways. Even though I had done some stupid things, I refused to be ignorant. I learned how to control my rage that bubbled up in me anytime I felt threatened.

Looking back over what appeared to be wasted years from sixteen to thirty-five, I see that all the mistakes I made in those years served as lessons to teach me the gifts of compassion, tolerance, and self-love. The utter joy of knowing intense love and all-consuming hate, the ability to feel utter fear and self-defeating depression, showed me all sides of the human emotion. I had lived with each emotion on a very intimate level.

Before reaching my mid-thirties, I was looking for a reason to simply "be", and I endeavored to do every last thing I wanted to do. I enjoyed breaking wild horses, singing with a rock-and-roll band, driving fast, living faster, drinking a lot of scotch, and having sex with a lot of men. What can I say? It was the seventies!

I worked in a veneer mill for years and time just flew by. I really don't remember very much of those years. It's hard to remember anything when you're hungover every morning. My life was flying away from me.

One day I realized my psychic gifts had been put on hold. I'm sure the Karmic Council figured they better keep them from me until I grew up enough to survive or took myself out of this body.

Don't take me wrong. There were wonderful periods of my life I would never change for the world. At the age of thirty-one, I was in love with an ex-CIA agent. Although he was married, this turned out to be a very intense and fulfilling part of my life. He taught me what spiritual, physical, and emotional love was; how to share your mind, body, and soul with another person. I regained my psychic abilities, and I found I could meld myself into him perfectly and wholly.

This also taught me that sometimes, no matter how strong the connection, how wild the love, how great the sex, or how deep the need, you can't always be married to the one you love, not in this lifetime anyway.

When he left me to follow his dream, which has made him a millionaire today, I declined to go along with him and his family. I had learned to want more, I deserved better than being second to another life he had. And at that time, being a very jealous woman, I could no longer be the other woman.

Instead, I made the decision to move to a different part of the country and start over. Looking back, I realize he was sent by my guides, teachers, and angels to reconnect me to my destiny. No matter how long I live, I will always thank him for his love and the way he helped me get out of the rut I was in—allowing me to move forward to the life I had waiting.

The point I need to make to you is simply that I was poor, not entirely uneducated, and I was most certainly no saint, far from exploring my spiritual side when I moved to Atlanta, Georgia, in the fall of 1983. Broken-hearted and flat broke, I drove into my mother's driveway in an old Ford which only ran because I prayed it to. I unloaded my few belongings and started over.

In the 1980s I married my fourth husband, John, and we lived a quiet life together for 32 years, until his recent death. I'm slowly adjusting to this new life I have on my own.

I'm also doing the work I was directed by the creator to do. The very strict religious belief systems of both my mother and grandma had turned me off religion of any kind.

Grandma might have practiced the Wiccan faith but "by Georgia" we went to the neighborhood Baptist church every Sunday, even though some people never spoke to us. Many of the people who ignored my grandma at church would come to her home for healing help on the sly.

As I grew up and became a responsible person, I studied Druidism, a peace-loving belief. In these ancient studies and past-life regressions, I found memories of past lifetimes spent in worship to the God/Goddess. My psychic abilities that I had ignored for so long came back to me as if in the wink of an eye.

I also learned to channel healing to plants, animals, and humans as a Reiki master. I found my guides, teachers, and angels waiting for my reawakening and ready to help me in this life's work. They instructed me in the many ways I was to help humanity, to teach others how to access their personal power. To help humankind find Divinity within them, no matter what religion, no matter whom their God figure was. I strived to teach compassion on all levels of human existence. Please don't take this statement as that I believe we have to be doormats. I am all for protecting myself and the ones I love, human and animal.

I worked very hard to awaken this lifework with plenty of prayer and meditation. In 1996, I found myself working as a self-employed professional psychic and clinical and metaphysical hypnotherapist. My normal days were filled with appointments and I was thankful. My clientele had steadily built by word of mouth. I was booked up from 10 a.m. until 6 p.m. almost every day.

On one of those days, my last appointment was a past-life regression which lasted two hours and revealed many past lives of a client who desperately needed answers to help her in this life. I was drained. I couldn't even speak by the time she left my office.

My clients have no idea that I travel with them into their past lives, seeing what they see and feeling what they feel. It takes its toll after a while. I left the office about 6 p.m. and headed home. I then knew I had to slow down the number of clients I saw every day. So that's what I've done.

Home is a small brick house located in the suburbs of Atlanta, Georgia, where John used to wait for me to return from my day of "mystic hocus pocus." (He always said that with a smile). With good humor and a little disbelief, he and I survived our many years together.

One thing that has always been important to me is spending time with other psychics and healers. As I write this, my excitement builds because tonight the girls are coming over! Today is the day before the Full Moon.

Full Moon is the most magical time of the month for us. There are five of us who feel powerful and hardly able to contain ourselves. We feel able to leap tall buildings; smite down our enemies; banish evil entities; send demons straight to the light or the pit, whatever they choose; right wrongs; and create good! A smile spreads across my face as I think these thoughts, knowing that not one of us would hurt a living thing God created, except in self-defense.

This group of professional psychics and healers used to meet every month, until we all moved too far away for visiting that often. But we still meet when we can, which makes this gathering all the more special. We all have found that helping others is fun and fulfilling. We work with angels, goddesses, saints, ancestors of our tribes, and each of us has been selected and has trained in different works. Each of us has been sent into this lifetime to continue our work.

A lot of the problems we are seeing as spiritual counselors are the lost ones, souls that either did not know how to ascend to the light or just refused to go out of fear. These souls have forgotten that the creator is, above all else, pure unconditional love. No one is turned away from his love or his help, no matter how wicked their earth life has been.

However, I do believe that there are and have been souls here on earth that should not ever be let loose on mankind again.

After our spiritual work is completed, the girls and I have food and a glass of wine, catching up with each other's lives. We bid each other goodnight and everyone heads home.

I have the feeling that all my lives have always been charmed and, believe me, I appreciate all the help my angels have sent to me through the years in this lifetime. Each morning before I get started, I give each of the other four psychics a call. We seem to keep each other grounded on this plane. I love them all more so than sisters. Ours is a connection of ancient secrets and long forgotten promises and blood vows. After checking in with each sister, I start my day.

Every day is a challenge for some people. They have to make difficult decisions about their lives. A lot of the time it's almost impossible for them to let go of ego or fear long enough to make an informed decision. Consequently, I always have special clients that I just have to help more so than others.

You'd be surprised at the people who show up at my door—especially the professionals who won't admit in public that they believe in my kind of spiritual guidance. But I understand why they visit me in secret. I know all too well how hard it is to be treated with disrespect and disregard for your beliefs.

My clients, some that I've worked with for many, many years, come to me seeking personal advice. I help people with their marriages, pregnancies, cancer and other diseases, divorce, death of a loved one, and so much more. Sometimes they want to explore their spirituality. They almost always end up talking about their relationships. Some want to know what to do in their careers. Occasionally they just need an understanding shoulder to cry on. Sometimes it's a laugh riot over the silly things we've done in life.

And sometimes this work is deadly serious. For example, a number of years ago a woman came to me out of desperation when her nephew was murdered and the police had no clues. She wanted to know who had brutally shot her loved one in the parking lot of a convenience store. I called my psychic sisters and together we came up with details, including images of the murderers. The police took our descriptions of an old dark car with "fins" and five people, including two women with "weird, curly hair," and put them in their file only because they had nothing else. Two weeks later when they caught the killers, they were stunned that our information was completely accurate. Two women with big, curly hairpieces and three men, all who had been in an old navy blue 1950's car with fins, went to trial and then jail.

One man is still there for doing the shooting. These evil people hadn't even known the young man; the shooter just felt like killing. The police, who hadn't believed in this "psychic stuff," kept my phone number. I've done other police work, too. It's so satisfying if I can ever help give families of victims at least a little resolution and closure.

For years after that incident, my client, the victim's aunt, continued to come to me for Tarot readings. She's a writer and felt as if our sessions helped her with story ideas. A couple of times I tried to get her to do a past-life regression, but she said she didn't believe in past lives. I finally talked her into a regression anyway, but she was sure it wouldn't work. She fell into that hypnotic trance faster than anyone I've ever seen.

The past lives she experienced were astounding. I believe she relived her past lives; she believes she received visits from others who have lived before. It doesn't matter; no matter how it happened, there were beautiful life lessons. And she has turned each of those people from the past into amazing characters in her books. So it worked out great, though not like either one of us expected.

I have learned to help myself as well. I've worked to be less judgmental and more open-minded of others and of myself. Today I am very thankful for every stupid move and foolish action I took when I was younger. Because without my past, I would not be the woman I am today. I am looking forward to the future work here on earth and when I pass into another dimension.

Was my life directed by destiny, a plan that was pre-determined before I came into this life, or by fate, just accepting whatever came my way after I arrived here on earth? Or was it a little bit of both?

You decide.

WHO'S TALKING ... *Deborah Alexander has always accepted the fact that not everyone understands her gift. Many do, however, and as a popular intuitive psychic advisor in the Atlanta area, she enjoys a large following. www.myatlantapsychic.com*

24: COUGAR ON THE PROWL
LOUISE, 69

I AM ALMOST 70, BUT I WANT TO RAVAGE THE YOUNG MAN WHO sells me running shoes at the Athletic Shoe Factory. I want to grab hold of the collar of his shirt with my teeth and drag him out to the parking lot and have my way with him. And leave him for dead. Or drag him home and chain him to my bed.

This is embarrassing. I don't tell anyone.

It all started when it was perfectly acceptable for me to have sex with young men. It was the '60s, and we were all sharing this wonderful free love, albeit while trying to ignore our moral compasses; studying; going to classes; saving the Earth; and protesting the war in Vietnam. It was an exhilarating and dizzying time. "Make love, not war," we said.

I met my first husband in college, and when I stayed over, his roommates would congratulate us on the number of times they heard us make love. "Wow," Brian would say to Richard. "Good job last night."

When we got married, we made love every morning and every night. That's what I thought married people did, and besides, it's a great way to start and end the day. You love each other, and you're married, and you're already in bed. I settled into a wonderful routine.

One day I had lunch with my girlfriends and we started talking about how often we had sex with our husbands. Twice a month, said Stephanie. Maybe once, said Sharon. Sheepishly, Laura admitted she and her randy husband had sex almost once a week.

I was mortified. Surely, I had some sort of nymphomaniac disorder. Of course I didn't tell them the truth. I mumbled something like 2-3 times a month maybe, and the conversation drifted away to hemlines or something equally benign.

The marriage didn't last, though. We lived about an hour from Manhattan; and while he was happy with the newspaper, the television, and a Barco lounger, I was busy getting tickets for the ballet, the symphony, Broadway plays, and museum exhibitions. I tracked down the best restaurants and street fairs. I wanted it all.

But Richard hated New York, and I always felt that the City knew that. He could never find a parking space; he always got tangled up in traffic. One time, we missed a performance altogether because he gave up, turned the car around, and drove us back home. It was like the City was having a fight with him.

We still made love, though, even that night, but the sex wasn't enough to keep us together.

I fell in love with a man who lived in the City. He left his wife for me. I divorced my husband, sold the house and my car, quit my job, moved to the City—and the married man went back to his wife.

Just a darn minute here! That was not the way it was supposed to go. This left me heartbroken, not even thirty yet, single, and with a sense of entitlement to unlimited love-making to handsome young men.

And the City was ripe for it.

Those were the years of Studio 54, piano bars, and Upper East Side singles bars. The economy was booming, coke was practically free—well, always free for girls. The '70s were pre-AIDS and before the "This is your brain on drugs" campaign. We did lines of coke off the bar at after-hours clubs and on hand mirrors in our offices. There were discos with dark corners where you could pull off a quickie. Wall Street was a shitshow of excess. Good-looking guys in European-cut suits and expensive ties owned Manhattan.

We girls were voracious, and the men were prey. Fresh from the Women's Liberation Movement, we had no qualms about going to bed with anyone we chose. I remember being out with a man friend of mine and a handsome young man entered the restaurant. My friend nudged me. "There's one for you," he teased. The handsome young man approached the coat check.

I bet my friend $100 I could get the young man to leave with me in less than two minutes. Tony took the bet. I went up to the guy, put a hand on his elbow and said, "I wouldn't bother checking my coat, if I were you."

I collected my $100 and left the restaurant with the young man. We went out together for almost a year. I don't remember his name.

I was in a stage of arrested development. I had fallen in love with two men in their 20's, and there I remained, stalking the nightspots for handsome young men in expensive ties, culling handsome young men from parties and art openings. When my girlfriends and I graduated into our 30's, it became a game, and my girlfriends joined in. It became a competition, who could date the youngest guy. We called our age bracket "the dirty thirties."

I kind of thought I was the winner, hands-down, especially when I dated a man a decade younger who hardly spoke English, a few points extra. I met him at a party. "Does he belong to anyone?" I asked. "Can I have him?" A delicate blond, he was Finnish and adorable and universally sexy. That lasted a while. Long enough for me to teach him about several American holidays that the Finns don't recognize. St. Patrick's Day was amusing, ("I now know how many Irish people live in Manhattan!") but Valentine's Day was the best.

After explaining the concept of the holiday to him, he went off, pensive. The next day, he called me at the office. "Lou, I am so sad. I not sleep all night, thinking."

"What's the matter, Harry?"

"I think and I think, and I am so sorry."

He was so very, very sad. "Sorry for what?"

His voice seemed even sadder. "I think and I think, and I think I cannot be your valentine. I am so sorry."

"Oh, Harry." Bless his heart. He thought being my valentine was some sort of marriage commitment. I let him off the hook.

My friend, Nancy, did me one better. She married hers. Then Ann, who said she was only playing, fell in love with one younger man who broke her heart, and then years later, married the next one.

I was being beat at my own game. I decided I would grow up and date men my own age.

I married one. He was handsome and fit and funny and smart, but unfortunately, taking on the challenge of a woman who believed all the crap we women were fed during Women's Lib was too much for him. When we divorced, I fell back into my old habits, but I was nearly 50 by then. Now, dating men in their 20's was a little creepy.

I had to expand my parameters. I still lusted after good teeth and smooth skin and blindingly good sex; so when, on enchanted evenings, whenever I saw a young stranger across a crowded room, and the exchange was charged with sex and future, I went for it. But this time around, the men were in their 30s. Anything less than a 10-year difference didn't count. Only when you got into double figures were you really dating a younger man.

And so there was Zoran. We locked eyes in a hotel where he worked as head of security. And for months, I was happier than I had been in years. He was mad for me. We'd meet in the City and have a late dinner and coo at each other over wine at Elaine's. Then we'd try to drive to his place in Brewster, NY, but invariably, we couldn't make it home without stopping along the way to make love in the front seat of the car.

But a few months into the relationship, he announced that our personalities were too different. I was too overwhelming. The sex was too much; the whole thing was too much. Broke my heart.

Nearly three years later, I got a letter from West Virginia. He lived in a pup tent about six miles up the side of a mountain, where he wrote poetry and communed with the Great Spirit, whatever the fuck that is. He had given up sex. Tantamount to slowing down and peering at a highway accident, I wrote and asked if I could visit and he reminded me he is celibate and booked me into a bed & breakfast.

He took me to see his little tent, which was dirty and smelled bad, but I still wanted to pull him in there and make love. He showed me his little stove and box of books. He said he needed a new flashlight. If he had asked me to stay and sleep in his dirty tent, I would have stayed.

But he didn't ask, and when I got back in the car to drive home, I set my hands on the steering wheel and thought, "What the hell was that?"

I kind of lost my sense of adventure after that, but not my taste for younger men. Not that I don't try. I've even done the Match. com thing and met age-appropriate men, but there is something off-putting about bad teeth and nose hairs and whiskers growing out of their ears.

We women know about those unexplained hairs that grow out of our chins. They grow there overnight and they are impossible to pull out with our fingers. No matter how hard you try. They're slippery. We should carry tweezers with us, but we don't. We get nuts when we spot one in the rear view mirror and practically get into car accidents trying to yank it out; we make pacts with our girlfriends to watch out for them; we'll tell each other, pull them out. So why don't men do the same? Why do they think it is okay to walk around with whiskers growing out of their ears and hair growing out of their noses? What's up with that?

If all men looked like George Clooney, life would be good. Last I looked, he does not have whiskers growing out of his ears. Last I looked, he does not have flab hanging over his belt or from the undersides of his biceps. Last I looked, he doesn't have facial hairs that are so crowded into his wrinkles that he can't shave them.

But that's George Clooney. I know. I don't look like Meryl Streep, either. But I do not have whiskers growing out of my ears or flab hanging over my belt or from the undersides of my biceps, or facial hairs crowded into my wrinkles.

Walking around here in the real world, there are a lot of available younger men with good teeth and smooth skin. Most of them have no idea I have designs on them.

They are prey.

WHO'S TALKING ... *Louise Smithers, 69, is a Manhattan marketing executive who refuses to retire. She likes expensive restaurants, cheap wine, and young men.*

25: SEX?
RUBY, 73

"DO YOU WANT SOME SEX?"

"What did you say?"

"Sex. Do you want some?"

"Oh, I didn't hear you. No thanks, I just ate."

If you're 25 years old that might be insulting. But at 73, it's merely a part of life. At this age, conditions have to be just right for sex to be appealing. Nobody ever wants to admit that, let alone talk about it, but that's what you can expect as you age. In fact, I'll give you my take on sex for seniors.

First of all, don't ever blurt out, "Do you want some sex?" When Harold and I first married 53 years ago, that was all it took. Now it takes some preparation. Well, actually, a lot of preparation. It's sort of like being a teenager again, prepping for our first time. We planned copiously and talked about it a lot and dealt with angst and suppressed our guilt over sinning, and then finally did it. It's like that. But without the sin part.

What used to be the big bang is more like a very sweet whimper that takes time, prompts, and lots of lotions. And if nothing comes of it, it doesn't matter. We still enjoy being together.

When I began noticing the signs of aging like mottled skin, wrinkles, and cellulite, all of which seemed to attack when I was in my sixties, I worried that my husband wouldn't find me attractive anymore. But then I realized that he was at an age where once he takes his glasses off he's blind as a bat anyway, so he doesn't have a clue about those things. I just make sure he takes his glasses off before I shuck my clothes.

Much more often than not, though, we no longer do "it." The fun now is in the flirting, teasing, and touching that we recall from before our sex days. It's wonderful to come on to each other with no expectations. The innuendos, jokes, and back rubs no longer require sexual intercourse to be satisfying. It isn't like our younger hormonal days when all we had to do was look at each other sideways or accidentally bump into each other to feel compelled to fall to the floor and screw our brains out.

The things that lead up to the big event are what excite us these days, except now there are no expectations and only about one big event every couple of years. And that's getting to be fewer and farther in-between; although our last anniversary, with all of its fond memories, did bring out the best in us.

Will we miss sex if we don't do it anymore? We laugh at that question. After only-God-knows-how-much sex and five children, we figure we've probably used up our fair share of physical shenanigans. My feet are never again going over his shoulders.

Do we worry about whether or not we're "normal" for our age? Hell, no! We're both far beyond the point of giving a rat's ass about what anybody else is doing in their marriage. That's their business, not ours. It doesn't matter if another couple has sex until they are 100 years old or haven't had any in 50 years. We don't care. We do care about what is best for us. Period.

Something that happened to me that my gynecologist says happens to a lot of women as they age is that my vagina walls have thinned and become tender. Thank goodness Harold isn't as—well, this is embarrassing but I think women should know—hard as he used to be. It works out just right. That's why I think all of that hormone phooey and those "erectile dysfunction" pills are bone stupid. Nature is taking its course. Let it be. Stop pretending to be something you're not—young. Embrace the joys of being the age that you are.

That's what Harold and I have decided to do. We love each other, have weathered many a storm together, and intend to continue to do so until we croak and the coroner sticks those tags on our toes.

I've written this under a fake name because I'm rather old fashioned and have never talked about this to anybody except Harold and my closest women friends, but I think all women should know that they don't have to feel like something is wrong with them if they're not living up to our society's stupid expectations that we're supposed to try to be the same young person all of our lives. What's the point of living if we never grow and change? That's not for me.

I hope it isn't for you, either.

WHO'S TALKING ... *Ruby Stone is the pseudonym of a usually private woman who is tickled at her own brashness in talking about sex. Her husband is delighted. They both hope that her chapter is helpful to other women.*

26: GETTING A FACELIFT
NORMA, 65

WHEN I WAS 52, I HAD SOME COSMETIC SURGERY DONE ON MY face. That decision truly surprised me. As a person who likes and respects Mother Nature, I had long ago tried to make it my business to like my physique as it came, warts and all. I figured that liking one's body, one's hair, one's coloring, one's boobs, was mostly about attitude. I didn't have any serious ugliness, and in fact, tended to feel lucky in general when it came to looks. I didn't really think I minded aging a little; seemed like it earned a little respect (whether deserved or not).

Other people were surprised, too, because anyone who knew me would have thought that a boob job would be far more appropriate. It turned out that there were other unexpected aspects of the whole experience. Not bad, particularly, but still unexpected. By the way, I don't write this as a cautionary tale; surely anyone venturing into cosmetic surgery has her own reactions, her own experiences. This is simply my personal experience.

I had begun being repeatedly distracted by the face of some woman who appeared to be really pissed off ... and she was in my mirrors! She did not seem like me anymore. It was weird, because I wasn't in the habit of checking my appearance in a mirror all the time. I'd put makeup on with a mirror, of course, and probably give myself a good once-over when getting ready for a special event. But once that was done, not so much. Spinach could cover a tooth, a smudge of food could be on my face, my hair could be sticking up on top, and I wouldn't know it 'til that night, if at all. I could wash my hands in front of a mirror and never glimpse myself in it. Thus, when that seriously pissed-off lady kept showing up in my peripheral vision, I was truly taken aback.

This foreigner's face had significant vertical ruts between her eyebrows, giving her the look of a tiresome, aggravated, grumpy woman. An angry woman. I grappled with the fact that it was a mirror, and therefore, dare I say it, that grumpy woman was me.

I think that those canyon-like furrows were due to a frequent barrage of pretty terrible migraine headaches that came along with menopause, which, for me, went on for a difficult ten years. For many of those years, I didn't have the right medicine to help with those headaches, either. They would sometimes last for days.

I hate to complain about menopause, because in most ways I was lucky. I experienced only a few hot flashes, I tended to get pretty decent sleep, and I managed to have a pretty decent sex life throughout.

Still, the duration of the process wore me down like an old shoe. I experienced a roller-coaster of depression that bounced in and out of my life. Sure, there were life causes for some degree of depression. I had been divorced for about eight years and I was still coping with responsibility for raising three not-so-simple children. Since I had my last one at forty-two, I was still especially hands-on with my ten-year-old. My terrific mother had come to live with us, and she came needing all sorts of support, mostly with respect to her health. But on the whole, I felt successful in meeting the challenges.

But the hormonal depressions were different. They seemed to come from out of nowhere, they were much more severe, and I found myself slammed with a feeling that didn't seem much like the usual occasional depression of my past. Once I realized they were hormonally controlled and not really mine, I managed to survive the major dips fairly well. These frustrating rough spots were ultimately not really my own depression, but rather the jerking around by Demon Hormones. Understanding that really helped.

The other thing that happened around that time was that a good girlfriend, one with whom I had played tennis for years, had some cosmetic surgery that was truly amazing. She looked absolutely like herself, wasn't particularly changed at all. She just looked relaxed and rested. Refreshed, but herself. She seemed to have weathered the procedures very well, and I might not even have known that she had done anything if it weren't for her openness in talking about it. The fact that she looked like herself, unchanged, was pretty impressive!

So I began to consider getting some cosmetic surgery for myself. While I was at it, I thought I might want to ward off a threatening turkey neck. My mother, who after all was eighty-five at the time, had a serious dangling waddle, and there was clear evidence that my neck skin was on its way to the same fate. Why not just find out about it?

I went for an exploratory appointment with the same plastic surgeon my friend had used. It was incredibly interesting to me. The doctor was very willing to explain things, looking at me the way a sculptor must look at his block of marble as he's formulating ideas. He described various things he could do and came up with his suggestions. He wanted to do a jowl lift, which would help with the turkey neck, a brow lift, which would help with the furrows, and finally a lasering of my skin, which would smooth and refresh. He also wanted to do a bit of work around my eyes, which would be easy to do, as long as he was there. Made sense, at the time, even though I had no real concerns about my eyes.

Then we talked about cost. The dollar figures were high, of course, but I felt I could afford to do it. Then he cleverly offered a ten percent discount if I had it done right away, before the end of the year. Ten percent of a big number is a big savings, and having it done over the holidays sounded like a good plan for hiding from the masses during recovery. (Later I felt that this was inappropriate pressure from the doc, but it worked.) So instead of visiting other surgeons and getting other opinions, I took the plunge and signed on the dotted lines.

I decided to not tell people because I was hoping to have only a 'refreshed' look at the end of the day. I could get it done right after Christmas and lay low for a couple or three weeks during recovery. I realize now that this part of my decision was a mistake, but at the time, it seemed right.

I did it.

And the next jolt came along immediately.

My old face was gone and there was no turning back. Regardless of how things turned out in the long run, I had to say goodbye to my old, familiar, life-worn face. I had not foreseen this sense of loss, even though it seems so obvious in hindsight. I had to fall back on my basic philosophy of liking what I had, no matter how the face turned out, because the old one was gone. I mourned the loss, and I never saw it coming.

I don't want to relive the difficulties of the surgery and post-op item by item, but I must say that the recovery time, in my case, was much, much longer than expected. Surgeons make these predictions without much hands-on knowledge. They operate, but they don't live with the recovery process much.

During the first weeks, I could have been cast in a zombie movie, complete with bruises, red, oozing eyes, and very long-lasting peeling skin from the laser work, all without zombie makeup. I really couldn't go anywhere without frightening people, so I laid especially low and especially long. Many plans had to be changed to accommodate my hiding. And friends began to wonder what my story was, because I was declining invitations so often. Some even worried that I was unhappy with them. I never intended to create such mix-ups, of course.

One by one, my family and close friends were learning The Truth about my overhaul, each with his or her own reaction. It was upsetting to some of them.

Two of my children had a bit of a hard time with the change. I made a mistake by not telling them what I was doing ahead of time, based on the notion that there wouldn't be all that much change. But because the kids saw me fairly early after the surgery, I looked especially … well … bad.

That was upsetting to them, along with their realizing that I would look different now. It was difficult. I hadn't seen that coming, and if I had, I would definitely have explained more to them ahead of time, and perhaps waited to see them for a longer period following the procedure. I certainly hadn't intended for anyone to be upset, especially my children!

One rather lovely thing came clear, though. My mother, with whom I'd always been close, really didn't have a hard time with it at all. It was as though she hadn't noticed. Ultimately, I realized that it was because she didn't look at my face when we spoke; she looked in my eyes. She related to me, not to my face. What a gift that realization was.

As the peeling finally ended, weeks into the recovery, there was lingering fluid retention, and this brings me to the next odd reaction.

By this time, I looked mostly fine and still had my personal appearance features—the same nose, same eyes, the same general face. The waddle was pretty well gone (one of my favorite parts), and those not-me brow furrows were finally really gone. It was all good, really. I tended to wear more makeup than I generally liked in order to cover the remaining redness of the skin peel. I also tried to fix my hair up much more than usual, to distract eyes away from the facial changes during the transition period. In other words, I wasn't quite me.

But that pesky fluid retention—which lasted for around four or five months—had an effect: it ironed out nearly any wrinkle

I had ever had, giving my face a bit of a china doll appearance. In fact, someone actually said I looked like a china doll, and although they meant it as a compliment, I found the remark very difficult to hear. I wanted to be myself, not a china doll.

Because of the fluid, my face was 'sculpted' in a way that showed none of my life experience. To make matters worse, the doc had insisted on using Botox on my forehead, just for the period following surgery, so that my muscles wouldn't pull down the 'brow lift' he had worked on so diligently. I didn't care when he told me he wanted to use it for this purpose, but I didn't foresee the lack of a more natural facial expression. For one thing, I couldn't give my son "The Look" when he got into trouble.

I wanted to get rid of the brow furrows, of course, but I didn't want to look anything like any kind of doll, china or not. The word 'glamorous' came up a couple of times, too, and I simply could not identify with the feel of that word. I had no interest in glamour, being a practical woman. It's funny, I think, that I didn't like the term, even though it was clearly meant as a compliment.

In other words, the new face didn't exactly feel like me anymore.

Weeks after the surgery, I was just re-entering my more normal life, returning to the tennis courts to play with my friends. On the first day back, I was running a little late, so I needed to hustle my way from the car into the facility. I was wearing a tennis skirt, which of course revealed my legs. Most unfortunately, I looked down, and I could see exactly how my thigh skin looked with each pounding of my feet on the asphalt: it was wrinkling up like an Austrian theater curtain that rises in scalloped drapes! Ohhhh, noooooo! Now my face is one age, but my legs are of another generation!! What could I do?

It was a panic! But I am happy to report that before I actually got out to the tennis courts, I had realized that this question was easy to answer. I would do nothing. I simply figured out that I would never finish trying to get it all right and that I should relax and let things unfold as they would. It would be a hopeless, endless pursuit to fight aging, one body part at a time, so I accepted, on the spot, that I would just sit back and allow the old bod to do its best. It was a shock to come to this realization. I had never even considered that my face might be out of sync with the rest of me! For this early, fairly shocking realization, I am very grateful. It's kept me from making myself crazy with any the fruitless pursuit of an unnatural youth.

There was a side story, having to do with a mole, which I much preferred to call a beauty mark. It was under my left eye, and although I had been teased on occasion about it, I liked it. (I liked to compare myself to Marilyn Monroe in that respect.) The doctor asked me at the initial consultation if I wanted him to remove it, and I said no. How would I ever know which way was left if he did that?

As it turned out, however, the laser removed all the dark color of the mole, which meant that at the end of the day, what I had was more like a beauty wart. I lived with it for a long time. The doctor said I could get a tattoo to color it back in, but that truly would not have suited me. Finally, a couple of years later, I had the former beauty mark removed entirely. Now that was weird. No mole under my eye anymore. It was disorienting.

In the years since the surgery was done, I have recaptured many of my old, familiar wrinkles. As the surgeon told me, having the procedures done does not preclude ongoing aging. I really like and value those creases. I earned them.

But here's another unexpected surprise. Ever since I had the work done on my face, I've been uncomfortable with people complimenting me about how young I look. I try to just accept each compliment with a genuine, 'Thank you,' but often, folks pursue it. "No, really! You don't look like you could be sixty-five!" And, "Wow, really? I would never have guessed you were that old!"

When I made the decision to have the work done, I wasn't trying to look any younger than my age, so now that I apparently do, I find myself unwilling to just allow people to be so impressed. I can't help myself, and often find myself telling people, "Well, to tell the truth, I cheated." That, of course, leads to many fascinating discussions, but I just can't stand letting people be so misled. Who knew I'd have a moral dilemma with every compliment that comes my way?

I must say that I gained a lot of good things from having had the surgery. I did feel buoyed by the fresher appearance, especially once the swelling was resolved and I regained a few of my more natural lines. The Botox wore off, and I could once again give a good scowl to a naughty child. And I eventually outlasted the China Doll Dilemma.

I would also have to admit that having the work done enhanced my love life. Maybe it was just having a little more light-heartedness and a smidgeon more self-confidence, but whatever the reason, it's certainly given me a leg up over the years, even though I've aged since I had it done. The doctor didn't promise that I'd quit aging.

I guess that if I had it to do over again, I would. But I certainly hadn't anticipated the many unexpected surprises that went along with it.

WHO'S TALKING ... *Norma Kovacs is an Okie by birth, but now lives in Denver. Having had her three children late in life, she has only recently achieved empty nester status. She considers this an adventure. Norma is still trying to decide what she wants to be when she grows up.*

27: THE BODY
LOTTIE, 84

"LOTTIE THE BODY." THAT IS QUITE A NAME TO BE REMEMBERED by, especially at my age. Today I live a quiet life in Detroit with my husband of twenty years, Willie.

We married when I was in my sixties, a testament to the fact that it's never too late to find love. Willie is a retired chef and I feel blessed to have such a sweetheart in my life. Although he's a bit younger than me, we fit together perfectly as a couple. We have a lot in common, like a love of cooking, going to mass, and being with our friends and family.

But I didn't always lead such a quiet life. From the time I was seventeen until retirement at sixty-one, I traveled the world performing.

Born Lottie Bristow in New York, I studied ballet when I was a girl and loved it, so by age seventeen I'd quit school to become a professional dancer.

I performed with "Whitey's Lindy Hoppers," a dance troupe based in Harlem that worked all over the country. Herbert "Whitey" White formed the dance company in the 1930s when he saw that white folks were visiting the Savoy Hotel in Harlem, where he was head bouncer, to watch black people dance. Whitey, a black man named for the white streak in his hair, turned out to be a good businessman, taking the dance to the people. His shows were very popular through the 1940s. Famous for the "Lindy Hop," a dance that combined jazz, tap, swing, the Charleston, and more, groups of six dancers traveled around performing at events. That's what I did and that was the beginning of my dancing career.

The name "Lottie the Body" came early on when a sculptor, who was with a college in New York, made a sculpture of me. He named his creation *Lottie the Body* and the name stuck to the real thing.

At this age, I can admit that I was blessed with a great body. I was even known as the "Gypsy Rose Lee of Detroit" for the town where I eventually settled down. But although I loved the costumes and glamour and attention and fame, that wasn't what was most important to me. I wanted to entertain men and women through my love of dance. I wanted them to experience the joy of life that I felt. It was my love of people that made me want to make them happy. I know that sounds too simple to be true, but it is. I think that's the truth for many performers.

In the 1950s, after Whitey's Lindy Hoppers ran its course and closed, there was only one place for me to dance, only one place for a professionally-trained black dancer to make a living—Burlesque. It was either take off my clothes while dancing or don't dance at all. So I took it off.

However, back then it wasn't like it is today. "Stripping" meant ending up in a bikini bottom and pasties, more than a lot of women wear to the beach these days. In my kind of exotic dancing, it wasn't the attitude that dancers have today: "Look at what I've got that you can have." It was more like: "Look at what I've got that you can't have." That's what drove men wild.

Lots of couples came to our shows, too. I've been told that I was sexy and sensual but never offensive to women. In fact, a pregnant woman even came to me once to thank me. She and her husband had seen my show on the night they went home and conceived their child. I was so pleased at that.

Sometimes I didn't take my clothes off at all, either because the contract didn't require it or I didn't feel it was necessary. Now that really drove men wild. And made sure they'd come again the next night.

The way the shows came together was that all kinds of entertainers worked through an agent. The agent would send whatever kinds of acts the people wanted and we would sign a contract outlining conditions on both sides. It was decent money for that time.

I have too many stories to tell for one chapter—it would take a whole book—or two—so I'll share a few examples from my adopted home state, Michigan. I love this place.

When I first started performing in Detroit, I loved the music scene here. And the people are so warm. This Midwestern state isn't always automatically associated with the advancement of African Americans in this country, but long ago black people came here to escape slavery, later to work in the automobile factories, and eventually to participate in the music business. Many Southern musicians came to Detroit to work, and they stayed.

But let me start with a story that often surprises people because they don't know there was an area of Michigan, in the mid-western part of the Lower Peninsula, which was a vacation recreation area for African Americans from all over the country.

Black people moved there to live permanently, too, and to retire. I know, that sounds odd because it was pretty much out in the middle of nowhere. That was why some very smart black businesspeople like Phil Giles, Lela Wilson, and Arthur "Big Daddy" Braggs were able to take advantage of low property costs and buy up a bunch of land to develop a center for entertainment and business in the 1940s. It was a huge hit and drew crowds for years, until the early 1960s. Not only did the entertainment draw African-American audiences, white people from neighboring areas came, too.

I loved performing there. It was known as the "Summer Apollo of Michigan" and "Black Eden." It was like a Las Vegas show with singers, entertainers, skits, comedians, dancers, and show-girls. Showgirls just had to look pretty. We dancers had to work our tails off. Some of the acts were Della Reese, Aretha Franklin, B.B. King, Louie Armstrong, Jackie Wilson, T-Bone Walker, the Four Tops, the Rhythm Kings, Sarah Vaughn, Cab Calloway, Dinah Washington, Fats Waller, and more I can't even remember.

It was an exciting time. I adored performing with such big talent. Ziggy Johnson, a well-known choreographer, worked with us. Aretha Franklin and I became friends and she is one of the sweetest women you could ever meet. And she can cook her butt off!

I became part of "Arthur Braggs Idlewild Review" of performers he booked to work around the country, as well as in Michigan. We worked the Vagabond Room in Cleveland, the Black Orchid Casino in Toronto, and many more such clubs. Aretha and I were once booked into the Pink Pony in Indianapolis, a popular club "across the tracks" where there was standing room only; the place was always packed. We learned that the owner, Tuffy Mitchell, was known as the head of the Jewish Mafia and that the place also ran a numbers game. Life on the road certainly was an education for young women. As well as working with the Idlewild review, I traveled to other places to perform.

By the early 1970s, Idlewild's popularity waned because blacks could get into other places they had been barred from before. Then I often performed at the Golden Horseshoe club in Harbor Springs, Michigan. You can probably tell that the club had a western theme. I really liked the owners, kind people who were good to their workers. Harbor Springs is a resort town on Lake Michigan that has a long history of wealthy vacation homeowners from Detroit and Chicago. That area is popular in the summer with boaters, golfers, and lake lovers; and in the winter with skiers and snow lovers.

The Golden Horseshoe was popular with everybody. On any given night customers might include high-rolling big city businessmen, a famous singer or actor or two, a celebrity athlete, a few mobsters, politicians, fraternity boys, couples, locals, a bridal shower or bachelor party, a doctors' convention, and Vietnam veterans just returned from war…. You name it, they came.

I want to use this example because I know that people wonder what the life of a dancer is like, and they often imagine the worst. Well, I'm here to tell you that we are just like anybody else—all kinds of people with all kinds of beliefs and values.

A waitress at a club in Harbor Springs told me I was different from some of the dancers. I didn't go out with customers. I didn't get drunk. I wasn't a diva. She was surprised that I would sometimes go out with the workers for breakfast after closing. I certainly wasn't shy, but I wasn't into the wild life like some performers, either. I was a *dancer;* it was my profession.

I didn't even feel competitive toward other dancers. I didn't have time for that. There was no time to fuss. I was too busy concentrating on my job. Performing is demanding and takes a hard-working, honest person to do it well.

The most fun night of the week at the Golden Horseshoe was Thursday night because it was "butler and servant's night" off from work. House workers, almost all black, who came with their wealthy employees to their summer residences, came to the club to hear good music, dance, and watch a good performance. The Dixieland Band had some Lawrence Welk musicians on summer break from filming their popular TV show. They were great musicians. The energy in the place was electric! It was so much fun. The waitresses at the club said the butlers, maids, and servants tipped better than anybody else. I told them that's because they knew what it was like to serve other people and they appreciated their chance to be served.

Performers, including me, stayed in the servants' quarters of the Fisher mansion. It was the vacation residence of the Fisher family of Fisher Body, the automobile company that merged with

GM. In Harbor Springs there were, and still are, fabulous vacation homes owned by wealthy families, mostly from Detroit with connections to the auto industry, passed down from generation to generation. The Fisher home was a beautiful place to stay. On an exclusive private peninsula, we had to give our names to a guard who would open the big fancy gate to a fabulous world of old money, a world that few ever get to glimpse except from a boat on the lake. Being inside was like being in a movie—with lots of fabulous cars.

I had many experiences like that, staying in interesting places (some much better than others) and meeting all kinds of people. I danced for many more years than most in my profession, and over the years I traveled and met famous people and had experiences that most women couldn't even imagine. It was hard for me to imagine sometimes. Oh, I was famous in the world of burlesque but I was meeting politicians, actors, musicians, athletes, and high society folks who took fame to a whole new level.

For example, when Arthur "Goose" Tatum, one of the founding players of the Harlem Globetrotters, and I were a couple, I traveled with him and other team members to Cuba. This was the 1950s and Cuba was a totally different place from what we think of it today.

A young Fidel Castro met our plane and I thought he was a very sweet man. He was very gracious to us. I soon discovered that the casinos there were much more, shall I say, "liberal" than what I was used to in the States. There were back rooms with all kinds of "activities." You name it, it was available: women for men; men for women; combinations of whatever ... Goose disappeared in the back room of one of these casinos, so I waited in the bar.

And waited. For hours. Chatting with other people in the bar, I learned a lot about what went on there. I was told that not only did a lot of American men come down for female prostitutes; wealthy men would also send their wives for male prostitutes.

Sometimes the couples would come together. As I watched the unbelievably good-looking males and females come and go from the back, I had to admit I could understand the temptation. I'd never seen such gorgeous men!

Goose and I, by the way, didn't last.

Another interesting time was during the 1970s in the Philippines when I got to know Imelda Marcos, wife of the Prime Minister at that time. Infamous for being a designer shoe fanatic—she was said to own over 2,000 pairs—she took me shoe shopping and bought me some fabulous shoes. This was before her husband was ousted for absconding millions of dollars from the government, probably to pay for Imelda's shoes.

I had many experiences that I'll never forget, like being the first black woman to ever dance on television in Alaska, and cutting the ribbon in a big opening ceremony in Fairbanks. I was treated like a queen up there.

I was often treated very well wherever I went, respectfully by both men and women. In a day and age when African Americans were still not always welcome, I lived my own sort of Civil Rights Movement, making friends and connections in my own way wherever I went. Oh, make no mistake about it, there were also times when I was treated like a second-class citizen, but those times were rare. I wish I could say the same for all of my fellow African Americans.

My life was different and I know it. One my dearest friends whom I met while working was Christine Jorgensen, the first well-known transsexual in this country. We were both born around the same time in New York.

Christine was born a man but in the 1950s had sex change surgeries in Denmark. She returned to the U.S. and became a stage performer. I loved doing shows with her. I felt honored to be invited to perform in the Jewel Box Review with artists in drag and others like Christine. She was a great talent and a wonderful person. I especially got a kick out of watching her sing "I Enjoy Being a Girl." She did enjoy it! Christine passed from cancer in 1989 and I will always miss her.

I worked with many famous people in my day, all over the country, like singer Sammy Davis, Jr.; producer Billy Rose, who was once married to Fanny Brice of the Ziegfeld Follies; Theodore Mann, known for his off-Broadway productions; and Robert Levy, a producer of black movies then known as "race films." I worked with comedians Redd Foxx and Totie Fields. I'll never forget Totie's joke about dieting. "Always start a diet on Monday. That way if you miss this Monday you don't have to worry about it again for another week."

I've worked in many other countries, too: France, Australia, Singapore, Hong Kong, and countries in Africa. I've been given awards along the way, especially for my work as an MC for the Harlem Globetrotters. That's something I did throughout the years, traveling with them to many places, including around Europe. My most recent award was presented to me at Detroit Orchestra Hall, which I treasure, not for being Lottie the Body but for my body of work as a performer.

I don't hang on to my old things, including my dance costumes. I had some gorgeous clothes, handmade, beaded, sequined, feathered, and furred. I've donated the ones I kept for display in the entertainment section of the Charles H. Wright Museum of African American History here in Detroit. That's a wonderful museum that has all kinds of displays, including histories of the Underground Railroad and Motown music. And the events they hold at the museum are great. I can't go very often these days, but it's good to know that our history is being so well preserved. It adds to my pride of my adopted hometown.

I spent a lot of my life on the road and that can be hard, so people always want to know if I was ever married back then. Yes. I once married a well-known professional athlete in Juarez,

Mexico, and thought it was love. That is, until finding out that not only was he bisexual, he was on the lam from the police for having transported a minor girl across state lines. We stayed right where we were in Juarez, supposedly for our honeymoon, we got a divorce, and he left to go marry the girl to avoid being thrown in jail.

So I was thinking that maybe marriage wasn't for me. I hadn't done a very good job of picking out a husband.

But after that, for a long time, I was known as the wife of Bob Graves, a handsome man and successful buyer for a big department store in Detroit. We lived in a ranch-style house in a mixed neighborhood with black, Jewish, and white neighbors. The mother of Jimmy Hoffa, the famed Teamsters boss who mysteriously disappeared, lived just a few doors down. Bob's family, including his children, became my family, too. I love them dearly.

Truth is, even though Bob and I had the marriage papers, we never had the ceremony. We just never got around to it. I was always on the road. After twenty years Bob got lonely, I guess, and found someone else. He left our home and left me unable to pay all of the bills, so I lived for a time without heat or hot water. It broke my heart when he left, but in all honesty I could understand why. It's hard to keep the home fires burning when you're gone all the time. I'm a strong woman and I loved my career. I wasn't willing to give it up.

Unfortunately, the woman Bob chose was not a very nice person and would harass me, throwing eggs at my windows and doing other nasty things.

When I finally retired at sixty-one, Bob surprised me by showing up at my door, in the house where we had lived together for so long, with a big present for me. I invited him in and opened the box to find a gorgeous beige linen suit. I thought it was an odd gift but loved it. I put it on and modeled it for him, which delighted him. I asked him to sit down for supper and we shared some of my homemade stew. He said he loved my cooking, and then he said he didn't know how he could have been so stupid as to leave me. The other woman was no longer in his life. I didn't hesitate to forgive him. I still loved him. We found our way into the bedroom where we made love. Afterwards, we were lying there just like we used to, smoking a cigarette, relaxed and laughing about the Detroit Piston basketball team, who he did not like. Then, with no warning, Bob gasped and stopped breathing. Right there in bed beside me.

Frantically, I called an ambulance and his niece, who was a doctor. I tried to revive him. But it was too late. Bob was dead.

When his niece arrived she told me he'd known he was dying of a bad heart. It was then I realized he'd brought me a suit he wanted me to wear to his funeral. So I did.

How fortunate I am to have met Willie Claiborne, my present husband, a few years later.

Do I still dance? Well, every now and then if I hear some good music I might cha-cha into the next room, but you're more likely to find me in the kitchen. I love to cook! Willie and I watch television shows like *Dancing with the Stars*, attend mass, visit with friends, and go out to dinner. I loved the excitement of my life as a professional dancer. But that time has passed and now I enjoy a more quiet life. Lottie the Body may live on in fond memories but the truth is I'm too busy with today to give that much thought. I have no regrets. I concentrate on now. Just like I've always done, I live my life in the most loving way I know how, because that's what life is all about.

Lottie the Body may have brought me fame but Lottie the Woman has always cared most about the same thing: sharing whatever gifts I have to make people happy.

If I were to give advice to a young woman today it would be to live your dreams, just like I did. If I could make it in a time when there was everything going against me—a teenaged African-American female in a highly competitive profession during racist times—you can do whatever it is you desire to do, too. Just remember me, Lottie the Body. If I could do it, you can, too.

To all of you women over sixty, I pray that you may have the same kind of love and happiness that I enjoy. I send my love and God's blessings to you all.

WHO'S TALKING ... *All Lottie Claiborne ever wanted to do was dance and dance she did, from age 17 to 61! Along the way she earned her claim to fame. Find an 80-year-old man and ask him if he's ever heard of Lottie the Body. If he says no, he's lying.*

28: REALITY

LINDA, 65

SERENITY CAPTIVATES MY SOUL AND SWEEPS IT AWAY TO FLOAT through time and space, traveling on a cloud of splendid enchantment. This magic journey gently delivers me to a remote beach where I sit on pristine sand, soaking in the warmth of the island sun. The rhythm of the soft tidal symphony bids my body to slow down, breathe deeply, and simply exist. The scent of the jasmine flower in my free-flowing hair solidifies my tranquil sense of well-being....

The roar of a neighbor's friggin' leaf blower startles me out of my blissful sleep. It takes a moment for me to get my bearings. My back porch, not the beach. An old green hammock, not warm white sand. And the blaring noise of an evil contraption, not soft waves. When I become queen of the universe I'm going to outlaw leaf blowers, along with a lot of other stupid, unnecessary, obnoxious appliances. While I'm at it, I'll ban a number of stupid, unnecessary, obnoxious people, too. It chaps my ass that some folks are too lazy to wield a common rake or broom for the sake of the peace and quiet of the neighborhood.

I abhor the interruption to my wonderful dream but know it's too late to recapture it now, so I roll out of my hammock. LuLu, my small Sheltie, has been roused by the racket, too, and arises from her spot on the lawn. A herding dog, I wonder if she dreams of undulating hills dappled with flocks of sheep. That would be her version of heaven, I imagine. We look at each other in disbelief. I suspect she might be the only living being who shares my distress over rude interruptions. Everyone else on earth seems to own a damned leaf blower.

That dream felt so real. I could feel the mellow ocean breeze and smell the sweet flower in my hair. That woman who was back there on the beach is, I have slowly come to realize, the real me. I live in my head a lot these days with her, rather than with the stressed worker bee who blithely buzzes through my chaotic days in reality. I have become quite detached from that frazzled woman, not knowing quite how she invaded my body. Well, okay, I do know, but I don't like it.

I often ponder these things now that I've turned 65. It's as if that big birthday flicked a switch that turned a light on my life, one that makes it impossible for me to ignore the truth. It's like being interrogated by a big old Irish cop (I can say that because I'm Irish and because I want to) who shines a spotlight right into my face. I cower as he bellows, "Where were you on the night of your life?! What's your alibi for the time of the offense?"

The offense? Pick one: I wasn't paying attention; I was afraid to "be all that I could be;" I fell into society's trap of what women are supposed to do; I was narrow-minded; I fell in love one too many times; I lacked self-confidence; I had to make a living to support myself; and perhaps, just perhaps, I knowingly refused to face reality. Who can corroborate my alibi? Lots of women who are in the same situation. Maybe even you.

I am not the grown woman I imagined I would be when I was a girl. I thought, in fact knew for certain, that by this time of my life I would be settled, retired, and resting on my laurels after making a living off of my published novels. I would be that relaxed, happy woman on the beach. I would be the epitome of an attractive, healthy, mature, Zen-like, goddess writer. I would be queen of my universe. I would even eat my greens.

As I go inside my house, schlep to the fridge, and open a Coke, I consider all of this. I also contemplate whether or not to open a new bag of chips to go with my gut-rotting drink, but nix that idea in favor of making at least a half-hearted attempt to save my aging heart from clogged arteries. My body, with the extra twenty pounds it's been carrying around for about, oh, ten years, aches from my workout at the gym earlier in the day. I work out twice a week with a group of women, led by a gorgeous trainer named Dawn who looks like Stana Katic, "Beckett" on my favorite TV show, *Castle*. Our trainer teases that we're all "broken," each with our own injuries, achy muscles, and stiff joints. We work through the pain. At least that's something. I take solace in the fact that I'm not a total slug.

I also practice yoga once a week with a group led by Sue, the most calming person I know. The first time I did yoga class with her a year ago, when it came time for *savasana*, the ten minutes of silent relaxation at the end, I burst into tears. It had been so long since I'd spent time taking care of just me I didn't know what to do with myself. Afterward Sue told me that's pretty common, women are so wound up and stressed. I'm over the blubbering and do much better now.

But I'm still not the happy, healthy female I pictured when I was a kid. I chuckle at the insight I recently had in the dentist's chair while getting a root canal. It was my first such procedure, which was indeed as horrific as everyone always jokes about. It's like a street worker jackhammering in your mouth. Anyway, I was lying there clutching the blankie the assistant had kindly given me because I was quaking with fear when it suddenly struck me that I had become one of the characters in my novel *Becoming Jessie Belle*.

In the book, Haliakula is an aging Polynesian woman in the 1500s. She has wiry grey hair. Just that morning I'd noticed how wayward my grey hair has become. When left on its own, it sticks out like wispy cobwebs sprouting from my head in all directions. My island character also has sagging bare breasts. As I sat in the dentist's chair I could feel mine resting upon my midriff in spite of the aid of a bra. They always say a woman's boobs will "sag" as she ages. I thought that meant they would tip downward a bit. No one told me that not only would that happen, they would also slither underneath my skin in a fervid race to my waistline. It's as if they think they'll win something when they get there.

"Yay, I crossed the line first! Where's my trophy?"

I talked about this once in one of my women's seminars. An attendee noted that if a mature woman wants to ever again see the pert things her breasts once were she needs to stand naked in front of a mirror, jump up and thrust her arms in the air, and for a split second while she's coming down she'll get a glimpse of them like they used to be.

I tried it. It works. Alas, it doesn't last.

Haliakula, the character in my book, also sports a big, round belly, which in her culture signals a prosperous life. My tummy looks like a soccer ball has taken up permanent residence in there in spite of the fact that for most of my life I counted a flat abdomen as one of my best features.

But what brought me to my thoughts of this fictional woman as I sat in the dentist's chair was that Haliakula has no front teeth. I was wondering if I'd also have a big hole in my mouth when this was over. It sure felt like it. Maybe when I wrote my fictional character she was just an uncannily accurate prescient description of me.

Okay, so things ain't what they used to be. I come to my computer and stare at the pretty mountain scene on the desktop while sipping my Coca-Cola. Unable to conjure up a reason for being there, I aimlessly pad through my house and land in my clothes closet. Sitting on my little bench in there, I finish my Coke as I look at all of that drab stuff hanging around my head. I'm bored with all of my clothes, even the new ones. I know, of course, that this is partly because I'm unhappy with my body and therefore don't like the way clothes look on me anymore, but besides that, all of my culturally appropriate duds are a drag.

When I become queen of the universe we're going to be able to wear warrior goddess and steampunk costumes wherever we want, especially to work. Or shorts and tee-shirts, whichever our moods prefer. But no bland "business casual attire" will be allowed.

Thankfully—glory, glory hallelujah—the blasted leaf blower outside ceases its rude interruption of my world, allowing me to leave my depressing closet and lie down on my bed in an attempt to resume my nap. Apparently, however, the neighborhood yard workers have secret surveillance cameras hidden throughout my house and know precisely when to start up again to make certain I get no rest.

"Whoa! She's down again! Hurry! Get out the blower! No, not that one! The super-duper-ginormous one! It's louder!"

I give up, get up, and come back to my computer to write. When all else fails, I always write. LuLu, my sweet dog, clomps along beside me and settles into a ball at my feet. The herder in her makes her stay near so I don't fall off a cliff. I would indeed be lost without her. She helps me focus and not wander off into oblivion.

At the computer I consider two things I'm working on at this time: a new novel, *The House on Haven Island,* and this non-fiction book for women over sixty. I open this one.

I've been working with some of the other writers for this book and enjoy that a lot, but have had a hard time with my own chapter. My life has been so chaotic and exotic and…long. While staring at the page mulling over what to type, I decide it's all too overwhelming and I'll just record the events of the last half hour since my interrupted nap on the porch. I should be able to handle that. My thoughts meander so much anyway, there's no telling where that will lead.

While reflecting about what to write, it occurs to me that I need to decide what I want to be now that I can no longer ignore the fact that I'm a grownup. What do I really want my life, at this stage of my life, to be like? I know the answer before I even get the words written out: I want to be the women I thought I would be when I was a girl.

A fond memory pops into my head of when I used to do women's seminars and of an activity I would do with audiences. It went like this:

Close your eyes and imagine that you are walking down a pleasant sidewalk on a pretty day. There is no one around except for one small child way down the walk, coming toward you.

As you get closer, you see that it is a little girl. You draw closer and closer to one another and something about her seems familiar to you. Finally, you are close enough to see her face and are surprised to see that she is... you! It is you when you were a child. That girl has walked right up to the woman that you are today and is looking you in the eyes.

What do you see in her eyes as you look back at her? Satisfaction or disappointment? Happiness or sadness? Love or loneliness? Gently take that little girl into your arms and embrace her. Feel the rhythm of her breathing as she is pressed against your chest and revel in the joy of having her once again so near. The scent of her hair and silkiness of her skin bring back memories of her young innocence and hope and anticipation.

Speak to her softly and reassure her that you will always protect her. Tell her that you will not disappoint her. Tell her that you love her. No matter whatever happened to her between then and now, you will take care of her forevermore. Feel her trust in you with the synchronization of the beating of your hearts as she begins to melt into you until the two of you become one. She is within you. She is you. Take good care of her.

I don't want to disappoint the child within me. What about you? Are you as happy as the girl within you deserves?

Women in my seminars would sometimes cry at that question. My eyes tear up with it now. It's a tough question, but an important one. Especially at this age, knowing that we no longer have forever to think about being happy later, we need to contemplate this *now*.

It's now or never.

Oh, I know that many women, perhaps you, are entirely happy with the lives they have built for themselves. This time of life brings them sheer satisfaction at what their lifelong efforts have wrought so far. They are living their childhood dreams or perhaps even better.

Not me. I must confess that I am not as happy as the girl within me deserves and can see, because I just wrote it down myself, that it is time to do something about that. What do I need to do? I look at the pretty trees outside the window above my desk and think about this for a moment. It is, I realize, suddenly silent out there.

Thank you. In the welcome quiet I consider my lifestyle and know how fortunate I have been. That said, I don't give a whit about the big house or country club lifestyle that my husband and I worked so hard to obtain. Lately I find myself buying every "cottage" and "coastal" magazine I can find. That's how I want to live. I don't care about keeping up with the Joneses or anybody else.

I do care that I continue to have enough money to travel. I want to spend more time sitting at the seaside, like in my dream. I also want to sail the fjords of Norway, see Machu Pichu, take boat trips up major rivers in Europe, visit the Caribbean islands I've missed, and revisit the holy sites of Ireland. Hitting the big six-five has made me aware that I won't physically be able to do that forever. So I feel even more compelled to "get in" all of those places I have yet to see, even though I've already traveled all over the world. There are new adventures left in me, to be sure.

Now that—traveling—brings me to a conundrum: to retire or not. Many of my friends this age are at this crossroads, too. You may be, also, or may have already crossed over. I haven't actually been in my present career as a college professor for too long, at least not as professions generally go. Twelve years.

I stayed in my former career as a seminar leader for twenty years. I find that I think about that job a lot these days. I got into it because of a tragedy: My first husband died of cancer at age 33. With my world suddenly shattered and the door to wedded bliss slammed in my face, I started traveling to do seminars. I ended up working through a company that booked me all over the world. It turned out to be an exciting career of giving training programs on topics like stress management and leadership. I've worked with some amazingly interesting groups like Southwest Airlines, the Knights of England, and the staff of Lucasfilm, Ltd.

Southwest Airlines was the first big company to hire me to do contract training with their employees. I started with a "hospitality" program about customer service. I had so much fun with the great people in that company, I was hooked. I wanted to do training programs like that forever. They have such a good reputation, and rightfully so, that once they hired me other contracts flowed in.

Doing a leadership program with the Knights of England, who were interested in the advancement of women in leadership roles, was an absolute treat. It was held at a five-star hotel in the breathtakingly beautiful resort town of Torquay on the southern coast of England.

Although I went in with a vision of Errol Flynn dashing about with sword drawn like in his 1930s movies, I was met by a roomful of charming elderly gentlemen, a few so elderly they had a hard time staying awake through an entire program. There was no rousting about, that's for sure. But they did indeed treat me like a queen for the day that we worked together. What a joyful memory.

For George Lucas' Lucasfilm Ltd., the *Star Wars* production company, I had the privilege of staying at his Skywalker Ranch, a working ranch in northern California. That was so much fun. I ran around musing over all of the big stars who had stayed there, and touching this and that. It's a gorgeous setting with thousands of acres of hills, forest, and pastures. And his staff people, unlike popular images of movie people being stuck-up, were some of the most down-to-earth folks I ever worked with. I wanted to move in.

I cannot aptly describe all of the beauty I've seen around the world. A winter night of stargazing in Fairbanks, Alaska, where the sky looked like something out of a movie, it was so unbelievably stunning. A summer night of flying over Canada and spending hours mesmerized by billowing neon towers of the dancing Aurora Borealis. Exploring the Great Barrier Reef off the coast of Australia. Wandering the highlands of Scotland. Trekking the Cinque Terre on the northwestern coast of Italy. Boating up the Black Sea. Getting lost in the great temples at Abu Simbel, Egypt. Buying local jewelry from a seller in Jakarta, Indonesia. And beaches around the globe.

My twenty years of traveling, ("road warriors" those of us in the profession called ourselves), took me to the most amazing places like that. I heard incredible stories from people everywhere and am sure that I learned more from them than they ever could possibly have learned from me. I treasure those memories.

I knew back then that I was fortunate to have such an interesting career and knew that I would miss it when I moved on.

There were, however, some hard times. Constant travel is anything but glamorous. There were times when I was treated like a star and times when I feared for my life. There were times when I cried from a broken heart for the things that sometimes happen to people and times when I laughed my derriere off over the hilarious absurdities. But after so many years of travel I needed to settle down, so eventually gave it up. Not before, however, meeting my present husband on an airplane. The best perk of that job, to be sure.

They say that as we get older we tend to remember the sweet and forget the sour, and that has happened with that job. I tend to remember the funny things the most. For example, I once had an experience I was sure would win me a prize. The company I worked with had over a hundred of us running around doing all kinds of seminars and we'd meet once a year for a conference in Boulder, Colorado.

One year we had a contest to see who had ever had the most embarrassing experience on stage in front of an audience. I was absolutely certain I would win. I'd had the most awful thing happen in front of 400 people. The contest started and people told their tales, trying mightily to outdo each other. Quickly we decided that going to the bathroom with your wireless microphone accidentally turned on didn't even count. Too many people had done that. Then it came my turn to tell my story.

I'd been doing a seminar in Baltimore, Maryland, with special guests in attendance from the U.S. Department of State who wanted to review my program for adaptations that might be necessary when I gave it to their group. I'd done lots of government and military work but these two people were new to me. So, of course, it was important to do a good job.

It was, as it turned out, Valentine's Day. Thus I had on a spiffy red jacket and felt pretty cool. I did my best and felt good about how it was going when, almost done, came question and answer time. A few people asked questions and I pointed them out in the big crowd by describing something they wore.

"Yes, the gentleman in the purple tie."

"The woman in the yellow scarf."

And then, "The man in the front row with the little red heart on."

All 400 people gasped in unison. They stared at me, as if in disbelief. I couldn't figure it out. I looked at the man again, sitting there with a little red paper heart, obviously made by a child, pinned to his lapel. He wasn't asking his question. Maybe he didn't hear me.

So I repeated myself. This time the room burst out in uproarious laughter. I still didn't get it. Finally somebody hollered that they'd thought I said "h-a-r-d" instead of "h-e-a-r-t." I actually had to spell it out in my head to understand. When the light finally went on in my head, I was so embarrassed! I wanted to crawl under the stage and not come out until they all went home. The guy in the front row turned beet red and never did ask his question.

The Department of State representatives thought that was hilarious but teased that I needed to leave that out of my government program.

To my shock, however, I did not win the "most embarrassing" contest at the conference. I only got third place. Second place went to a woman who had worn silk slacks with no underwear because she didn't want a panty line, and the button snapped off when she bent over to pick up something, and she mooned her audience.

First place went to a trainer who had, unbeknownst to her at the time, contracted food poisoning at lunch. She went back to her crowded seminar room oblivious to what was about to occur, and it hit her so unexpectedly and violently that she blew chow all over the front row of people. I must admit, she did deserve to win, bless her heart. How can you outdo that?

There have been many times in recent years when I've had a tough day and I've thought, "Well, at least I didn't puke on anybody. It wasn't such a bad day after all."

Those kinds of memories of that job always make me smile.

Not all of my employment has been that exciting, though. With that job and all of those since my first college degree at age 22 I've worked for 43 years. If I start with babysitting at 12 and include high school jobs as a camp dishwasher, at the Dairy Queen, and as a hospital candy-striper; as well as college gigs as a health center aide, waitress, cashier, bar maid, and secretary; I've worked 53 years. That certainly seems like enough. But all of those trips I want to take yet—I think my seminar job got me addicted—cost a pretty penny. And when one retires pennies do not fall from heaven.

Would I miss my present job if I were to retire now? In all honesty, not all of it. (Would you or do you miss everything about your job?)

I teach college education courses for future teachers and my students keep me going. They are diverse and bright and entertaining. They come in all ages and from all over the world. I admire their chutzpah and desire to contribute to future generations. They even give me great names for the characters in my novels. I never had children of my own—I do have stepsons and a daughter-in-law and grandson, all of whom I adore—and think that I gravitated back to education as my generative contribution to my community. It has been very rewarding work. I would miss students and colleagues, but not the job itself.

Friends on the cusp of retirement say the same thing. They wouldn't yearn for the work but would miss the people. I acknowledge that I would miss them more than they would miss me. They have kept me grounded, at least for the time being, so that I haven't yet gone off to live entirely in the fantasyland in my head.

But I do yearn for the work of writing, always wishing I had more time to hone this craft. I trust my time will come.

So maybe I should trust that I've done just what I needed to do. Maybe I need to let up on myself and accept that my timing simply isn't traditional. Maybe I needed all of those experiences and needed to meet all of those people in order to have more worthwhile material to write about. Maybe for me it wasn't meant to be until ... now. Maybe the child within me doesn't have to be disappointed after all. Maybe she has been patiently musing over the gore and the glory of my life, knowing that my time would come.

Now is that time. It's my turn to live in the world I always wanted to live in. The one the girl within me has always imagined, the one where I stand strong and good, and where I care more for thoughts than things. In my universe I may not be able to do away with those blasted leaf blowers, but I can write, travel, write, be with loved ones, get healthy, write some more, ignore negative people, and write again....

In fact, the older I get, the more I feel an urgent need to write. It isn't a feeling of having accomplished a great feat each time that I finish a book. It's a *relief*, like, "Thank my holy stars that one is finally out of my head. It was bursting in there. Now I can move on to the next one." It's as if I feel compelled to get all of these stories out of my noggin lest the grey matter in there someday turns to mush. But there's no question that being an older writer has its advantages. I have so much to tell.

Writer Elizabeth Gilbert; author of *Eat, Pray, Love*; once said, "Writing is not like dancing or modeling; it's not something where—if you missed it by age 19—you're finished. It's never too late. Your writing will only get better as you get older and wiser." Ah, yes, I am definitely older and wiser now.

Will I, this evolving wise maven, ever become the grownup I dream about? Will I become the woman the girl in me has been waiting for? Will I become that queen of the universe? My universe, yes. What about yours? Whether you're a woman over 60, or any other age, you've earned your place in this world. This is your time, too.

I decide that's a good way to end my thoughts here, so LuLu and I agree to go for a walk. I grab a bottle of water and we head for the door. That's a start for changing my life. One step at a time is better than going nowhere.

I'll get to all of those places I want to see yet. I'll write all of those books that are in my head. And I'll live in a cottage, maybe even by the sea.

WHO'S TALKING ... *When Linda Hughes was twelve years old she wrote in her diary that she would be a "writter" when she grew up. She is thankful to spellcheck today. Her wanderlust has taken her all over the world and she loves including it in her novels. www.lindahughes.com*

29: ERIN GO BRAGH
NANCY, 77

IT WAS THE LATE '60S. MY HUSBAND, DON, AND I WERE LIVING IN Morgantown, West Virginia, with our five children aged 3 to 14. We married when I had just turned 18 and he was 19. But we were doing okay for a couple who had married young with no money and who had a large family at breakneck speed.

We were in Morgantown for Don's job as CEO of a pharmaceutical company. We'd already been in the military with a stint in Japan and then a stay in Pittsburgh where Don went to college, so were accustomed to moving around.

During those years, because of the ages of our children, I was at home doing all of the things a mom with a bunch of kids does, like helping with school lunches and driving them to their various activities. I was very busy and very tired most of the time. Like so many young mothers, I often felt resentful at being "stuck." But we also had some great fun, attending all of the University of West Virginia football and basketball games. As with most things, it was a mixed bag of emotions.

Our house was just across the way from the business so there was no defined work or family space. That contributed to it not always being one of the happiest times.

Don had worked with a research team that developed a "transdermal patch," time-released medication through a patch put on the skin. That was a totally new concept at that time. He urged the board of directors of the company to get into research and development but they insisted that was a write-off and they were doing fine with contract manufacturing.

Suddenly Don turned in his resignation. He decided to "put his money where his mouth was" and start a research company.

Needless to say, this was a challenging time, but exciting at the same time for the opportunity. The environment in the U.S. was not good for such an enterprise. FDA requirements were much more expensive than we could afford or raise the funds for, so the search was on for the place where we could work.

We did not have any language skills and the children needed to be educated, so it needed to be an English-speaking place. England's industrial phase was tapering off due to the strong hold of the unions, but Ireland's revolution was just beginning and they had well-educated young people who needed work in their own country. Most of the university grads left the country—only four out of sixty engineering grads found jobs at home in 1970. The rest had to emigrate to find work.

So we sold our house in Morgantown, and everything we owned. On October 29, 1969, we arrived in Dublin with the five children and 60 pounds of luggage each.

No job—no house—no schools—no car—just the guts and determination to make it work. We piled into a taxi at the airport and the driver took us to the Pembroke Hotel where we stayed while we made our living arrangements.

People sometimes ask if I was afraid. No, I was never afraid. I guess I was too anxious for the new adventure. Oh, I knew Don had fears and that we all had big adjustments to make. But rather than being frightened, I focused on *how* I could do this.

We moved into a semi-detached house behind Herbert Park and the American Embassy. The location was good, but the house was old and on the shady side, and an old lady had lived and died there so no renovation had been done for a long while. We had been told there was central heating (very rare in those days) but after we moved in found that the "heating" was a three-bar electric heater which you could move from room to room and plug in. Because the house was old and the wiring inadequate, if the heater was plugged in and someone rang the doorbell, a fuse blew.

Remember we arrived in the fall: grey, cold, and damp. The daylight hours were from about 10 a.m. to 4 p.m. so it was dark and depressing.

After the house, the next step was schools. We enrolled the girls in Alexandra College and Dan in St. Andrew's. We shopped for all the necessary supplies and uniforms and spent several days teaching them the public bus systems, which is what they would have to use for school. This also meant that the girls were standing at the bus stop in brown mini-skirts with the wind and rain whipping at them in the grey mist of the day. Our son, Dan, could walk to school without having to cross the street. But he had no one to walk with and no friends yet, so in the beginning I walked with him, which was frowned on by the other boys in his class.

We were all pretty miserable, so miserable in fact, that *no one* dared complain. Don was having the same problem trying to set up an office. He said that when he started his morning each day he didn't know if he should shave or cut his throat.

One of the saving graces was that the house was in a well-established neighborhood and all of the children and preteens welcomed our kids and invited them to join whatever their activities were. It was a huge help.

We soldiered on and gradually began to get on better. We were in that house for about a year and found a better one in Black Rock, which had a lot more room, more daylight, and more yard, so we moved and were there for about eighteen months. Then we heard that a big old Georgian house was for rent due to a family dispute after Judge Lavery died (the Judge had not left a will). We moved again. This property had a big twenty-two-room house, acreage, a barn, a walled garden with fruit trees, a guest bungalow, and a large paddock just off the front drive. We got the kids a pony, moved in, and began to furnish the empty rooms. We hit the Dublin flea markets every Saturday morning picking up big pieces that no one could use because it was the era when small bungalows were favored. We were in the house only about ten days when Don signed our first pharmaceutical contract for the production and sale of a modified tetracycline product, an antibiotic. Half the normal dosage, half as often, with the same therapeutical results and fewer side effects.

That was our best news in a long time and so we had a party, inviting friends and business acquaintances from the U.S., Europe, and also local folks. There were about sixty guests and the party lasted three days and nights. The Irish know how to party.

That contract required that we find a manufacturing source. One was found in Athlone, a small town half-way between Dublin and Galway. So we produced the product Tetrabid in the ConMed plant using their equipment and labs and some of their staff. This was our bread and butter product for some time. We also used the small bungalow behind our rented residence for offices and research labs.

After a while, ConMed got in financial trouble and we bought them out and took over all their production, too. Then on the same property in Athlone we renovated another old building for more research labs and offices.

About this time, the legal issues with the Lavery House were being settled so we bought a house in the Dublin Mountains. One more move.

We needed more cash flow so we started a self-serve health and beauty aids chain called "Shop and Save." Prior to this time— it was the mid-1970s—chemist shops over there were small, family-owned, and offered only behind-the-counter service. If you needed a new toothbrush you had to ask the chemist for it.

The "Shop and Save" concept was open shelving (we did not do prescriptions), and the customer would put items in a shopping basket and finish at the check-out counter like it was already done in the U.S. But this was totally new for Ireland. We kept expanding this venture and eventually had twenty-four shops across southern Ireland. This improved our cash flow and we were able to further expand the pharmaceutical research company "Elan."

Since the children were all in school now, I started back to work and did all the purchasing for "Shop and Save." On the weekends and semester breaks, the children went to work with us and did chores to earn their pocket money. We eventually sold to Guinness Company of England, all but one store, and used the cash flow from that shop to pay the mortgage on our house. I ran that shop while Don concentrated on the research company. Again the children went to work with me on weekends. Donna (16) was behind the makeup/cosmetics counter, Danny (10) roamed around the two-story facility to report any shoplifting, and Andrea (8) would bag the items as I checked them out. Dena (14) and Lisa (12) both worked with animals on Saturdays.

After the house was paid off, we sold that shop, too, and again expanded the business in Athlone. I took a couple months off and soon got bored so I went back to work at Elan.

We had several research projects for American companies and they began to insist that we have a production facility in the U.S. to insure continuity of supply for their sales forces. This was a time of many dock and shipping strikes in Europe because of the unions' power. That "patch" idea, which Don patented, had really taken off and today is best known for the "smoker's patch."

So criteria were set and the hunt was on for a good location in the U.S. Don got an invitation to join a Red Carpet Tour of Georgia, which finished in Augusta during the Masters Golf Tournament. It was on that trip that Gainesville, Georgia, was chosen.

Land was purchased and a builder was selected and Elan was again expanding, but also expanding in Ireland.

During that time, Don was Chairman and CEO and I was Managing Director. He would find the business and I would mind the business. We grew and had subsidiaries in Europe, the Pacific Basin, and in California, as well as the new production plant in Georgia.

Elan was the first Irish company to go on the U.S. Stock exchange. When we retired, it had a bigger market cap than the major banks of Ireland.

Since "retirement" we have founded Chateau Elan Hotels and Resorts in Braselton, Georgia, U.S.A.; Saint Andrews, Scotland; and Hunter Valley, Australia.

Don has gone further to establish Elan Motors, building race-cars and racetracks. He also created the American LeMans racing format. He and our son, Dan, love cars and racing, and Dan has made it his life's work.

I continue to work with property development and have a number of rentals in a good community. These days I also spend a lot of time with my grandchildren, which is a delight.

I think back on those days in Ireland and feel so fortunate. One thing I loved about our adventure there was how close we were as a family. We lived and worked together like families used to do, something that is rare anymore. We learned about each other as well as about a different culture and lifestyle. And the education system there is excellent, so our children benefited from that as well.

I will always have a soft spot in my heart for Ireland. I hated the damp weather but loved the spirit and enthusiasm of the people. We built Paddy's Pub in Chateau Elan, our development in Georgia, in honor of our love of Ireland.

Going to Ireland gave us the opportunity to grow in all ways, with challenges in new ways of thinking and a new culture to offer our family. We met those challenges successfully and took on new ones.

Not too shabby a history for two small-town kids, married young, with no money. But we always had the will to take risks and work hard. And we had the determination to make *it* (whatever "it" was) work.

In December, 2014, we will be married 60 years. We have traveled to more than 75 countries; and lived in Asia, Europe, Australia, Bermuda, and the U.S.

Years of trouble, hard work, adventure, learning, and adapting. Years of tears, joy, and laughter.

That move to Ireland changed my life and that of my family. It made me understand that I can meet any challenge I am faced with. I encourage others to take advantage of their opportunities to meet the challenges that come their way, too.

Thank you, Ireland, for giving us that chance.

WHO'S TALKING ... *Nancy Panoz travels the globe with her husband, overseeing their various business enterprises. Her greatest pleasure, however, comes from spending time with her children and grandchildren, most of whom live in the southeastern U.S.*

30: EL AMOR CURA TODO
SUSAN, 72

SEPTEMBER, 1964. THERE I WAS, IN ALL MY GLORY, JUST ANOTHER Doris Day. Blonde beehive, white Samsonite luggage, lavender poodle-cloth coat, lavender silk dress to match and, why not, lavender silk spiked heels to top it off. I was at the airport in NY, waiting to get on my TWA flight to Spain, leaving all behind—family, friends, job, and bewildered ex-boyfriend. I had discovered another world. And I was going to love it!

Let me explain. One year before, after finishing college, a friend and I decided that we were going to "see the world" before settling down. So we got a job through a philosophy professor of ours to teach English to medical students at the University of Navarra in Pamplona, Spain. It was as good an excuse as any to set sail.

We never got to Pamplona. After staying in Madrid for a couple of weeks before we had to be up north, the people we met in Madrid assured us that Pamplona was a dead town except for July when the bulls ran on the street, that we would be considered "loose women" for living alone, and that if we wore red shoes we could be arrested for prostitution!

We were having a great time in Madrid and decided to stay for a while and sit in on history classes at the university to see if we could pick up some Spanish and some cute Spaniards.

In December, we decided that we had better set about seeing other countries before we had to go back to the States in March. So in January, we managed to book on a cargo ship that went around the Mediterranean. It had space for eight passengers. Forty-five days stopping at ports in France, Italy, Malta, Egypt, Lebanon, Syria, Turkey, Greece, and back to Barcelona. We had a fantastic time

That was where I met F who was an officer on the ship. He was tall, dark, handsome, and Spanish. Head over heels I fell. When we left the ship, my friend and I went to Paris and then to LeHavre to go back to the U.S. But I was hooked.

Back on the home front, when I finally returned to the fold, I told my parents that I had met someone and was going to return to Spain to see where it might lead. They were aghast at my decision to follow my heart, as we say. They asked if F was a bullfighter or a flamenco dancer.

OMG, a shipboard romance! My family and I decided to reach an agreement. I would stay home for six months, find a job, and then if my feelings remained the same, all would be respected and I would return to the beauty that was Spain and F. Six months was the most I could give because, after knowing F for only 45 days, more time apart would be ridiculous.

I was 22 and really could have done what I felt like but, remember, this was 1964 and things were not nearly as free as they are today. This was a big step for me and for my parents. Also F was on a ship, constantly moving around. It wasn't as if he had an office job and a place to live. I got a job, broke up with my boyfriend, and while all this was going on, F had been drafted for nine months and wouldn't be out until December.

So in September, I was boarding a plane to Madrid in my Doris Day outfit. I have to mention that the only places I knew in Spain were Madrid and Barcelona, and people dressed very formally in the 60's. I really thought I looked so elegant.

However, F was now doing his military service in Cartagena, a military port which was also a mining town on the southeast coast of Spain. This meant that when I arrived in Madrid, a bit crumpled but full of enthusiasm and ripe for adventure, I had to take a train to Cartagena.

I got on an overnight train filled with crying children, chickens, very noisy gypsies, and wooden bench seats that were, to say the least, a little uncomfortable after so many flight hours and the hour change. Somehow, I began to feel that I hadn't quite dressed for the part. My beehive looked like a bird's nest, my beautiful shoes were scuffed and stained, and my silk dress couldn't have more wrinkles. All of a sudden, beautiful Spain started looking a little less as I remembered it, and the reality of what I had done began to sink in. Of course, if things didn't work out, I could always go back home (the last thing my father said to me before I left). It was a long night.

Finally, we pulled into the station of Cartagena and there he was, my handsome official, dressed in the drabbest military uniform one could imagine. But under his arm I spied a parcel wrapped with a red ribbon and thought, "How sweet."

After our hugs and conversation struggles, my Spanish was nil, his English better, he told me that he had found a place for me to stay as he was stationed on the ship. On the way, I asked if the package was for me and he said that it was a spray for the bedbugs on the boat. Good romantic start in Cartagena.

He took me to a hotel in Cartagena that was more of a residence than a hotel. In those days, the tourism in Cartagena was nonexistent. The hotel was filled with old widows who were living off their investments or savings. I was a rare bird, indeed. They took me under their wings, and even though our conversations were almost impossible at the beginning, they thought my story was very exciting and romantic because they, as young women, never would have dared to leave home until they were married. At that time in Spain, boys could leave home at 21 but girls had to wait until they were 23 and had their fathers' permission. So I was considered a "loose" woman by much of the population there.

Since F was constantly on maneuvers, I decided I had to find something to do with my time. I tried visiting the school to see if they wanted English classes. Free. But no, since I was only going to be there three months, thank you but no thank you. I was really at wit's end.

I began sketching things in the town, but the only thing worth seeing was the main square with the cathedral. I remembered being very young and at my grandmother's house in her kitchen as she cooked. She always listened to a radio soap opera called "Our Gal Sunday". The introduction always said something like: "Can a young girl from a small mining town in the west find happiness in the big city?" For me it was the opposite. "Can a young girl from the big city find something to do in a small mining town in the east (of Spain)?"

One day, walking through the town, I saw a hospital. A few years back, when I was in high school, I had been a candy-striper at one of our local hospitals in Connecticut. So I thought, why not? I could carry trays and try to read stories (phonetically, at least) to children. I walked in and in my totally fractured Spanish said, "Soy Americana. Quiero ayudar."

I was soon to find out that the hospital had one doctor, two nurses (nuns), and a nurse's helper. I was taken to a room, given a white coat, and rapidly led to a ward where they introduced me to the doctor. I repeated my two short phrases: "I'm American, I want to help". He was very brusque. He looked me up and down. I smiled; he didn't.

He then grabbed a tray of injections and, picking up the first one, said in gestures: push in the needle, if blood comes out (he then slit his throat with his finger) "Muerto" and let his head fall dead. If no blood, he smiled, push, good. He pointed to the first bed and the first injection on the tray and left me with eight sick men. I was totally dumbfounded. But I had been in Cartagena for 10 days and was bored to death. I said to myself, "Do it!" So I did.

The first bed was overflowing with a huge guy, naked and smiling. I motioned for him to roll over, needle in hand. He thought it all was quite funny. He rolled over and I had a really big target. I gave a huge push, pulled, no blood, I pushed again and all went well. The whole ward applauded. I finished with them and from then on I was the favorite "injector" at the hospital. They all wanted the "Americana" (which is all they ever called me, never used my name, not even the doctor).

Of course, I was a novelty there, young, blonde, cheerful, and totally naive. The nuns had seen it all and took no nonsense and the nurse's aide was very timid. Her name was María and she lived outside the town with her parents and many siblings. When we could communicate better, she told me she was dating someone but had to leave him at least 100 yards from her home when they went out. If her father saw him, he would invite him in and, in that case, they would be officially engaged! Fathers in those days in Spain were very anxious to marry off their daughters, especially those with big families and a lot of girls.

Spain was just coming out of its postwar period following the terrible Civil War and many parts of the country, including Cartagena, were so poor. People had their work clothes and one Sunday outfit. Some people pawned their Sunday clothes to get through the week and redeemed them for Sundays. I was outraged one Sunday when I went to Mass at a small church and the people were giving what little silver or gold they had in cutlery or pins to the parish priest in order to make a new crown for the Virgin!

After being there about a month, I met an American woman whose husband was stationed at a Naval Base outside of Cartagena. She invited me to a Sunday dinner at their house. I was amazed to see that, just a few miles from where I was living, a "little America" had sprung up. There were pre-fabricated houses that were quite nice. Just like a suburban American neighborhood. There was a school, a PX where they could buy everything they needed, a movie theater, and social center. When I spoke to them about what I was doing and where I was living, they were amazed. They had NO contact with "the Spaniards" except for the people they employed on the base to clean, etc. They were completely isolated. Their children were learning nothing of Spanish culture, nor were they learning the language. It was such a lost opportunity, but that is how it was back then.

Anyway, as the days passed, I rapidly progressed at the hospital, simply because they needed me. It was rough.

Cartagena was a copper-mining town and there were accidents. I assisted at amputations, even learned to do spinal taps. During the first operations I assisted at, when the doctor asked for an instrument, I would hand him the whole tray because I hadn't a clue of what he was saying. He would give me an exasperated look and yell out the name of the instrument as he held it in front of my nose, for me to repeat it. But we got along quite well. He was an incredible surgeon and did wonderful work with the very little means at his disposal. He saved many lives.

I was really a "girl for all seasons:" I gave injections, helped feed people, assisted in delivering babies, and held people's hands when their relatives were dying. I even helped with the fittings of new limbs that gave people hope, and the response of these people to a smile or a hug was so warm. People died and babies were born. I worked mornings for almost three months but never could eat until dinner time because you really had to have a strong stomach to get through the morning.

In the meantime, I was receiving mail from my friends in the U.S. Many of them were now working in New York or Boston. They described their jobs, the people they were meeting, the places they would go at night, the plays, the concerts, and the clothes they were able to buy now that they were on their own and making good salaries. I was on a different planet!

I have always been a fun-loving sociable person, but I began to have a perspective that was completely new to me. I found myself able to do, and wanting to do, and realizing I *could* do so many things that had never occurred to me. These were lives so completely unlike mine had ever been, but they were complete and happy and valid, with values that I only began to discern. Things that had always seemed important to me didn't seem as important now. Things that I had taken for granted began to have enormous worth. It was as if I were outside and looking into a window at my actions, my priorities, my motives.

My days in the hospital ended, unfortunately, with my contracting hepatitis and spending three weeks in bed, with my old widow friends showing me how to embroider in the morning. In the afternoon, F and his shipmates would sit around my bed and teach me how to play *mus*, a very entertaining card game that relies on tics and gestures to win.

I left Cartagena in December, but my time there made my life richer, gave it a new perspective, and gave me an intimate look at the country I have now lived in for almost fifty years, and have seen change so incredibly and rapidly.

I look back at those three months and know that what I did there, what I saw there, what I learned and intuited there changed my life. Since then, I have done things that I never would have dared to do had I not stayed at that hospital and "done it"!

FYI: I married F.

WHO'S TALKING ... *Susan Noonan is an American writer in Spain who has co-authored books for children, and educational materials for parents and teachers, in Spanish and English. View her offerings at: www.sac-o.com.*

AFTERWORD

WHAT DO YOU TALK ABOUT WHEN YOU'RE SITTING AROUND WITH your family members or friends? Everybody has a story to tell. What's yours?

Our hope is that this book encourages you to share your inspiring, funny, and most telling tales with those who mean the most to you. Or to willing strangers; or to anyone else who will listen. Personal stories are the fabric of the relationships that we weave into our lives.

Sherri Daley and I were college roommates 47 years ago (gulp!). She, by the way, was the glamorous one back then and still is. We've stayed connected over all that time and across hundreds of miles by getting on the phone every now and then, and laughing and crying together. We may not know everything about each other's lives, but we know the best parts. I picture us ninety-five years old, shouting at each other into new-fangled phones that we can't figure out.

A couple of years ago we had a reunion with our two other college bunkmates. It was absolutely amazing how much each of us had changed and how much we had not. We went to a restaurant and coincidentally sat next to a table of four young college women who were roommates. "Look," we said, pointing to ourselves, "this will be you in 45 years!" They appeared to be horrified and didn't look our way again.

Ah, we can only hope that they, too, will build the friendships that we have. May you do so as well. Go ahead; do it right now.

Decide which life story is the most important for you to share, the one that will be helpful or amusing to someone else, and then tell it. Write it down, illustrate it in art, or talk to a friend over a cup of coffee. What you talk about is what makes up your life.

- Linda Hughes, 65

ABOUT THE AUTHORS

Sherri Daley has established herself among editors as someone who will write about anything—from new forms of cancer treatments to the lives of Broadway stage hands, tuning up your own oil burner, that new car smell, blueberry jam, and Joshua Bell's violin. She's the author of a book about commodities traders and a ghostwriter for business motivational texts. She has written freelance for national and regional publications, including *MORE* magazine, *Car and Driver,* and *The New York Times.* She's appeared on dozens on television talk shows, interviewed by, among others, *Oprah, Phil Donahue,* and *Sally Jessie Rafael.* www.sherridaley.com

Linda Hughes is an award-winning author with honors from the National Writers Association, Writers Digest, and the American Screenwriters Association. For twenty years she traveled the globe in her career as a trainer and has been a subject matter expert for MSNBC, Fox News, and TNN. For a good chuckle, watch snatches of her interviews on YouTube at "1980s Hairdos with Linda Hughes." Her most recent novel, *Becoming Jessie Belle,* is about visits from dead ancestor spirits. She enjoys writing about living people, too, and especially enjoyed working with the lively ladies in this book. www.lindahughes.com

CPSIA information can be obtained at www.ICGtesting.com
Printed in the USA
LVOW07s0824091016

507941LV00001B/2/P